A Topical Survey of English Literature

R. N. Sarkar

ATLANTIC PUBLISHERS & DISTRIBUTORS

Published by
ATLANTIC PUBLISHERS AND DISTRIBUTORS
B-2, Vishal Enclave, New Delhi - 27
Phone: 5413460

Sales office
4215/1, Ansari Road, Darya Ganj
New Delhi - 110002
Phone : 3273880

Typeset at
APD Computer Graphics
B-2, Vishal Enclave, N. Delhi - 27

Printed in India at
Mehra Offset Press

PREFACE

The present work is planned to serve a double purpose ultimately to the immense help of the students of English literature; a well-marked stage by stage development of literature and language and at the same time meeting the practical needs of examinations in Honours, M.A., I.A.S. and other State administrative examination courses of Indian Universities and Public Service Commissions. The Introduction part in this connection is a brief consistent history of this evolution, more or less abstract in presentation so as not to get it beclouded in the massing of concrete instances. I have even avoided frequent mention of dates in the Introduction not to make it a little thorny for a mediocre understanding to follow the course of literary history in its psychological and philosophic sequence.

In the preparation of this work I have been taught well as to the manner of treatment and the selection of topics in my long years of teaching of the subject, and considered positively some of the suggestions made available to me by my students and some fellow teachers of different colleges and universities.

I have included in this survey Shakespeare criticism and criticism in general covering also the classical landmarks in the field, and included even the Greek literature in relation to the English course in different stages of college and university curriculum and the intake of foreign words in the history of the language.

I do finally tell my readers that the book is prepared only to serve practical needs, and therefore the treatment cannot claim comprehensiveness, it is selective and limited to its set purpose.

All my thanks are due to my colleagues and students for their encouragement and finally to my publisher who has taken all possible care to make it a good production.

R.N. Sarkar

INTRODUCTION

Anglo-Saxon Period

English literature has developed from the earliest period of Romanised Britain to the latest 20th century fracas of unreached destination. One should at least have a clear idea of this sweep. The Anglo-Saxon period of English literature has a plain history of Christian and pagan elements, sometimes separate in existence and sometimes mixed up.

Jute, Angle and Saxon these three Germanic tribes came to Britain (it was then called so) and made a wholesale massacre of pagan Britons. They came as marauders from Germany across the English Channel, the tribes started invading the land from 449 A.D. roughly on Bede's authority. The uncultured savage people of Britain saw them exposed to terrible incursion by stronger invaders from across the Channel, they were left long alone by Caesar's legions who left the land in 49 B.C., left alone twice over again later before St. Augustine came there. The conflict between these two peoples, Germanic and Pagan Britons, was one-sided and came to so sad an end that there is hardly any parallel in history, so total was the extirpation of the Britons. So nothing remained of their language and whatever oral literary cultivation they may have had. English literature started from the settlement of the Germanic tribes in England (the land was also named after them – Anglo land England), the language too was theirs (Anglo ish English). But their language and literature came to be invaded by influx and incursion from outside. So English literature and language could not retain their original sanctity.

The first incursion after thier permanent settlement in England, a land left yet entirely to themselves, was not by means of an armed conflict, not by means of any conflict at all, but by means of a missionary campaign from Rome. St. Augustine landed on the southern tip of Essex in 597 with the New Faith and at the Synod of Whitby in 664 the authority of Rome was acknowledged in the whole of the Island against the claim of the Irish Missionary. The whole land came under the sway of the Christian Faith and with it her literature though not completely rid of her pagan heritage.

The Christian monasteries became the centres of cultivation, or at best their clerks compilers, of old and already mouldering maunscripts. In the process of compilation of old materials they must have interpolated something of their own sentiments and ideas, particularly of their newly awakened fervour of faith. The whole of the Anglo-Saxon literature then has essentially its manuscript sources, four in all of later discovery. The pre-Christian literature too has a Christian tint owing mainly to later compilation by the Christian clerks. The Christian literature of this period too is only consciously Christian in the choice of subject, but in its unconscious revelation something pagan.

The prose literature of this period was neither by choice Christian nor pagan in unconscious penetration, it was utilitarian in motive and purely worldly in outlook and approach, and of course of later development mainly under the guidance and authority of the Saxon king Alfred. The necessity arose for writing mainly historical accounts and moral exhortations in prose from a motive of racial unity between the Danes and the Anglo-Saxons inhabiting the same land side by side long after the Danish settlement. King Alfred had little time before the treaty of Wedmore in 878 to write or translate works in prose for his people, or for peace between the embroiled races.

The battle of Hastings in 1066 opened the door for yet another commingling of races and languages and for a new shape of literature now under the influence of Norman French. The already blended Saxons and Danes, formed into a strong English race, had a strongly built language and a literature written in it. But in the late 11th century the language was being shelved away gradually and the literature either being replaced or thoroughly changed. This leads to the next stage of development of English literature.

Middle English Period

From the 11th century onwards Norman French began substatially to disturb the already more or less settled language by its vowel system and a new influx of French words into the fabric of the language. English remained for about 1399 the language of the natives and French ruled the whole culture and the upper class, mainly Norman aristocracy lately settled in England after the conquest. It was a different language invading the Anglo-Saxon citadel. But ultimately the native language asserted itself when in 1399 in Parliament too French was finally replaced by English, although this English doubly invigorated by fresh French blood.

It has, therefore, become a landmark in the formation of language as it has no longer been either before or after. Literature too has absorbed some curious French elements in its evolution. Thus the Norman trouveres lent their theme and narrative pattern and also their sunny Provencal mood to the known and unknown poets and scops of this period. Hence quite a good number of romances and ballads formed a substantial part of literature of this period. Even the Church of England came to be dominated by the French monastic movement and principles. *Romań dè lá Rosé, Romań dé Renart* and *Sansoń dé Rolańd* held greater sway upon English literature now and formed the greatest poet of this period Chaucer as he is and gave the greatest inspiration to its formative principles. English literature was more genuinely formed as the language under the Romance language and literature as pre-eminently Chaucer was. Moral, didactic, allegorical poetry and secular romance were all derived from French literature, even native elements in contact with these foreign matters were a fresh look as they did in Chaucer's *The Cantérbury Talés*. Chaucer emerged as 'the well of English undefiled' and the first successful national poet.

From Chaucer onwards English literature was striving for a national status, to be replenished by European elements, but yet to maintain a true English character, which Chaucer succeeded in doing and Gower only felt envious of his success. That envied imitation is no doubt his *Confessió Amuńtis*. The development of the Mediaeval Drama shows this gradually attained freedom from foreign language and domination of the Romanised Church for a true human and English spirit, of which the culmination is to be marked in the next stage.

The Renascence Movement

From the death of Chaucer in 1400 to 1516 the date of publication of Thomas More's *Utopiá* is a period of sincere striving for language adjustment and of course for a national status of literature, mainly by imitation of Chaucer, then by evolving a new species of literature through Mysteries, Moralities and Miracle plays to drama proper.

The European contact, mainly through translation and adaptation of masterpieces of literature for a special kind of humanism in this period, is however to ensure European status of England. More is the first leading figure in this effort. European contact of course is not all, the whole nation was up in a desperate bid to explore whichever corner of the globe they could reach for new wealth, knowledge and power. This was a new awakening that gripped the whole nation and led it to fresh activities, so it was called quixotic romance.

The contact with various parts of the world through voyages of the navigators in one way and through studies of their literature in another resulted in a rich possession of wealth, power and ideas which enriched the land and its literature. Blank verse and Sonnet were imported from Italy, drama was enriched by classical examples when it got rid of the shackles of the Church and endowed with humanistic outlook and sentiments; both poetry and drama ultimately, either in Blank verse or Sonnet form, developed their own originality and surpassed even the European excellence. The Sonneteers like Sidney, Spenser and Shakespeare, and dramatists like the University Wits and Shakespeare and Jonson surpassed all their masters on the continent. Another new species that enriched English literature of this period was Essay, only initially inspired by the French model. Bacon, however, developed his art independently and marked wide difference from the French essayist.

Shakespeare's drama far exceeded all principles of the art in the past; he broke laws because he was law himself. Marlowe in one way and he in another are the true emblem of the Renascence spirit, Marlowe by his unlimited aspiration and he by his still uncomprehended mystery of depth and understanding. No better word has yet been pronounced to explain this excellence of Shakespeare than what Matthew Arnold pronounced in his sonnet, 'Others abideth our question thou art free.' This freedom to build everything anew is the true Renascence spirit. The whole of the Renascence movement attains the zenith of its glory in Shakespeare's hands. Shakespeare critics from his days till today have explored that all transcending mystery yet found no final word.

Even the prose of this period was intoxicated prose, drunk in the spring of Helicon, as the prose style of Lyly and Sidney in *Euphues and Arcadia*. Thomaas Deloney's prose is the other extreme, an exploration in the opposite direction, as in *The Gentle Craft*; Dekker's too the same; the first unconscious step into another new field in English literature, the short story. The poetic prose of the one set contrasts well with the dramatic prose style of the other.

The poetry of a different class has a new line of development, again something of a venture into yet another new field, that really Metaphysical poetry is. Donne, Herbert, Crashaw and Vaughan, all exploited new learning, new discoveries of science as potion to their passion; love or devotion whatever it is the language is inspired, inspired with conceits, in the pattern of style, and in their passion-prodded, well-wedded eccentricities.

The Restoration Period

The post-Shakespearean period of English literature is a natural reaction of tired-nerved creativity, in which creation is dull imitation of the central luminary, and a relapse into the old principles newly revived or imported from abroad. The best creative effort in this phase of depleted energy, in the imitation of Shakespeare without Shakespeare's genius, is in the hands of Milton, not in his drama, in the early poetry neither, but in a different category of verse, the only successful attempt in this field in English literature till today, the epic poetry, the universal theme after twenty years of contemplation chosen and cast in the Homeric mould, which is exactly *Paradise Lost*, if not its close sequel *Paradise Regained* on a smaller scale.

The Restoration of Monarchy in 1660 after nearly twenty years of chaos and uncertainty, the uncertainty too laying impact upon life and literature, restored certainty in the very historical change, to the political organization, which reinforced vitality and energy in literature also, as in Milton's Epic and in a new creative principle which ultimately took shape in English fiction. Obviously it is a new shift from drama to the detailed account of life and society, realistic or invented, worthy to be thoroughly read and contemplated, as the novels of Richardson, Fielding and Sterns are, in the closet, rather than viewed upon the stage in wild excitement and performed by actors and actresses.

The French influx of culture and intellectual revitallization under its impact, and a new mode of habits and manners all due to the king's French retinues dominating the court, gave rise to a new type of drama, called artificial comedy, the comedy of manners, and heroic tragedy modelled also on French pattern; even Milton's *Samson*

Agónistés as late as 1671 is the best British illustration of classical principles of drama adopted for the treatment of a Bible theme only suited to his personal problem in life.

Artificiality of manners and habits mainly under French domination at court and in society, although not exactly as it was after the Norman Conquest of England affecting mainly the language, invited covert or open criticism of follies and incompatibilities in British life, and satire became the normal form of both verse and prose style; Dryden, Pope and Swift and Dr. Johnson in a different way, came to lead the trend; covert method of bringing to book the repulsive follies and freaks of manners formed the essayists' style, the style of humour as in Addison and Steele. *The Spectator, The Tatler* and a little later *The Rambler* were born to serve really this end. The whole literature had a critical rather than inventive turn more or less. Even Milton with his epic grandeur is not an exception. The 18th century then became a prose dominated reason promoted age in English literature, the novel took its rise normally replacing drama with enormous scope for social criticism in a still more genial form than satire and essay.

The Romantic Movement

In English life as also in literature there is a sharp reaction to this trend of prosaic rationalising, the reaction was already there in the 18th century which revived classicism because they wanted principle rather than passion, purity rather than diversity, reason rather than romance, and called the revival neo-classicism. To this trend too there has been a reaction, first a sort of withdrawal from the patterned and well-laid principle and a back home type of return to indegenous enrichment, for which authors have adopted any means in their possession including falsehood and pretension as Macpherson, Percy and Chatterton did; Thomson developed a sense of nature that cares very little for external principle or precept. Chatterton's *Rowley Poems*, Macpherson's *Ossian* and *Fragments of Ancient Poetry*, Percy's *Reliques of Ancient English Poets* and Thomson's *Seasons* bear evidence.

A more advanced group of poets than they took the direction of their mind and feeling and made no scruple of its sanctity for anything outside or acquired from any source however authentic. Young's *Night Thoughts*, Collins's *Ode to Evening* and Gray's *Elegy* mark this attained distiction. All these poets, either of pretended authenticity of matter or of private passion or meditation are better called precursor of Romanticism.

The two other still more advanced poets, Burns and Blake, if we are not ready to include Scott, are already within the ambient of Romantic inspiration, though not clubbed with the five great Romantic poets. The originality of sentiment and sensibility leads them farther away from the 18th century pattern and convention. They are unconventionally unique, one with a personal intensity of awakened passion and perspicacity for all that common life and nature offer him, the other with an incomparable and evocative vision of mind that sheds a new glow upon everything he views. They are Romantic by nature and without any doctrine.

From Wordsworth on Romanticism is treated and applied as a philosophic principle, which is explained by Wordsworth in one way and by Coleridge in another, although both of them and all the three of the younger generation of the great Romantics were led into their own respective corners by the same faculty of Imagination, a term that was subject of study in Wordsworth's Prefaces and Coleridge's *Biographia Literaria* as also its fit language for communication. The five great poets of this period have their own provinces all equally evoked by the one unique faculty, Wordsworth has Nature, Nature outside and Nature inside Man, for his world, Coleridge his supernaturalism, Shelley his glorious future and idea, Keats his world of beauty and Byron his self-conceit. For their journey the vehicle is Imagination.

The two major novelists of this period, Austen and Scott, and thc two major essayists, Lamb and Hazlitt, all taken together represent the movement by addressing themselves to a self that guides, Austen back to the family unit with a satirizing effect of 18th century sentiment and convention and style of writing, Scott farther away into the heart of antiquity to explore its wealth and bewitchment, and Lamb into pathos of his life and humour, and Hazlitt into his virility and vigour of mind and feeling.

The Victorian Period

The Romantic movement is distinct with an exaltation of soul which breaks the barrier of the set code of conduct for a distinction sometimes known and sometimes not known at all, sometimes the voyage is all, rather the reached port of disillusionment. It is a flight up into the air for the scorn of the old dead earth, but the flight tires the wing and makes the fancy bird seek support of the nest. The Victorian reaction is duly for such a nest, the nest is not directly in touch with the soil though the tree that holds it is.

The Pre-Raphaelite movement in the Victorian period is like that, the flight of fancy is a little restrained and brought not down to the earth but half-way down to art. D.G. Rossetti, Christiana Rossetti and William Morris, they had their support upon art for a vision of beauty. This middle point is discerned attained in Rossetti's *Blessed Damozel* in the passion for the union of the earth-born with the denizen of heaven.

The three great Victorian poets, Tennyson, Browning and Arnold, mark a deviation from the Romantic values of the earlier period, but the deviation is not of nature that claims its diametrical opposite end to reach. None of these three poets reached in his reaction the opposite extreme of realism as in the 18th century, they stopped short and turned towards an unattained standard of values, in their helpless state of unreached destination. Tennyson and Arnold lament their lost luck, the luck of the age or humanity, in a sort of 'sick hurry divided aim' state, and Browning remains content with a philosophy made out of this gap, out of failure itself, 'try and test' type of attitude accepted as a philosophy of life as a matter of course. So the first two are the great elegiac poets of English literature and the last of robust optimism.

The Victorian literature is highly porductive of fiction as the Romantic age of poetry, because of a curious evolution, in the Victorian age the evolution of a craved balance, a sincere attempt towards that end: so fiction too differs from the 18th century fiction in quality, and non-fictional prose of this period becomes philosophical. The age can boast of as many as six internationally famed novelists, Dickens, Thackeray, George Eliot, Hardy and the Bronte Sisters, and of prose writers of the standard of Carlyle, Pater, Ruskin and Macaulay.

Fiction of this period is not exactly realistic, nor sentimental, as it was in the 18th century; it is steeped in antiquity neither, nor confined to the values of the age; it is philosophic, moral, satiric, dramatic representation, entertaining and doctrinal account of life wherever which can be; every novelist has his or her particular end in view, just a point in-between the rude surface of the earth and the free flight into the air. Hardy's then is a shot beyond realities, Dickens's novels are entertainment though in a moral world, Thackeray's *Vanity Fair* is not realistic like Fielding's *Tom Jones*, only real life in satiric coat, the women novelists are lifted a little above real life though still breathing the air of this earth.

The Modern Period

Queen Victoria died in 1900 and that was the beginning of the modern period, first formed under the weak rule of her son up to 1910, thereafter under the impact of as many as two World Wars at an interval of 25 years only, and still vitiated under the threat of yet another more terrible global war. Literature has already left far behind the Romantic exaltation and also the Victorian solidity, yet calm calculation of values not all still within sight. Some new problems, economic, political and aesthetic hoodwinked the peace and prosperity of human culture, the British culture most. All these at once laid an impact upon literature of this period.

Poetry, prose fiction, prose or verse plays and critical writing, whatever the form might be the mind became all too critical either of the present undirected aimless state of life or about the unreached destination of some yet unknown values or at least about any kind of reached disillusionment. Yeats' *Sailing to Byzántium* and *Byzántium* together can offer this last experience, far different from Wordsworth's *Yarrow Unvisited* and *Yarrow Visited* experience. In this unsure stage of life and culture the creative mind is normally after symbols and suggestions and also other such varied experiments and newer artistic manoeuvres, at times borrowed from the continent or invented out of the native resources. Some new ideas of human progress and inventions of science also offered new subjects of thought and contemplation yet not for any final judgement or decisive conclusion but only for new engagement and acuteness of artistic experience.

Symbolism and Surrealism imported from France are only weapons to fight the new problems of undirected humanity with lost values, it is what Eliot's *The Waste Land* really does; even in novels it is attempted as in James Joyce's *Ulysses*, significantly published in the same year with *The Waste Land* (1922) obviously in the more problematic inter-war period of English life. Human psychology is even more deeply explored in this period, novelists too took it into their consideration, the Stream of consciousness novels of Henry James, Virginia Woolf and others take an inward turn in the study of man when they find no sure step beyond individual mind.

Just the opposite tendency in the study of man in modern complexity of social problems and some other new unnamed problems of the day is also noticed in modern literature mainly in drama and fiction. Huxley's idea of New Romanticism is therefore at play in our literature and life. A reaction to this tendency is not also a rare phenomenon in the modern world. Literature today is passing through sharp contrasts and contradictions with no definite end in view either in life or in literary delineation. So only a temporary and phased inquiry and attainment is possible in literature. That is mainly why One Act play and short story and short poems and short novels dominate the field today, every small fragment made into an artistic whole, as the Short Story is defined 'a mount of a moment'.

CONTENTS

CHAPTER I

THE OLD ENGLISH AND THE MIDDLE ENGLISH PERIOD

Old English Elegy: Early Anglo-Saxon Trend

The whole of the Anglo-Saxon literature is a mixed development: its Pagan and Christian elements are quite evident. Now whether it is Christian in origin or not in the early part of the Anglo-Saxon literature the supreme sway of a note of lamentation was considered the most profound element.

In the early Anglo-Saxon literature man saw himself completely helpless in the hands of fate. There was again sorrow out of complete isolation from the thegn or the human Lord. The earliest elegiac poem in English is really *Widsith, Lament of Deor* comes under the same category. It is the human Lord that one is seeking for, that gave rise to a great travel in this poem. The poem is, therefore, entitled *Widsith* which means a great traveller. The scop was moving from place to place to find a Lord in his desolate mind here. We then find a long list of Kings and monarchs in this poem. Among them we find the name of the king of Goths, Attila, the king of the Huns, and Albion, the King of Lombards, and of course a great many others.

The Lament of Deor narrates a different story. It is the story of sorrow, clearly defined, the sorrow of a similar scop who may have been thrown out of favour and led into an eager search of a new master.

There are other poems also in which elegiac note is quite clear. The examples are *The Ruined Burg, The Lover's Message, The Maid's Complaint, The Wanderer*. Death, danger, desolation could easily come into the texture of such poems of the early Anglo-Saxon period. Love can be the moving force of such lamentation, the lover or the maid whoever he or she can be can wake up for love and lament the sad lot of separation.

There is a different class of poems in which the mourning note is only a stray element, for example the lyric *The Seafarer*. The sailor in the poem does not have any great theme of lamentation like love or betrayal; yet in the poem human destiny is without any bright future. Man's lot is not within his careful calculation. There is something outstanding human authority. A description like this in such a poem is quite significant:

Over went the winter on my wanderways
All forlorn of happiness, all bereft of loving kinsmen.

Even in *The Lay of Beowulf*, the longest poem of the early period has something mourning about it. The poem is not an elegy, it is a heroic poem of epic tradition, but gloomy mood and lugubrious imagination loom large in the poem. It is the Christian seriousness, a call for the deeper understanding of life which the new faith sounded, that ultimately guided and controlled the outlook and sentiment of the possible writer and the later compiler in the dark nook of a Christian monastery. No poem of this period, long or short, heroic or unheroic, could escape this overall preoccupation of mind.

Anglo-Saxon Christian poetry

Christianity was preached in England during the 7th century. In all Anglo-Saxon literature, mainly preserved in four Manuscripts, preserved by Christian monks, the ardour of the new converts was either systematically recorded or casually reflected. Even the pre-Christian literature of the period must have been carefully collected and in some cases amended by the clerks of the monasteries. In the style of preservation and compilation the Christian strain is inevitable in all sorts of literature of the period. Christian poetry proper with a distinct stamp includes two very outstanding names, Caedmon and Cynewulf, and some other minor works of still untraced authorship. Christian poetry of the Anglo-Saxon period is therefore a conscious record of the Faith and the passion of the new converts.

Caedmon is the first recorded poet of England. There is a good account of how he became a poet while living in the monastery of Whitby among other brothers. The story is recorded in the pages of Bede the historian. Caedmon began to sing under the inspiration of God he met in a dream. His work includes the translation of the passages of the Bible. The only original work of Caedmon is his account of his dream.

His translation of *Genesis* and *Exodus* by the order of the Abbot is symptomatic of the early stage of the style of writing in the still formative stage of the language. Thereafter Caedmon began to write and sing all those things he had in dream and also those parts of the Bible he had not.

Cynewulf is the second writer known to the world of this period. He writes about Christ and the lives of the Saints. In the first poem in three parts Cynewulf describes the Advent of Christ, his Ascension, and his Second coming at the Last Judgement. *Christ* along with *The Life of Saint Juliana* was noticed in the Codex Exoniensis Manuscript, the other two poems *Saint Helen* and *The Fates of the Apostles* were found in the Vercelli Manuscript. These two poems are of doubtful authorship though they contained runic signature of Cynewulf. *The Phoenix* and *The Dream of the Rood*—these two poems are full of Christian outlook and sentiment, but cannot be made sure whether they were by Cynewulf or not. Only there is a clear evidence of Cynewulf's style.

The Christian Saints and Apostles are of a good number. Some of them no doubt are of exotic origin, such as St. Juliana, St. Helen and St. Andreas. Whether the Saints are exotic or of native origin they express the same Christian sentiment and fervour. Whether the account included the lives of the saints or the paraphrase of the Bible they were charged with a new spirit of a faith not very long preached among them.

One thing is clear that Christian poetry of the Anglo-Saxon period is not an unmixed literary production, rather Christian outlook and sentiment remained inseparably blended with the Pagan exoticism and temperament. Sometimes Christ appeared in the armour of a tribal chieftain.

The Lay of Beowulf: the first epic of English Literature

In Anglo Saxon literature *The Lay of Beowulf* occupies an important place. It is comparable to the Germanic epic *Nibelungenlieder*. The work is of later compilation by some Christian monk no doubt, although its subject takes us back to the first half of the 6th century. It narrates the victory of the Franks over the Goths. It occurred about 512-20. In this battle the hero Beowulf took part.

The story of the poem is of three parts. First of all Beowulf is a valiant Geat who comes to the help of Hrothgar, the king of the Danes. The king's palace of Heorot was every night raged by a monster called Grendel. Beowulf engaged in hand to hand fight with the monster. The giant was defeated in the fight and one of his arms was torn off.

The next story relates a fight between Beowulf and the monster's mother, in which he fought her down to her abode. Beowulf came back to Heorot in triumph bearing Grendel's gigantic head. He became the king of the Geats.

The third story is about Beowulf's encounter with another dragon who guarded an ancient treasure. Beowulf stole some jewels from the treasure to the terrible fury of the dragon. The dragon sets out for a fresh attack upon Beowulf's land, and lays in waste the entire land burning it with his pestilential breath. Beowulf slays the dragon and saves the people, but he is himself mortally wounded during the encounter by the monster's venomous teeth. The hero dies nobly consoled by the thought that he has sacrificed himself for his subjects.

The three stories together form the subject of the epic. The account is of varied temperament and outlook; no doubt the Christian element is mixed up with the pagan outlook and sentiment. The heroic story has practically nothing of the Anglo-Saxon life, although the form is essentially Anglo-Saxon.

The epic cannot be called Teutonic in origin; there is no mention of the land near the Elbe which the Anglo-Saxons inhabited previously. The scene is by turns the Danish island Sea land and the country of the Geats or Goths in the south of present Sweden. The unknown Anglo-Saxon poet was commemorating his forbears of Scandinavia when they were still pagan and pouring in upon the shores of Great Britain. This gives rise to a hypothesis that the story is based on some Icelandic saga partly supported by the fact that the chief incidents of the story of Beowulf recur in the Icelandic saga of Grettir.

The story of Beowulf is full of some customs and habits of the people who came down to Great Britain from Scandinavia, and, from Germany earlier to Sacandinavia, to settle permanently there. But the people must have already lost the violence and wildness of their habits and temperament undoubtedly as a result of their conversion to Christianity. Their barbaric cruelties and grossness yielded place to a predominantly moral tendency no doubt derived from newly preached Christianity. It is in fact a mixed and slightly artificial production, foreign materials in the national form. It compares with the Scandanavian *Edda* and Greek *Iliad*.

The epic is the only surviving thorough account of the people who came down to settle in Great Britain, their manners, habits, temperament and daily round of activities, all kept intact with a silver lining of the Christian idea of man's ultimate source of power and safety in his submission to a higher power far beyond this life and existence.

Anglo-Saxon prose literature

The earliest Anglo-Saxon literature must have been in poetry, and prose literature is found to be of later evolution, although in the very development prose had hardly any break or any stumbling block in its way. The earliest record of prose is the Laws of Ina, a King of the West Saxons, the laws which were promulgated at the end of the 7th century. The landmark, however, in Anglo-Saxon prose literature is the writing of Alfred. The other two important phases in evolution are the writings of Aelfric and Wulfstan.

The inspiration behind writing in prose came from a serious purpose of instruction and inculcation of his subjects. The king himself took the initiative and that is why he became the leading prose writer of this period.

Alfred can be termed the father of English prose. As king of Wessex he was inspired by a utilitarian motive to educate his people and instruct them in their mother tongue. About 800 A.D. the king noted a kind of gained supremacy in the south-west of England over all the Germanic groups settled in the Island. Now it is the king's duty to look after the unity and integrity of the people. Alfred started two types of writings: his original writing in prose and translation of other writers into the native language.

Alfred himself is credited with the translation of the *Universal History of Orosius*. The translation work was difficult; Orosius a Spanish historian of the 5th century wrote an obscure Latin. Alfred's other translations, not all by his own pen, sometimes done by others at his instruction, are the *Ecclesiastical History of the Angles* of Bede, *Pastoral Rules* by Pope Gregory the Great and *Consolation* of Boethius. His outstanding original work is of course the early part of *The Anglo-Saxon Chronicle*. Here Alfred is more like a modern chronicler even with the style of narration of his age.

Alfred's translation of Bede's Ecclesiastical history was a great help to his people for the achieved unity of races. Aelfric is no great author like Alfred; his prose is neither very utilitarian in its manner of communication nor accommodative in style, rather it is a bit too ornate to serve properly any such purpose. Aelfric was a pupil of the monastic school which Aethelwold founded at Abingdom. He wrote in the early part of the 11th century. We owe to him a *Colloquium* for teaching Latin by conversation. This can be called the first Latin-English dictionary. Aelfric of course made his name by his *Homilies* which are partly compilation and partly translation from the Father of the Church. Unlike the prose style of Alfred Aelfric's is almost rhythmic-like verse. His writings are more stylistic than the writings of either Alfred or Wulfstan.

Wulfstan was the Archbishop of York from 1002 to 1023. He was a preacher, his *Homilies* dates from 1012, when the English were suffering the ills of the Danish invasion. It is Wulfstan who proclaims the advent of the great Chastiser the Antichrist. Unlike Aelfric Wulfstan gives his language a popular lively touch.

The three outstanding figures in Anglo-Saxon prose writings present varied colours in the development of the prose style. The central monument of the early prose literature was of course king Alfred, himself a great admirer of academic excellence. They together made English prose quite viable.

The Norman Conquest: its impact on literature and language

The battle of Hastings decided the fate of England and her literature and language so completely as nowhere in the early period. The character of the Norman Conquest is completely different from the Danish invasion of England. First of all the Northmen who came to inhabit the northern part of France were originally of the same German blood with the Anglo-Saxon people; but they came down to France purely to be conquered by a superior culture.

When these Northmen came down to England with William the conqueror, they were by then fully acclimatized in the Roman culture already refined to elegance. The Norman people now dominating

England gave therefore to the conquered nation a culture, a language and also a literature that formed their own literature far different from the earlier Anglo-Saxon evolution.

The first impact of the Battle of Hastings upon England was the accepted superiority of the conqueror. The English people almost willingly made them subservient to the Norman lords. The language they spoke became already the official language of the land. In school, college and court, as also in Parliament the conqueror's language definitely ruled up to 1362. In Parliament it reigned up to even 1399. The English language ultimately won its victory, and won with much French elements to its ultimately improvement.

The literature too came definitely under a French outlook and sentiment; even in literature in their native language the English authors always vied the lightness of heart and free motive and movement from the contemporary French literature. Chaucer perhaps could have been less enjoyable without a French movement to impinge upon him. Perhaps Chaucer's difference from Gower is mainly due to a vigorous French impact upon him.

Anglo-Saxon literature came mainly under the Germanic influence. The Teutonic manners and habits silently controlled the writing habits of the Anglo-Saxon period, but the Norman conquest of England set a different note, it is altogether a passage from gloominess to light-heartedness, from fate to free nature, and of course, from a constraint of prejudice to purity of heart. The best fruits of all such changes would be at once noted in the writings of Chaucer.

Both the language and literature left the already gained solidity of Anglo-Saxon period for a new venture under the impact of the Norman Conquest. Both language and literature formed themselves anew to a greater strength. Some new elements came to assert themselves in the life of the people as also in their literature hundred years after the conquest. From the 9th century to the 14th England witnessed a vigorous development of both her social and political life on the one hand and literary consolidation on the other.

The Middle English Romance : its importance in English literature

The Romance in Mediaeval literature is a whole evolution under the impact of the French literature. In the earlier period there was practically no impetus to write anything like that. The whole outlook was changed in contact with the French people and their literature. Romance is the product of the Middle Ages.

It is very difficult to assess the whole course of the Middle English Romances. The source of the romances of this period is to be traced in the three strands of literature conveniently arranged as the Matter of France, the Matter of Troy (Rome) and the Matter of Britain.

The Matter of France deals with the exploits of Charlemagne and his followers. The French epic, *The Chanson de Roland,* is the great source of romances, in which Roland (Hero) figured. Earlier the epic was called *Chanson de Geste,* because it was originally a string of short songs celebrating the deeds of well-known popular heroes. Later those various songs concerning one hero were gathered together and the result was *Chanson de Roland.*

The matter of Troy consisted largely of tales from Greek and Roman sources. The two great cycles of these romances deal with the deeds of Alexander and siege of Troy. They compare with the *Arabian Nights.*

The Matter of Britain deals with the exploits of Arthur and his Knights of the Round Table. It is the richest store house of romances which English literature knows. There were many cycles of Arthurian Romances, the chief of which are those of Gawain, Launcelot and Merlin, the conquest of the Holy Grail and the death of Arthur.

After the Conquest the writers of England took great interest in the romances and the exploits of the Knights who came to England and all those cycles which they imported into their land; their primary interest was in the exploits of the native heroes.

The romances of the Middle Ages had mainly three subjects: love, religion and war. These three elements broke the barrier of racial prejudice. The romances thoroughly exerted their influence upon their minds. The England of these days breathed the free and sunshine air of the country. It is a literature that bespeaks a new change.

In England this change brought in its wake other many romances, as for example Layamon, a Saxon with his remote German blood turns the French rhyme of Geoffrey of Monmouth into English. The result was Layamon's *Brut*. He added a number of things which neither were in the Latin version nor in the French, yet were highly interesting in their original form mainly from Wales.

There are other two romances, *King Horn* and *Havelok*, which appear to have founded the national English tradition coming down from the time of the Danish wars, although originally deriving much strength and force from their French parallels.

The styles of romances are of course various as their sources. In the Auchinleck manuscript of Edinburgh there are two romances, *Sir Orfeo* and *Sir Tristrem*. The stories are of the two best known in the world. Sir Orfeo is Orpheus. The romances are quite of interesting lot which foreshadow the rise of the novel in the later years.

Chaucer: his contribution

Chaucer appeared in English literature a giant among pigmies. He came with the varied knowledge and experience of life which his great contemporaries, mainly Langland and Gower lacked. Chaucer's dominant position must be assessed in comparison with three great contemporaries, Langland, Gower and Barbour.

The first startling point of Chaucer's contribution is a complete break with the Anglo-Saxon tradition of English literature. Chaucer started with a French spirit deeply imbibed in his soul under the impact of French literature he thoroughly read. In this period the most outstanding influence upon him is the influence of *Roman de la Rose*. Chaucer acquired the language as also the spirit of the French literature. In translating *Roman de la Rose* Chaucer not only derived French uniqueness of style but also gave English literature a new outlook which was really lacking in Anglo-Saxon literature.

Chaucer borrowed elements of other European literatures and replenished the lean flood of native literature. Chaucer was under Italian influence and derived the best that was in that literature to augment the already depleting flow of the native reservoir. Chaucer must have studied Dante, Petrarch and Boccaccio. He is more indebted to the last although he borrowed from all of them extensively.

Most of his tales were either written in imitation of Boccaccio or under his influence as also some other European authors. Boccaccio's *Decameron* supplied Chaucer with the form of his masterpiece, *The Canterbury Tales.* Perhaps Chaucer's development under the Italian influence gave the first impetus towards writing good stories in English literature. Chaucer's *Troylus and Criseyde* is the best example of a half adapted translation of an outstanding story of Boccaccio, *Il Filostrato.*

Chaucer is not all imitation of other European writers, not at all totally French, he had his originality not acquired by any other contemporaries then nor by any immediately later. It will take at least hundred years for anybody to attain Chaucer's status in English literature.

Chaucer derived the best of English and French, the combined effect of his acquisition is a landmark of English literature. He is a French cut of an English coat in literature.

Gower wrote *Confessio Amantis,* a collection of stories, but Chaucer's collection of stories in *The Canterbury Tales* is not only a different world but also of entirely different interest. The *Tales* is no doubt the masterpiece of Chaucer's contribution, it far exceeds the excellence of Chaucer's other works, as for example *The Hous of Fame, The Legend of Goode Women* and *Troylus.* The *Tales* is what Chaucer can be both as a man and as a writer. As a writer Chaucer is essentially realistic, observing the facts and trend of his contemporary life as also foreshadowing the essence of future evolution, and as a man accumulating the varieties of his experience with the zest of a carefree trouvere.

The Canterbury Tales represents his English period. He has gathered together a lot of Canterbury pilgrims giving all of them stories to narrate just compatible with their habits and temperaments. The Prologue to the *Tales* seems to be a gallery of pictures of varied colour and costumes, new in English literature, unattained even later with the same excellence of dramatic suspense and surprise yet with the precision of an unfailing eye.

Chaucer offers English literature a new tone which is the quintessence of his humour. He gave a finished language which was the need of the hour and which supplied the basic structure of future development. The literature came alive with a new human touch already liberated from the bondage of Mediaeval preoccupation of religion and sentimental reaction.

Chaucer's humour

Chaucer belongs to the Mediaeval period, but he is in many ways a little ahead of the general trend of his age, not only in literature but also in life style. His sense of humour is a natural evolution of his life and experience.

Chaucer is a man of varied experience, and as a writer of varied interest. It is perhaps he among all his contemporaries who assimilated deeply the best of the European literature. All these resulted in a habit of life and an outlook on literary activities. He started his career by translating *Roman de la Rose* in which there were things that fed the flood of humour in him.

Chaucer wrote in the early period some very short songs and roundels which are now lost, and which must have been the stray and unorganised reflection of his sense of humour. Chaucer's power of enjoyment of the varied things of life was very great, his excellence as a writer lies in his power to make all of them enjoyable to others.

There are imitation and adaptation from other sources, foreign and native both, but his power reveals itself in his skill for organizing all of them to an effect of humour. Dream and allegory were the two very substantial elements in his early poems and in some of his late. These elements are the evidence of his sense of humour. Chaucer's allegories differ from other allegories of the Middle Ages, and the difference lies in his extraordinary power of humour.

We may cite in this respect one very interesting poem, *The Parlament of Foules*. It was practically an allegory calculated to serve a practical purpose—celebrating the betrothal of Richard II and Anne of Bohemia. The assembled birds are urged to make the choice of their mates, while the queen bird Eagle would avoid the base and pick up the best worthy to keep her company. It is highly interesting for the humour in the presentment of the real in the garb of an allegory.

Chaucer's *Hous of Fame* is charged with a humour of a completely different kind, truth is made enjoyable by the very act of the author's skilful handling of it. There is dream, there is allegory, and ultimately there is a truth which becomes highly enjoyable for the treatment; the author fully exploits the real link between the earthly life and its unreal aspiration.

The Legende of Goode Women was written as late as 1385, Chaucer is then mature. The Prologue to the *Legend* is full of Chaucer's best humour which is derived out of the poet's power of enjoying love and its freakish manifestation. Chaucer is always concrete although he often uses dream and allegory as instruments.

Chaucer is no doubt at his best even in respect of the evolution of humour, in his masterpiece, *The Canterbury Tales.* Here he passes far beyond the humour he has exploited in the *Troylus* piece. The Prologue to *The Canterbury Tales* is concretely a picture of life as thorough as it could be in the Mediaeval period; but it is even more truly a close manifestation of Chaucer's sense of humour derived from his wide experience of life and ways. The Prologue is an account of all Mediaeval professions and liberal life; Chaucer enjoys varieties with a zest that can be termed as humour and can make them enjoyable to others with the same gaiety of heart. No doubt in the whole of the Mediaeval period this sentiment is rare, as for example it is awfully lacking in his great contemporary Gower.

The Contemporaries of Chaucer

Chaucer in his age outdistanced all others, so a sharp contrast with his contemporaries brings out the excellence of his genius. Chaucer apart the whole of the Middle Ages is a literary slump. Chaucer is, therefore, an exception, or better say, like Shakespeare a maker of a golden age of literature out of a picked up heap of commonplace materials.

At least a few of his contemporaries must be named to appreciate the spirit of Chaucer's time, man like Layamon, Trevisa, Mandeville, Wyclif, Langland, Barbour and Gower. Layamon is a true historian who with his pure German blood took himself the noble task of unification of a mixed race, following the example of Wace. History of this kind was written then with a utilitarian motive. He forgot his German blood and proclaimed the Britons as the true owner of the land. Barbour did the same thing with his Scotch blood in *Bruce*.

Trevisa, Mandeville and Wyclif are the three prose writers of the period of sharply different interests. Trevisa is a translator, but translator of a significant book, Higden's *Polychronicon*. This original is really an account of the state of language in England then. The incursion of French into the native language seriously disturbed the unity of the races and their languages. Trevisa translated it and made his own commentary on the change already secured of a time when he felt people must know it. Wyclif is an Oxford man, a man of letters, a reformer. He is the first Protestant and the first translator of the Bible into English. His translation of the Holy Book in the native tongue for the common people to understand their religion is a protest against the Church authority.

John Mandeville is a true writer of romance under the pretence of a traveller, he pretended to write an account of his travels in the East, but the extravagant description of the wonders of all types is only suited to romance, romance really it was in the form of a travelogue.

Alliterative verse that was long discontinued was started afresh in an anonymous collection written in a dialect of the Lancashire area; in that collection *Sir Gawayn and the Grene Knyght* is a secular romance. From a different dialect came Langland's *Piers Plowman;* dialect variation in the Middle Ages is very sharp. *Piers Plowman* represents the west Midland dialect. It is a social satire, perhaps the first of its kind. The allegory, although very loosely constructed, teaches people the truth of good work. The author's dream opens to his view a whole field of folk waiting to be led and taught by Piers the Ploughman who knows labour and truth as the secret of the path of God.

Piers Plowman is of the nature of a Morality Play, particularly the two almost detached episodes within its framework are; there is in the literary work of the Mediaeval period an evident moral and religious bias, whatever the form. The poem in itself is a social record in the contemporary conventional form.

Gower is no doubt the greatest of Chaucer's contemporaries. Chaucer stigmatized him as 'moral Gower'. He is a foil to Chaucer's genius. He wrote mainly in French and Latin, in those days the language of the aristocracy to which he belonged. When he came ultimately to write in the native language he wrote in King's English, *i.e.*, the East Midlands, like his rival Chaucer.

Both Chaucer and Gower belonged to the same area, but Gower was poles apart from Chaucer. He is last in date an Anglo-Norman poet, writing first in French as in *Speculum Meditantis* and in few other love pieces. Then he tried Latin as in *Vox Clamantis* in which his anti-people reactions are quite evident. The Peasants' rising of 1381 taught him a lesson which went fully against the democratic outlook of Langland and Chaucer.

Only in the last stage of his writing career, Gower, evidently envious of Chaucer's success, came to write reluctantly in London Dialect, as he pretends, at the instance of the King. *Confessio Amantis* is therefore the only work Gower wrote in English. His difference from Chaucer is clearly marked out in this work. It is like Chaucer's *Canterbury Tales* a compilation of stories. It starts with allegory, Venus who has little fondness for him asks him one day to make his confession to her priest Genius. His confession of sins with illustrative stories is out of his moral and spiritual motive which is contrasted against Chaucer's motive in *The Canterbury Tales.*

The Mediaeval period is almost a blank without Chaucer and his direct contrast Gower. The age has its own tradition and genius, which is best illustrated by the authors noted above and by the romances of varied kinds and ends.

The Evolution of the Drama in the Middle Ages

The Renascence is the blossoming period of the drama in English literature, but it began developing long before it attained the highest point of glory. In the Middle Ages drama was only an extension of a form of preaching of Christianity.

Drama is really to be called a handmaiden to the Bible. It was in the form of tropes or declamation in dialogue that drama made its first appearance. It came round about the Norman Conquest. Christian missionary took it unconsciously as a form of preaching the truth of the Bible. First of all the Church people declaimed the passages of the Gospel in pure Latin; but the dialogue became a little more dramatic when declaimed in the vernacular.

The best known example of the transitional stage is *Adamo* which was originally written in French. A Norman or Anglo-Norman scholar must have translated it and performed in England. It is the story of a highly dramatic conflict of passion and faith in the first parents of mankind, which later may have influenced Milton in his studies of the character of Eve in *Paradise Lost*. The sin of temptation the crux of the plot.

Ultimately the Anglo-Norman poets abandoned not only Latin but also French, and adopted in their place the native language. The whole England observed the Church rituals by means of tableaux at Christmas and Easter. The feast of Corpus Christi is also celebrated, though a little later, with elaborated dramatic tableaux. The drama came now to be divided into some cycles. It was not then the custom to perform a play on a fixed platform as later in the Elizabethan period. At the initial stage all the dramatic dialogues performed inside the church premises. Then it came out of the Church premises and got out of hand of the clerks. Yet the performance remained purely conventional.

The Easter and Christmas cycles were first in date, the Corpus Christi cycle came later in about 1264. The stage was moving scaffolds at a stage when the Church authorities wanted to enact the stories of the Bible by moving from one place to another. On Christmas and Easter days the crude stage became stationary much later.

The cycles of plays all detailing the stories of the Bible in their closely related phases in some selected cities of England, and the cycles got their names from the cities where they were presented. There were mainly four such cycles—York, Warwick, Chester and Coventry.

Some of the important plays of this period are *Nativity* and *Noah*. These plays are called Miracle Plays. In the body of such a play at times secular matters were introduced, sometimes it assumed the form of interlude; allegorical though most of them were they paved the way for secular drama under the head the Morality Plays. The important examples of this class were *The Castell of Perseverance, Mankind;* the most outstanding in the whole lot is of course *Everyman*.

During the Middle Ages drama showed only a limited progress. It originated in the Church building with the set purpose of preaching the Bible. The language in which it was first performed was Latin. The actors were then all clergymen. At the next stage drama developed a secular character with the introduction of outsiders as actors and with the shift of the place of performance from inside the Church building to the porch, then gradually from the porch to the market place and the streets.

The usual trend of preaching the Gospels underwent a change, secular matters were introduced and drama became an independent branch of literature. The earlier stage of Mystery plays passed on to the Miracle and then Moralities, from the text of the Bible to the lives of Saints and then to the abstract principles of human morals, with the commingling of the serious with the lighter elements in the interludes to a stage of purely human interest.

Decadence of the Drama in the Elizabethan Period

Great enthusiasm was shown about the spectacular tableaux of the four major cycles of Miracle plays, and even the Moralities attracted a huge crowd in those major cities, and up to 1520 plays were more or less in the Christian convention even though played outside the Church premises. Thereafter drama fell prey to her new masters, although she no longer remained handmaiden to the Church. This is then the beginning of a new fall of standard.

Drama became a new tool for argument and use against enemies. It became impregnated with the Renascence and Reformation spirit. From this time on the authors of the Moralities who could be easily traced unlike in their earlier stage of evolution made them serve only their controversial ends and cared never for the literary value. John Skelton's *Magnificence* written about 1516 represents only the transitional stage of this evolution. The play aimed at a mere moral lesson, the first specimen of a laicised morality. In the succeeding few plays the Renascence spirit of the new conquest of knowledge is fully at play. In them the ugly devil is ignorance. The morality play of *The Four Elements*, printed in 1519, written under the influence of the great navigator Amerigo Vespucci, strikingly imbibes the spirit of More's *Utopia*. The same ardour to instruct and acquire knowledge fills John Redford's pedagogic Morality *The Play of Wyt and Science* which dates from the end of the reign of Henry VIII.

The Reformation too took the stage to preach their ideal and poured venom upon its enemies. The first in date in this group was one by David Lindsay. His *Satire of the Three Estates* was played in 1540 at

Linlithgow before the King of Scotland, the bishops and the people. It is a mixed dish, of both politics and religion. Lindsay's attack is mainly against the Church.

Bishop Bale uses the ready instrument of the Morality to strengthen his Protestant bastion. Tragedy, comedy and Interlude whatever he may have written he made it serve his faith. To this end he makes a free use of history distorting historical veracity as in *King'Jehan.* In this play he paints John as a man misunderstood, a noble victim, the first Protestant.

Interludes which attained an independent form already came to be handled by a master artist of this period. Heywood seems to stand out this doctrinizing craze of drama, perhaps the only distinct attempt. Interludes were mainly for fun and farcical effect. He was original in avoiding Morality plays and in having no purpose but to amuse. They are mainly scenes from fableux and modelled on the French. The most commonly known interlude of Heywood is *The Four P's,* in which four persons, their names with initial P's engaged in a contest for greater lies. The Palmer wins because he says in all his travels he has seen no woman lose temper.

Up to 1550 the drama played second fiddle to some other motive than the motive of art and simple innocent amusement. From 1550 onwards it started progressing steadily gradually undoing its slavery to doctrinization but came under the repressive authority of the city administration when it left the premises of schools and colleges. Then professional company of actors required letters patent for performance in the city or patronage of the wealthy nobility. The first Company to obtain letters patent was Leicester's Company in 1574. Some of the Companies therefore built their permanent theatre houses beyond the city area on the other side of the Thames yet within its easy access to avoid interference by the local authorities. The first such house was built in 1576.

CHAPTER II

ESSAYISTS UPTO EIGHTEENTH AND EARLY NINETEENTH CENTURY

Renaissance element in Bacon

The Renaissance spirit made Bacon what he was, but did not obviously make him as it made Shakespeare or Marlowe or even Sidney or Jonson. His was not quixotic Romance as it was called, neither was he charged with nationalistic outlook as most of the writers of the age were. He can be defined satisfactorily by another very significant characteristic of the movement which can be regarded as the Gospel of the age—homo mensuro, man is the supreme measure.

This last agreed well with Bacon's personal and very private qualities, it could even support his private morals as it could no one's. It could explain Shakespeare only to some extent, but it explains Bacon totally. For Bacon man's personal interest is the highest measurement perhaps the only measurement, it explains his own personal case, as it can also be extended to his utmost philosophic end.

From *Novum Organum* to *The Advancement of Learning* Bacon's development is really very varied, but the essential Bacon is nowhere so totally revealed as in his essays. That is mainly so because the Essays brings out clearly both his age and his private self. The whole nation was then groping for new fields of excellence with a spirit of conquest, in Bacon too there can be seen three such new interests from abroad readily made his own, Montaigne's Essays, La Rochefaucauld's aphoristic style and Machiavelli's *Il Principe* and his morals.

All these strands are uniquely blended in his Essays yet leave him free to imbibe the Renaissance spirit and give vent to it in, everything he writes and mostly his essays of diverse kinds. His essays were published as early as 1597, as many as ten essays in a collection, thereafter they were reissued next year, and finally all the essays in one collection in 1625.

In 'Of Studies', the earliest of Bacon's essays, quite in a Renaissance spirit, Bacon deals with the practical aspects of reading books that may better serve the worldly need of man. He is a classical scholar and the author of *The Advancement of Learning*. 'Of Studies' in particular does not bear testimony to an unqualified love for knowledge but to a Renaissance care for earthly equipment for well being '...natural abilities are natural plants that need pruning by study'.

'Of Friendship' which begins with almost a philosophic enquiry into the subject turns ultimately essentially utilitarian in the service of human health. The Style is humanistic, quoted elaborately from classical history and literature. 'Of Ambition' could have been a highly philosophic essay, but in Bacon's treatment it never scales beyond its worldly limit. Bacon takes up the issue of ambitious men, no doubt under the overall Renaissance impact of concrete realities of human life. Love in the Renaissance period came to mean embodied human beloved. So does ambition in Bacon's essay.

'Of Superstition' does not, however, explore like Shakespeare or Marlowe or Greene the Elizabethan types to their own end; it is a study of the general causes and ultimate results of such illogical elements in life. Bacon's study always aims at a human effect and mundane adjustment as if in no way he can ignore the basic human utility, a Renaissance preoccupation of mind, in Shakespeare in one way in Bacon in another.

Bacon's 'Of Truth' is the latest version of his attainments, in a highly tense philosophic reorientation of Renaissance values, Wherein Bacon's personal qualities have a significant part to play. Bacon is Machiavellian even in his interpretation of truth, mixed with falsehood it attains its extra effective quality on the one hand and on the other it offers greatest security and highest pleasure to observe the world's bewildering pyrotechnics of error. Such an estimate of truth is partly due to his private morals and essentially to the overall Renaissance spirit of his age with which Shakespeare too worked in his own province.

Bacon's Renascence preoccupation is further to be noted in his style and allusion. Just like one of the humanist group of the Renascence Bacon explores what the ancient classics of the European literature have in store for him to use. Bacon uses them in his style, vocabulary and even in imageries and allusions. He draws upon the Bible as in 'Of Truth', not for sound morals but as for effectiveness of expression, upon Greek and Roman literature freely, adopts the title of essays from Montaigne, and sometimes the Latin construction of sentences as widely the classical proverbs and adages. All these are due to Bacon's conscious and unconscious Renascence predilection.

Bacon as Essayist

A literary genre called Essay is introduced in English literature by Bacon for the first time, and that is his greatest importance in the world of letters. Montaigne has already introduced it in France, but Bacon has not imitated him although there is evidence enough in his essays that he took particular note of his French contemporary who dies in 1592 when he was simply rising as writer. Montaigne's *Essais* was Translated into English by John Florio in 1603, and Bacon of course started writing his essays towards the close of the 16th century, from as early as 1597.

The very characteristic difference between Montaigne and Bacon is the difference of the English Renaissance. Bacon's Essays bear the stamp of the Renaissance and Montaigne's *Essais* clearly does not. Montaigne's *Essais* almost all has the colour of the mind that informed it, and every piece in it can be explained by a Johnsonian phrase 'the loose sallies of the mind'. Bacon is something quite different, he borrows only the name from his French counterpart, and takes note of his contribution in his essays, as in one of his later essays 'Of Truth' (1625) : 'And therefore Montaigne saith prettily, when he inquired the reason why the world of the lie should be such a disgrace and such an odious charge...'

The form that Bacon follows in his essays is something intermediate between Montaigne and La Rachefaucauld. His outlook is as utilitarian as that of Machiavelli. The classical and European trend of his writing may have been due to his deep classical learning. In his other works too, particularly *Novum Organum* (1620), Bacon remains a true classical scholar, The Renaissance spirit gave him the direction of his genius, his utilitarianism is only a combined force with 'humanism' of a special kind. Even those few essays in our selection are evidence enough of the quality of his art.

Bacon subtitled his *Essays* as *Counsels Civil and Moral.* He did it under the Renaissance influence of serving a utilitarian purpose. Bacon recounts the practical utility of friendship in his essay 'Of Friendship', especially two kinds - 'peace in the affections and support of the judgement', and he wrote this essay to serve a practical and, exactly at the request of a friend Toby Matthew in 1623. The classical references in the essay are all too numerous, as if all efforts were carefully made to cast a utilitarian subject into a literary mould. This trend is almost everywhere to be noted and it has supplied a new flavour to his dish.

Bacon takes almost the Mediaeval view of a faculty like ambition in 'Of Ambition'. Ambition is sought to be explained pseudo-philosophically in terms of the Mediaeval humour theory, there it is of the category of choler fad that even physically affects the subject. Although the subject could have been a true philosophical and psychological discourse. Bacon does follow none of the course, rather he makes a utilitarian pastiche of the two in which his true quality of style presents itself.

One of the earliest essays, 'Of Studies', first published in 1597, is self-evident of Bacon's witty and aphoristic style not really the marks of immaturity of the creative mind, but of the native trend of its creativity. The mind is basically analytical, quite obvious from the initial classification of three different ends that studies serve - 'Studies serve for delight, for ornament, and for ability', it remains ever so all through the essays, only in aphoristic generalization the mind is able to make a synthesis as here 'Reading maketh a full man; conference a ready man; and writing an exact man'.

Bacon differs not only from his French counterpart, but also from all those later essayists, particularly Steele and Addison of the next rallying point, in one clear view that his utilitarian outlook is never prompted by any public criticism of private follies. The essay 'Of Superstition' could very well be an 18th century essay published in the *Spectator* or the *Tatler* or of one in the still later *Rambler*. But Bacon's representative treatment makes it quite different. Bacon's is not a social duty done in vein of humour, criticism fictionalised in form. Here is superstition studied as a universal or general theme, as a part of human nature doing harm as it does in every individual, more than atheism.

'Of Truth' represents Bacon's later stage of writing. The essay was published in 1625. The treatment is a little philosophic, of course it is not of the philosophic inquiry of *Novum Organum*. Bacon's Latinism in construction and expression is no hindrance to a clear pursuit of the mind's movement. Truth is a realistic study in philosophic terms. It is better joined with lie or falsehood to serve its worldly purpose, 'that mixture of falsehood is like alloy in coin of gold and silver, which may make the metal work the better, but it embaseth it'.

Bacon is aphoristic in expression and utilitarian in outlook, although he does not take a social view of his art as do the two 18th century essayists in English literature. He is quite abreast of classical learning in language and style. Essay in his hand is really a reflection of his Renaissance mind and the strength of his personality. As a prose stylist in his essays Bacon is more pliable than he is in his *Advancement of Learning*.

Addison: a critic of manners

Addison and Steele share a critical outlook with the satirists of their age, particularly Pope and Swift, although they adopt a different method, not the method of satire but exactly the method of humour. Both the essayists write periodical essays and get them published in the *Spectator* and the *Tatler*. Of the two Addison is more acute a critic of manners which exactly do not fall within the scope of satire and under the category of social offence.

Addison is a master of humour, he knows the true measure of humour, one that does not hurt, nor offers anything that can be published by law but something that can easily excite a sense of enjoyment by exposition of incongruities. All his Coverley parers are full of this enjoyment. The Author himself is in the role of the Spectator. Sir Roger de Coverley is himself, a good study of society. He is a young man grown old crossed in love by 'a widow of the next county to him.' He remained a loving and loved bachelor the rest of his life, a Squire Western type without marriage.

Sir Roger and Will Wimble together make a good pair of upper class reduced opulence, particularly Will Wimble. Addison makes humour of their position and this making humour is a sort of lively criticism. A passage from the conclusive paragraph of the essay, 'Sir Roger...' will make it clear:

> Will Wimble's is the case of many a younger brother of a great family, who had rather see their children starve like gentlemen, than thrive in a trade or profession that is beneath their quality. This humour fills several parts of Europe with pride and beggary.

Addison's criticism is paired with lively humour always, 'Women and Liberty' is a humour of the position of women more free in England but to little advantage to morals. A party is well replenished where there are fair women. It seems to be a pleasant banter upon the political parties and role of women, a modest criticism of suffragettes long before its time. The conclusion of the essay is a good pointer: 'Thus may the fair sex contribute to fix the peace of a brave and generous people...'

In 'The Man of the Town' Addison makes fun of the upstartism of the town with no knowledge of book and pedantry of the bookish scholars, both equally withdrawing from nature and geniality of life. It is in the name of the knowledge of the world that the towns people hate bookish knowledge and in the name of the knowledge of books the pedants ignore knowledge of the world. Addison recommends neither of them, this reaction is recorded clearly. 'The worst kind of pedants among learned men, are such as are naturally endowed with a very small share of common sense, and have read a great number of books without taste or distinction.' The political Upholsterer is yet another funny character that Addison paints to underline the oddity of his attitude. He thinks more of the problem of the kings and potentates of the world and completely forgets the problems of his own home, as for example the marriage of his grown up daughter: 'None that I heard of and asked him whether he had yet married his eldest daughter. He told me, "No, But pray... tell me sincerely, what are your thoughts about the kind of Sweden...".'

One of Addison's sincere criticism is of the prejudice and superstition of his people. He takes up this subject in a vein of gossip under title 'Omens'. Addison's essays are mainly popular gossip in form and style. He is often gossipy as particularly in this essay. Whatever Addison's criticism of manners of society it is not hortative like Dr. Johnson's criticism in his Rambler essays. It takes exactly the line of humour.

Addison as Essayist with special reference to The Dream

Steele and Addison are friends and contemporaries and as essayists hold a significant place in the development of the art in-between Bacon and the essayists of the Romantic movement. From Bacon to the 18th century essayists is an enormous progress, a progress towards the flexibility of the style which can, and very well did later, accommodate fiction. To this style Addison's contribution is greater than that of his friend.

Bacon's compactness is gone, the attained flexibility in the method of presentation makes room for various stray elements and does it in a manner that represents Addison's humour better than anything else. As a good example we have here the essay 'The Dream' in which Addison's style is expressly allegorical. If one can ignore sense or its underlying implication the essay reads like a story. But sense is impossible to ignore, Addison is socially very conscious, not less conscious than his friend Steele, the adopted technique is only an effective means to his end, though the means is quite interesting.

The dream is the matter, but not like the dream of Charles Lamb closely personal, it is of the 18th century character, essentially objective, objective in the author's treatment. The author is only a disinterested observer. Addison's Coverley Papers are Spectator's papers. What Addison observed in society and life at large is delineated with the touch of his brush, so the picture cannot but produce an effect. The dream of humanity is thoroughly probed and delightfully painted, the humour lies in the painting. In the dream of the author a vast heap of human deformities and infirmities is gathered mountain high in a field, they are shaken off by every description of men and women, 'but there was not a single vice or folly thrown into the whole heap'.

The *Tatler* and the *Spectator* were meant for extra social duty of literature, but they are not in Addison's hands dry moral disquisitions as almost all the *Rambler* essays in Dr. Johnson's hands were. Addison does his moral duty and at the same time invents his own instrument. He makes essay a pleasant treat, not simply effort in moral and civil counsels as in the hands of Bacon, and paves the way for another literary genre called novel. 'The Dream' fully redeems this side of the author's quality. The essay could have been a satire, a good play of Jonsonian character, but it has not been owing to the author's abiding sympathy for the people who make themselves ludicrous by seeking to shed their present deformities in exchange for yet more unbearable infirmities of body and mind.

At least half the duty of the author is a reformer's duty, but the duty is discharged in his artist's role. Dream is only a cover for exposing the human illusion of unreal happiness. The real happiness the author suggests by Patience is contentment and is with one's own lot. Addison has not projected his own personality as Lamb has done in most of his essays, but he has in perfect agreement with his age objectified his stand with only a stamp of his personality in his style. 'The Dream' bears it out thoroughly:

> '...the phantom, who had led them into such gross delusions was commanded to disappear. There was sent in her stead a goddess of a quite different figure...'

exactly to rule the people's mind. This is how Addison does his social duty by suggesting a solution stylistically.

Addison: his The Man of the Town

Addison is a good critic of his age, but a critic with a good sense of humour, humour that reveals truth with pleasure. He does it best in 'The Man of the Town'. Will Honeycomb is only a fictitious character introduced in several of his essays which foreshadow Dicken's *Pickwick Papers,* a book that improves upon the *Coverley Papers.* Will Honeycomb is introduced as the friend of Mr. Roger de Coverley who is again Addison's own representation.

The Man of the Town, Mr. Will Honeycomb, is only a type of affectation which Addison hated most, a figure of humour whose life provides not exactly fun but humour. He could have been a good Dickensian character had he been reserved for him. The only difference is, Addison makes him a true object of criticism, lively humour though, not harsh or morally pungent as in the *Rambler* essays; but Dickens precludes all criticism, because he wants only to understand and enjoy.

Will Honeywomb does not come within the reach of the arms of the law, all his offences are only follies, all city-bred follies. The humour is, those follies he makes use of to ward off another great evil, pedantry. Addison seems to be more offended to pedantry than to the folly of adventurism. Addison's art is making humour of fighting one evil by another while himself remaining non-committed to either with broad simper upon his lips.

Will Honeywomb's coming in contact with a coquette and writing misspelt letters and trying to cover up his lack of education by means of his pretended or real hate for pedantry are humour enough, even subtler than the humour of Dickens, undoubtedly of Ben Jonson.

In The Man of the Town Addison makes fun of the upstartism of the town with no knowledge of books and pedantry of the bookish scholars, both equally withdrawing from nature and geniality of life. It is in the name of the knowledge of the world that the towns people hate bookish knowledge and in the name of the knowledge of books the pedants ignore knowledge of the world. Addison recommends neither of them, this reaction is recorded clear, 'The worst kind of pedants among learned men, are such as are naturally endowed with a very small share of commonsense, and have read a great number of books without taste or distinction.'

Addison, however, shows his essential sanity of outlook by an indirect revelation of a solid support to a culture that strikes a perfect balance between book learning and knowledge of life.

Addison's Art of Characterization

Addison and Steele made their contribution to the two major Periodicals, the *Tatler* and the *Spectator* in the first few years of the 18th century. Addison has made his purpose clear in the very first paper of the *Spectator*, he makes it clear in the last half sentence of the Paper, "for the inspection of all such papers as may contribute to the advancement of the public weal."

Addison and Steele kept intact their social purpose in all their writings, particularly Addison as the observing eye of the whole club. He made his observations through a spectator, he observed not only the social background of his contemporary age but also the human manners and activities by means of some characters. Steele of course describes the major characters of the club in Number 2 of the Coverley Papers; the characters then seem to be social types. In the treatment of Addison all those characters attain some sort of individuality.

Addison makes Sir Roger De Coverley really a curious character, a figure of humour. He starts from where Steele left him. Sir Roger was a Baronet, a gentleman of Worchestershire, of an ancient family. Steele describes him as a bachelor 'crossed in love by a perverse beautiful widow'. Addison develops him further into a full figure of humour.

It is Addison who makes a unique company of Sir Roger and Mr. William Wimble. It is an odd company which by forces of interaction develops both the characters. Will Wimble came down to stay at Sir

Roger's house for a whole week, he was a typical younger brother of a Baronet and 'descended of the ancient family of the Wimble' Sir Roger was then fifty-six and Mr. Wimble was between forty and fifty. Sir Roger represents one type and Mr. Wimble another, a curious type of impoverished landlord, not exactly landlord but younger brother of a landlord, 'bred to no business, and born to no estate'.

Addison covers a wider canvas of the early 18th century society in the countryside by means of a number of characters, Sir Roger and Will Wimble are of course the two major types representing the two tiers of upper middle class, now in the current of changes not all to their liking. Sir Roger at the church is really a figure of fun sometimes elevated to the plane of humour, as his odd manners offer enough enjoyment revealing at the same time a universal truth of nature.

Addison did not simply confine himself to the study of the countryside, he also made a choice of characters from town. The Man of the Town is a typical character of town snobbery. He poses for a man of wide knowledge. He is too much gossipy, in his gossip he includes all the trivialities of life. He seems to be a true relic of Chaucer's Canterbury Pilgrims.

Another curious character represents the political predisposition of the age. Addison's political upholsterer makes a fun of all his political efforts. He is vainly trying to keep up his position by means of a show of his deep interest in matters political, although at home he is completely an unsuccessful man. He has a scrambling family, left uncared for, because he has no time to do it. There is simply a touch of irony in this leader earnestly requesting the author to lend him half a crown.

Addison in his studies of character clearly maintained his sense of humour and his keen insight into the manners of activities of his own society. His characters are mainly types, the major types of the ancient tradition and modern interpolation, although he does not end simply there. His selected types do also attain some sort of individuality in their responses and reactions to others. By means of characterization and his true knowledge of life in society Addison foreshadows a new species of literature called fiction.

The Superannuated Man: Lamb's autobiographical style

Lamb is in most of his essays, particularly personal essays, thoroughly autobiographical. The presentment of autobiography in different essays is quite revealing of Lamb's quality of humour. Personal essays Hazlitt too has written, but Lamb's difference from Hazlitt is mainly to be noted in this personal relevance to his humour. Hazlitt often laughs at his readers but Lamb simply laughs with them and shares their enjoyment.

The Superannuated Man fully reveals how self-projection of the author can be the guiding force of his humour. The essay is apparently an account of the pathos of a superannuated clerk, essentially Lamb's own life. Everyone knows Lamb had no University degree, he was early in clerical service directly from school, as the clerk is here. *The Southsea House* is a personal essay in which Lamb talks of his colleagues more than himself, but *The Superannuated Man* is a little different as an autobiographical account stylistically more mature and in point of humour more inward. It differs from *Dream Children* because it avoids the mask of a dream, it deals with something more penetrating than dream.

The essay is almost a close literal parallel to Lamb's life, Elia rightly replaced by Lamb as the plan of the *Essays of Elia* has it. Thirty-six years of service, the service of a dreary type, made the clerk feel like Lamb and the early release from his dull duty led him also into a crisis of feeling, very common in such life of uninteresting daily round, but nowhere so thoroughly brought out with so unsurpassed a personal pathos as here. Lamb's humour lies in a close representation of his own life in the life of the clerk and in the equal problem of his life of work and of his life of uninterrupted leisure. Lamb proves himself a great artist by his ability to depict it so lovingly.

Lamb's London is Wordsworth's nature, we know it. The clerk's life in service and his life of idleness can be very well a common lot of every clerk; but the clerk's London life during holidays is specific and undoubtedly Lamb's own experience. His love for the busy week-day London with the prospect of old book shops opened for exploration and enquiries is Lamb's love, the absence of that treat on holidays and Sundays is a source of annoyance that can be only Lamb's.

The name Elia is only a cover for Lamb who is always in search of an opportunity for mystification of his own case. Lamb would not like his great contemporary Hazlitt project his personal history, as in *On going a Journey* or *The Fight;* he has a different taste, a different humour, always offering his readers an extra dose of enjoyment in their applied efforts to detect him under cover however thin it might be. In this essay the cover is thin and delightfully penetrable.

CHAPTER III

ELIZABETHAN SONNETS

Wyatts as a Sonneteer

Wyatt is a true connoisseur of lyric verse, in his love for poetry he found new areas and yet unknown energy during his travel abroad. In 1527 he brought to England a new form of verse from Italy, which later supplied vitality and force to Elizabethan lyricism. His master was Petrarch not always successful. He only blazed the way for English sonnet.

Petrarch's sonnets were original, the inspired rendering of passion, passion that was his own; but Wyatt's sonnets were formal imitation, passion also a part of his imitated form, obviously not all out of his personal experience though he too had a mistress. Even his close imitator Surrey became a better artist, he at least detected the secret of Petrarchan sonnets, the poet's love for Laura. So he sang his love of an imagined lady in his sonnets.. Wyatt sang of love, but was not sure of his lady, the king's with Ann Boleyn was not a sure case. That was really a set-back in his song of passion.

Wyatt is a pioneer of the early stage, and all his immaturities are attributed to it. His seriousness and sincerity are really that of an innovator. He is neither like Sidney nor like Spenser who perfect the form in their own way and pave the way for even a better artist Shakespeare. Personal passion, out of their own experience, made them truly passionate and supplied them new strength. Wyatt had really to overcome the lack of that opportunity, his mistress is hardly within his reach. He had no lady to fall in love with as easily as others had, nor had he like Surrey conceived the necessity of a love inspiration for full sincerity. So love has hardly any passionate sincerity in most of his sonnets.

Wyatt's sighs and supplications are almost formal in imitation as it were of Petrarch. He is himself in most cases less chivalric than Sidney, he can tell his mistress hard truths. It is possible for him to bid farewell not only to his mistress, but to love also:

'Farewell love and all thy laws for ever;
The baited hooks shall tangle me no more;
Senec and plato call me from thy lore.'

Wyatt's 'I find no peace' sonnet is a close representation of his excellence as a sonneteer at the earliest stage of its inception. He recalls in this sonnet some tremor of heart of Philip Sidney. He does not know how to address his mistress, it is very difficult to address a king's wife as such, a king who was ill-reputed for a wife-killer in history! He has only to undergo a crisis of feeling heart-throb, which has no definite end, either sorrow or solace.

The poem is, therefore, full of contradiction in terms of expression. The poet is full with an experience, 'Likewise displeaseth both death and life.' He only knows that love is the cause of his crisis - in other words, 'my delight is causer of this strife'.

The side of form is also less perfect, especially in relation to Sonnet's later development in this land in the hands of masters like Sidney, Spenser and Shakespeare. Wyatt at times imitates Petrarchan form not all correctly, his imitation even in this poem is not really very regular; the Octave and Sestet parts are regularly formed, but the rhyme scheme is sadly irregular, as for example 'done' ill-rhymes with 'on'.

I find No Peace: Analysis of its theme and style

Wyatt has not written too many sonnets, not more than 20 in all. The present poem is quite representative, though with all the signs of a beginner, more care is paid to the side of form only lately imported by him from the Continent. The sonnet 'I find no peace', though carefully modelled on petrarchan form, seems not to be absolutely successful, again marked with the inconveniences of a pioneer.

The rhyme scheme is not really very happy, 'ice' rimes but ill with 'wise', such instances are not rare in this poem as also in others of the poet. The sonnet of course has a clear division of Octave and Sestet, the last two lines form a couplet. The poem shows a rhyme system that can be represented by ab, ba, ab, ba, cd, cd, ee.

The theme of the sonnet is of course Petrarchan love, but love of a kind that discards exact Petrarchan parallelism. It is not exactly as Laura's lover heaved a sigh, it is all too bitter for that. The treatment of love here betrays the fact that the poet can also write satires. Wyatt is eventually a satirist. The poem seems to be full of self-accusation, a sort of self-satire and finally a satire on love itself.

The poet is only sure that he finds no peace, but really he is not sure of his success in love, nor in a mood to dedicate himself completely to the passion and the lady. The concealed remote suggestion is that the lady is beyond his reach, he only a victim of a passion that takes away his peace of mind, leaves him in a deplorable condition. Really his lady was a king's spouse, the king of Henry VIII's status who ultimately sent him to the Tower.

The poem gives no idea of any high and noble status of love, but only points it as 'causer of the strife', destroyer of peace. No high value of love one can derive out of this poem, perhaps it is so because the poet's mistress from a higher station remained only as a source of pain, not the kind pain Sidney felt, but the pain that finally leads to self-pity.

Wyatt's treatment of love

Wyatt was not merely a dreamy lover like his friend and junior Surrey, Wyatt was really a lover, but his love is not like Sidney's. Sidney's lady was only married to a different man, Lord Rich, not at all above his station in life; Sidney's love for Penelope Devereux is a straight development which begins before the lady's marriage and continues after her marriage elsewhere. Wyatt's love is of an irregular kind, a sort of adulterous relation with a king's married wife, unchivalric and undignified.

This difference between Sidney's case and Wyatt's lends peculiarity to their specific cases and controls their treatment of love in their sonnets and their ideas. Petrarch exerts influence upon both, but the influence on Wyatt is more on form than on the very sanctity of love. Wyatt's is purely a court calumny which of course not Sidney's although he is more in the court circle. No exaltation of passion is noted in Wyatt's 'I find no peace' as it is to be noted in *Astrophel and Stella* series, particularly, in 'Loving in truth' piece.

Actually Wyatt had no higher idea of passion, it has not found any link with peace, passion here does not necessarily invite purity of heart, does not perhaps prove creative in force as in the case of Sidney. Love in Wyatt's sonnets is a disturbing passion, purely personal as later it would be found in Byron. It is no extension of passion to an ideal world of vision. If Sidney can be compared to Shelley Wyatt must be to Byron, of course Sidney lacks Shelley's Platonic view.

Wyatt is purely personal. He renounces love, as in 'A Renouncing of Love', love's integrity is nearly unknown to him, he has only intensity of passion, but no exaltation, no peace. He renounces love for peace, peace in his study of Seneca and Plato, curiously enough he never finds that Platonic ideal that lifts love above from the earthly mire of the body.

It is very difficult to form any idea of love from Wyatt's sonnets, because he has no philosophy of love, as Browning has, he has only personal reactions, and those reactions are often ironical or satiric. 'I find no peace' is neither philosophy nor chivalry, it is the 'causer of this strife', it is better comparable to Byron's 'When we two parted'.

Sidney and Wyatt: their treatment of love theme

Wyatt is the pioneer of English sonnet and Sidney the first step in excellence in the art. Both belong to the same period, only Wyatt a little earlier. Their theme is the same, but their difference lies in their treatment of it. Both deal with love, but they are poles apart in their reaction and approach to it. Perhaps their private experience is mainly responsible for this divergence of approach and attitude.

Ann Boleyn in the life of Wyatt was a bitter dish, but Penelope Devereux in Sidney's life was expressly a source of pleasure in pain, of which true creative inspiration is the ultimate result.

The nature of their love makes all the difference. One loved a king's wife, particularly a killer king's, the king who sent him to the Tower, the other missed the chance by his wanton folly, Sidney must have explained it so to himself when Penelope was married to Lord Rich. The result was repulsion for one and impulsion for another. Wyatt's sonnets bear evidence of this repulsion and Sidney's *Astrophel* series is better called impulsion-inspired.

Both Sidney and Wyatt are in the circle of the court, Sidney more deeply. Watt is only a treason of love, so he could write 'Renouncing love', Sidney's is true fidelity that even marriage to another man cannot change its colour and character. Significantly Sidney can write 'Loving in Truth' Sidney's is true love, Watt's is passion which is still to attain its true sanctity. Wyatt knows how to deviate from it for a better substitute, from passion to Plato. 'I find no peace' sonnet depicts a peaceless state of passion, it is better not called love –'I love another, and thus I hate myself.'

Sidney's 'Loving in Truth' is true love that becomes creative. Love causes no frustration, but deepens into a sort of pain, pain that ultimately proves creative, just the Indian view of Sloka out of Soka. The poem is not only a good study of love that knows no frustration but shines ever brighter. The origin of sonnet is love, it is just so in this sonnet. Sidney first wanted to write about his love in imitation of Petrarch, but later he detects his folly. He finds imitation hardly able to match his passion. He sees passion itself is expression enough. It is wrong to imitate other's art to bring home to others one's true feelings. His discovery is 'look in thy heart and write'.

Love, as it is in this sonnet, is truth itself. It is never an undirected folly, it is too genuine for that, it is sacred. Love is here chivalric, almost in the Mediaeval tradition of heroic nobleness. It differs essentially from love in spenser, and completely from that of Wyatt's experience.

Loving in Truth: Sidney's love theme

All the sonnets in the Elizabethan tradition, from Wyatt down to Shakespeare, have love as their theme, of course in Shakespeare it has a curious originality. Sidney wrote sonnets to weep his woe out, obviously his life lies behind it. Love in Wyatt, Spenser and Sidney has three different reactions, Sidney's perhaps the most benign, and in the chivalric tradition.

'Loving in Truth' is really filled with the graceful dealings with love. Penelope Devereux could marry the poet, but the poet's initial neglect turned it otherwise, her marriage with Lord Rich left his charged with a powerful feeling which came out in the noblest possible renderings in the form of sonnet. The present poem is a record of one such moment of feeling. Love in Sidney is equivalent to truth. Love gives rise to pain, which is purely the poet's experience, but pain can inspire poetry as in India the first verse came out.

Love is the cause of all delicate feelings, a man's love for a woman is not simply sentimentalized in the lines of the sonnet, it attains the consummation of a divine feeling absolutely free from the conditions of the mundane outlook. Browning individualized love sentiment, Sidney did not, he only rarefied the sentiment— 'I sought fit words to paint the blackest face of woe' – the poet writes, but woe does not end in woe. Love is woe to him but not an ordinary woe, it turns to inspiration, it gives voice to feelings.

Sidney's love is original, personal and not conventional, essentially creative. When love can make one weep so nobly and gracefully, woe of loving does not remain ordinary sorrow. That is why the lover remains an Astrophel and the lady his Stella. In Sidney's 'Loving in Truth' sonnet love is inseparable from excellence of poetry. The poet does not want any extra-terrestrial heaven, the passion itself, fulfilled or not, is heaven on earth. On this point Sidney's treatment of love betrays some supra-chivalric quality. In the cult of chivalry there is no refusal, no betrayal, but in Sidney's poem betrayal also attains the beauty of creative ecstasy.

It is neither Spenser's case nor Shakespeare's; yet Sidney knows love is not an end in itself, although the lover may think so, or for the time being feels so. Love in Sidney's poem and life leaves the lover free to utilize the trail of passion to some other better end, as in the present poem the attainment of literary glory. When the glory is attained love then seems to be attuned to a higher end. Thus worldly love is at times considered the stepping stone to heaven. Sidney of course does not directly attribute that quality to love, he ends in this poem in love supplying the power of creativity as in the quoted last line –'Look in thy heart and write'.

Sidney and Spenser: their treatment of love

Sidney and Spenser both explore the wealth of sonnet and pave the way for Shakespeare to perfect the form and improve the approach to the theme, the theme of love. *Astrophel and Amoretti* series of sonnets are two landmarks in the developments of the borrowed art of Italy in its native English glow. Both originate from the personal experience of passion, essentially of two different kinds, and both taken together mark a sharp contrast to Wyatt's case.

Wyatt's is almost forbidden love which invited the king's wrath, making mistress of another's married wife is neither the case of Spenser nor that of Sidney, though the latter's case could have been but for its highly idealized character. *Astrophel and Stella* series of sonnets is Sidney's address to a married woman, Penelope Devereux, Lord Rich's wife, whom he missed by youthful indecision. It differs from Wyatt's case because it is all too idealised for a bodily contamination of sin and from Spenser's case because it attains its true grace out of disappointment of a hope for marriage.

Spenser's love is a fulfilment, his courtship of Elizabeth Boyle comes to a happy end. So it could not have been so idealised as it has been in *Astrophel* series. Spenser writes actually to immortalize love, the name of his lady, Sonnet No. 75 is a clear testimony:

'My verse your virtues rare shall eternize,
And in the heavens write your glorious name.'

But Sidney has just the opposite course to take, love is what makes him write, it is his truth, it immortalises his verse:

'Loving in truth and fain in verse my love to show,
That the (dear She) might take some pleasure of my pain'.

Both the poets got their inspiration to write in this form under the influence of Petrarch, but were ultimately guided by their own respective cases. Spenser could write a prologue and an epilogue like Prothalamion and Epithalamion respectively to the actual sonnet series, in the glorification of love and marriage, his own and his friend's. Spenser's special case induced it, his love realised in marriage held him tight to mundane fulfilment and earthly satisfaction.

Like Kalidas's 'Meghdut' Spenser sends spring and flowers as messengers to his love to tell her 'the joyous time will not be stayed unless she do him by the forelock take'. The lesson of love as in Sonnet No. 70 of the *Amoretti* series is simply impossible in Sidney's case. Such an attempt would have been desanctifying to his idealised love. Spenser can idealise love as much as he can by means of his verse, so sinks a little lower than Sidney's love which has strength enough to idealise his verse. Spenser knows as in Sonnet No. 75, his lady cannot die when his verse know how to eternize her. Shakespeare differs from both. Shakespeare's is an easy escape from the very claim of idealization. Like his plays the sonnets are life.

Shakespeare: as Sonneteer

What actually prompted Shakespeare to write a vast number of sonnets, as many as 154, is not known for certain, except from internal evidence of the series of sonnets. They were written over seven years between 1593 and 1600, and collected by Mr. W.H. from Shakespeare's private friends, and numbered later by the compiler when published in 1609. The sonnets are of two series, the first series of 126 addressed to a friend, the rest to a Dark Lady who is a cause of bitter feeling between the two friends.

Up to Spenser Elizabethan sonnet has a steady development, Shakespeare does not really belong to that stretch of evolution, he is a world apart, and that is the uniqueness of his position. He differs from all other Elizabethan sonneteers, particularly Sidney and Spenser, in the choice of his themes, which is unconventional. Shakespeare has no lady to love and to address his sonnets all tempered by the quality of his passion for her. In the second series of sonnets the lady is only a Dark Lady for whom the poet has only hatred.

Mystery gathers about the true 'begetter' of the sonnets. The source of inspiration is a young friend, critics are yet uncertain about his identity, now opinion is more in favour of the Earl of Southampton than Pembroke. Critics are still more uncertain about the identity of the Dark Lady. I think Bernard Shaw's view is more curious in his indirect suggestion in the play, *The Dark Lady of the Sonnets*. It is certain that Shakespeare's *Sonnets* has a special status with an autobiographical interest more concrete than any of his plays.

It is sure Shakespeare did not imitate anybody, not even Petrarch as most of the Elizabethan sonneteers did. Shakespeare's case is unique. He develops his own apparatus and is guided by his own sentiment and outlook. Not only his rhyme scheme is a little different and the 12 lines of the sonnet are concluded by a couplet almost in every case, but also the love theme has a strange character. It is a love for a friend, the spoilage of whose beauty he laments and whose excellence he evokes in glowing terms. Even more excitingly exceptional is Shakespeare's lament of the alienation of his friend by means of the Dark Lady and his deprivation of place and honour by a rival poet.

These are all new elements of personal experience exciting bitterness of feeling in the Sonneteer. Shakespeare is a master who does not feel really like Sidney nor like Spenser that anything else can either prod his pen or his pen seeks to idealize it. He is of this world and makes love a thing of this world, life itself is his ideal. Even his idea of love as in some of his sonnets, particularly Sonnet No. 116, is not unearthly idealization. It is the true discovery of its essential nature - 'Love's not time's fool, though rosy lips and cheeks within his bending sickle's compass come..'

Shakespeare's contribution to the art and theme of Sonnet as against other sonneteers of his age

Wyatt and Surrey completed the first phase of English Sonnet the next phase is started by Sidney and continued by Spenser. Shakespeare only perfected the form in his own way. Shakespeare is always unique, whether in plays or poems or in private composition of sonnets. These three Elizabethan poets are essentially personal in their sonnet, Shakespeare rather elusively. With regard to Sidney and Spenser the history is known to all, but Shakespeare's case is a mystery that requires to be explored.

Sidney and Spenser had their sources of inspiration clearly defined, they had to write their series of sonnets under the direct influence of love, love of two different kinds, one Romantically unavailing though inspiring to an Arcadian vision, the other only a suspense resulting in a more romantic success. Shakespeare's is none of it, neither the Arcadian passion nor success more enjoyable by suspense. Love in Shakespeare's two series of sonnets belongs to a different order, he makes it earthly but does not make it as Spenser does.

Shakespeare is always on the hard surface of the earth, the surface that has mystery enough. Shakespeare is subjective in his sonnets; he 'unlocks his heart' here, but not as the other two sonneteers do, they adopt more or less the Italian form to evoke their personal passion, but Shakespeare only adjusts his own passion to his own frame. The passion is also less romantic and perfectly under his control. He had also a mistress, the second series suggests, but he is less romantically passionate, his passion is also a mystery, at least curious, only fascinated by a Dark Lady who ultimately deceived him with his friend.

Love in his first series of sonnets is contrasted with the Time that changes. Shakespeare's view of love, a permanent element, confined to woman question neither. It can be very well a man's love for a man, such is Shakespeare's case. The mystery of such a passion, as Marlowe's Edward II's for his friend, is not yet adequately probed. Equally mysterious is Shakespeare's relationship with the Dark Lady. None of the contemporary sonneteers had the mystery about his sonnets. Shakespeare has extended the area of sonnet. So long sonnet was the true vehicle of love, Shakespeare made the first step towards its being more accommodative a vehicle. Already he introduces a different kind of love than one for a woman. Even his love for a woman is not like that conventional love one may deal with in sonnets. Shakespeare's treatment of love in second series is more like sarcastic banter.

Form of Shakespeare's sonnets is also revolutionized. Sidney and Spenser more or less kept the Petrarchan form metric system was also not varied. But Shakespeare makes the form more pliable and a little more free, the example is Sonnet No. 116. Shakespeare is more used to Blank verse, rhyme scheme is a little more relaxed and paves the way for Milton and Wordsworth.

Sidney as a sonneteer: Loving in Truth

Of the three great sonneteers of the Elizabethan period Sidney is undoubtedly one; his standard of attainment is surpassed by only Shakespeare. He obviously differs from his great contemporary Spenser, the difference is mainly due to two different kinds of experience in life. From Wyatt to Spenser all those sonneteers are more or less under Patrarch's influence. Shakespeare is of course an exception, his originality is unquestioned.

Sidney is Petrarchan only in form and love theme; Sidney is perfection of Petrarchan form. 'Loving in Truth' is a 14-line sonnet of the rhyme scheme – Octave ab, ab, ab, ab, Sestet cd, cd, ee, – regular Petrarchan form, no trace of Wyatt's rhyming defect. Theme of his sonnet is love, personal love as Petrarch's was, but yet the quality of reaction is highly individualistic. His reaction is exceptionally chivalric.

Sidney is the author of *Arcadia*, even his *Astrophel* and *Stella* series is not far removed from Arcadian idealism, of course idealism is not borrowed, it is in his blood, personally experienced. There lies his difference from the continental outlook. More than any one in the whole of the Elizabethan period he wrote from his heart, even Shakespeare did not do it with the same intensity of passion as Sidney did.

'Loving in Truth' is a representative sonnet of Sidney. Perhaps no sonnet better explains Sidney's quality and mood. Sidney was all along noble, of the very temperament of a Knight, no less noble in love than in anything else. As to a Mediaeval Knight so also to him love is equivalent to truth. Love a theme of honour. Even Shakespeare has not known this nobleness, loving a woman with all seriousness and sincerity. Lord Rich's lady can never be a Dark Lady. Her denial can inspire no bitterness as in Shakespeare it has done. Love's woe is also like enjoyment, refusal like yielding.

Sidney knew from his own experience, there is a clear statement of this knowledge, that love itself, when it is sincere, can be a great source of creative energy. For this knowledge Sidney did not require any European lesson. As Petrarch was self-taught, taught by his own experience, so was it also to Sidney. Sidney in that sense Elizabethan Petrarch.

Penelope failed him because she married another man, but she could not fail him as a great source of inspiration. The sonnet 'Loving in Truth' gives one the idea that Sidney was well-read in European sources, but it did not serve him as well as own experience, his own heart, 'look in thy heart and write'.

Shakespeare's treatment of love in his sonnets

Love is a major theme of Shakespeare's plays, particularly comedies; love is again the theme of his two long poems, *Venus and Adonis* and *The Rape of Lucrce*. In Sonnets, however, love has assumed a new form. Neither the idea of love nor its treatment in Shakespeare's sonnets parallels those either in Sidney or Spenser, nor can it be explained by Platonic idea.

Shakespeare's Sonnet No. 116 is really an account of a love which should better be called friendship. There is woman in Shakespeare's concept of love elsewhere, in his comedies as also in his second series of sonnets, but not in his first series. Here Shakespeare differs from Sidney and Spenser. Both Sidney and Spenser had personal experience of woman's love, Shakespeare had it or not is not known. Shakespeare's married life is not the source of inspiration behind even the second series of sonnets.

Sonnet No. 116 accounts for a love which is a general law of human nature and not specific although the friend whom he addresses here is an individual, may be either Southampton of Pembroke. His love for this man equals a man's love for a woman. Shakespeare has done more than

Sidney or Spenser has done for a woman. Sidney's love for Penelope Devereux remains unchanged even after her marriage with another man. In respect of his friend Shakespeare makes a similar trial of love. The meeting of the two minds, if it occurs, must endure in spite of obstacles.

Shakespeare's mistress, a Dark Lady who came to cause separation between them and strain their relationship, does not contribute to Shakespeare's idea of love as in this sonnet No. 116. Shakespeare sets love against time, time that changes everything, he finds his love not 'Time's fool'. It is like the fixed star that directs the course of the ship. It leads and directs human life upon its proper course. At least in this sonnet love is not so much a passion as it is a directing force. It is all good, force that steadies life. Shakespeare knows no further philosophy, far less Platonic philosophy.

Shakespeare's love in his sonnets is really not the love in this comedies. It is of one kind in the first series, the appreciation of beauty, and a feeling appreciation of qualities of another kind in the second series. The poet's mistress has no beauty yet she could be his mistress, she must have Cleopatra type of bewitchment that can enthrall the poet's mind and heart. It is passion not asexual as it was in the first series. Here Shakespeare is just upon the hard crust of the earth. Shakespeare's relationship with the mistress is highly psychological, becomes more so when it acts as a divisive force between the poet and his friend. Shakespeare's love is not comparable to that of any other poet's life of his age. Wyatt's bitterness of feeling could have been his, but Shakespeare's satire in the second series of sonnets attains almost the quality of humour and thus marks a wide difference.

Love and Time: The twin principles of Shakespeare's sonnets

Shakespeare's treatment of Time in his sonnets has a deep implication particularly when estimated with love. Love and time run parallel in some of his sonnets, especially sonnets of the first series. Time is the eternal force that has seen the end of everything. In Shakespeare's conception only Love remains outside its influence, such is at least the idea of Sonnet No. 116.

In Sonnet No. 116 love is regarded above the influence of time, it is not 'Time's fool'. Everything changes in the course of time, but true love does not. Shakespeare's love for his friend must not he feels. But in the second series of sonnets the idea has a change, Shakespeare's love for the Dark Lady has a mixed quality, time has introduced a new element of hatred, yet love remains, because love is a psychological fascination in spite of contempt.

Shakespeare's love for his friend, of course, is of a different force. In the second series it is psychologically very complex by the intervention of the Dark Lady. It seems to be Time's ravages. Even in Time's ravages love retains its hold, the poet finds it 'in my mistress eyes'. He confesses 'I, my mistress' thrall'. 'Love's fear heats water, water cools not love.' In spite of changes in the poet's mind for the mistress love still remains, but this time love is a passion, a passion that is completely different from that of the first series. Time cannot kill it, but can change its nature and character.

In the first series time is guiding force in the Universe, Shakespeare reminds his friend of the inescapable force of time, reminds him urged by his personal interest. The poet feels his friend is already forty, time will not halt its march if he does not utilize it in the proper moment. He can still make an indelible mark upon the canvas of time which the poet's verse cannot even ensure. He pays a glowing tribute to his beauty, but he is afraid the ravages of time will not spare it. So he must take to an alternative method to eternise his beauty and thereby escape the erosion of time.

Time is painted in this series of sonnets as 'Devouring Time', it is 'Old Time', though it proves 'bloody tyrant Time'. Youth, honour, and the beauty of the body are within the stroke of 'Times scythe' - 'Nothing against Time's scythe can make defence'. The poet asks his friend to perpetuate his youth and beauty in a new form exactly as his own by marriage and by having children through consummation of marriage.

In Sonnet No. 116 in this series Shakespeare places love beside eternal march of Time. The force of true love alone survives the assault of Time, a love like his for his friend. Shakespeare perhaps demonstrates it in the second series where in spite of sufficient reason for love turning gall it retains its hold upon his mind and heart. Even for friendship and love he can forget the changes Time has brought about in their relation.

CHAPTER IV

ELIZABETHAN DRAMA AND SHAKESPEAREAN SCHOLARSHIP

The Tempest: Is Caliban a born devil?

The agreed date of *The Tempest* is something before 1612, December 27, the date of the betrothal night of Elizabeth of Bohemia. And the very occasion has to some extent influenced Shakespeare's pen and the pattern of the play. The play belongs to the last phase of Shakespeare's writing, the play itself seems to be Shakespeare's valediction. The Caliban episode in the play should at least be viewed in the context of this change of attitude in Shakespeare.

The name Caliban must have been taken from one of Montaigne's essays in translation 'Of Canniballes', from which Gonzalo derived his wisdom. Florio's translation of Montaigne was first published in 1603. Now the name Caliban is an obvious distortion by means of transposition of letters of the word cannibal. Shakespeare has more or less maintained the native savagery of a cannibal in the character.

Caliban has been overphilosophized by the critics of Shakespeare, a poet like Browning supports them. We have already noted, Shakespeare had a practical purpose to serve with this play, the occasion is evidently a betrothal, so the tone is a little light and the mood is less serious, rather sportive in the play. Shakespeare's creation of the character is more or less comparable to another significant character of *Henry IV*, Falstaff.

Perhaps Maurice Morgann's estimate of Falstaff should have been transferred to the character of Caliban for a right judgement of Shakespeare's treatment of it. Shakespeare did not paint any of his characters with absolute disgust, rather even the most beastly character of his play is not deprived of Shakespeare's full sympathy. No doubt Caliban has not been. Quiller Couch tells us none of Shakespeare's readers 'would be disinclined to pay him on the head with "good dog good monster".

Caliban in the play of *The Tempest* is a savage character, we may not call him a 'noble savage'; Shakespeare differs much from Rousseau. Shakespeare's purpose with the character is fully served in the play. He has not made Caliban another Falstaff. He is a deformed creature and deformity goes even deeper than the physical deformity of Richard III. Again the evil that is in him is less revolting to Shakespeare's audience than it was with regard to Iago. Caliban is rightly to be assessed in the company of two other characters in the play, Stephano and Trinculo. Caliban is a savage below the level of humanity, and a sharp contrast to two other villains from a civilized society. Caliban is without any form and without a moral standard, whether he should be considered as a fish or simply a lump of flesh with human voice or what, Trinculo did not know. Devilish humanity in Trinculo and Stephano pairs well with Caliban's inhumanity, and Shakespeare's purpose with them is to ensure light enjoyment that the occasion of the play demands.

Trinculo, Stephano and Caliban are brought together in the play in a highly entertaining scene where Shakespeare has entirely discarded the moral view of things, so there is hardly any question of devil and deformity. The three characters are in their drinking bout and forget almost everything but their plot against Prospero and his daughter. Stephano offers him significantly 'to remove his fit': "He shall taste my bottle, if he have never drunk wine afore, it will go near to remove his fit." And Caliban offers him to lead him to the mastery of the island.

The entertaining scene of high treason and secret plot against Prospero is only an enjoyable light scene without any serious question of moral judgement. Shakespeare has done with any such issue as he has done with Falstaff and similar other characters, particularly in his comedies.

Caliban in Shakespeare's play of *The Tempest* is not a character that could be brought into the area of moral judgement. The occasion of the play absolutely precludes an issue like this. Again Shakespeare's all-embracing sympathy with every bit of his creation conflicts with such a moral view of his characters. Caliban is then a comic element with his shape, sound and unavailing revolt and also the timely revelation of his beastly savage predisposition.

King Lear: Storm Scene

Of all the tragedies of Shakespeare *King Lear* is undoubtedly most elemental; in tragic intensity it compares with the Greek tragedy of Sophocles and Aeschylus. The gloom that gathers in *King Lear* is nowhere to be found in Shakespeare's canon, only *Timon of Athens* comes nearer to it in the same effect.

In *King Lear* the most controversial scene is the storm scene. Perhaps no scene in *King Lear* provoked so widespread a debate among the critics as did the storm scene. Shakespeare's purpose in the scene is variously interpreted by different scholars of Shakespeare, as sometimes the role of the Fool. The storm scene is no dobut the climax of Lear's sufferings, and if the significance of the scene is sought to be explained, it must be explained with reference to the ultimate end of this suffering. It is commented often that 'through suffering Lear learns wisdom and attains salvation.'

The storm scene is dramatically very significant, it exhibits Shakespeare's dramatic excellence, the scene made to serve as the meeting point of three persons betraying different degrees of madness in them. It is here that Lear, the Fool and Edgar meet in one hovel and under the same inescapable atmosphere of the elemental fury of a storm. Even in the source play we have 'thunder and lightning' which appeared to be the voice of the divine intervening to save Leir and his friend Perillus'. That was no doubt a faint suggestion of an external stormy weather having an impact upon human destiny. Shakespeare of course took the suggestion and made it a great source of dramatic excellence serving to point out human regeneration.

Lear's sufferings outside curiously coincide with his suffering within himself; this dramatic coincidence of the external conflict with the internal is the true excellence of the storm scene, the manner in which Shakespeare transforms his source material in the scene is the true stamp of his genius far excelling the genius of his predecessor.

The central point of the storm scene is the attainment of spiritual health through the patience and endurance of suffering which is taken up as the starting point of close examination by Professor Jones Campbell. Professor Campbell of course covers in his analysis the Stoic philosophy and Christian humility in the very spiritual reawakening of King Lear in the storm scene. Professor Jones Danby of course takes exception to this particular line of interpretation and modifies the view by simply suggesting a clear difference between the suffering that is Stoic in nature and the suffering that is essentially Christian. Danby suggests a finer spiritual purpose that is achieved by a sort of Christian patience which is detected in King Lear in the storm scene.

Professor Heilman makes a significant observation in an article 'Reason in Madness' that Lear is mad but this madness has deeper reason which has a close parallel to the reason in the foolish jargon of Lear's Fool close beside his master. The coming together of the three madnesses in the same place is strikingly in agreement with a true spiritual purpose which Shakespeare must have served with the scene. Lear's coming to his senses even in his madness is clearly to be seen, particularly in the passage Act III, sc. 4, lines 106-9:

> Here is three on's are sophisticated: then art the thing itself. Unaccommodated man is no more but such a poor, bare, forked animal as thou art. Off, off, you lendings! Come, unbutton here!

Of the three Lear is no doubt really mad, Edgar only pretended madness and Lear's Fool made mad admixture of true philosophy with his foolish conceits. Lear is mad, mad for all his mistakes in his earlier life and for wrong decisions - all those errors in the judgement of true nature; but now sufferings led him to the extreme point of madness which gave rise to a sort of spiritual reawakening that gave him eyes to see things in their true colours, see with an all-embracing love. Shakespeare handles the storm scene in *King Lear* to serve a true artistic purpose that ends in inevitable spiritual effect.

The Fool in King Lear

In King Lear's tragedy of life Shakespeare has adopted a sustaining dramatic device— the device of parallelism and the device of contrast— the first by means of a unique sub-plot, the second by means of the striking role of the Fool. Professor Knights is right in pointing this out in his remarkable study of *King Lear*.

By the touch of Shakespeare's mighty genius most of the Elizabethan bricks were transformed into marble. The character of the Fool in *King Lear* is a wonderful example of such a transformation. The conventional Fool of the Elizabethan stage is transformed into a philosophical spokesman with a running commentary on the tragedy. The Fool enters, thanks to the master dramatic craftsmanship of Shakespeare, just at the moment when his presence is dramatically and most urgently needed. Lear is be fooled and the Fool answers the befooled King - 'Youth's a dog must to Kennel',- because the ways of the world are smooth enough to bear the presence of the truth. It is indirectly a comment on the first two daughters of King Lear who have cheated their father. The Fool sighs when Lear divided his kingdom between his first two daughters on the merit of their mouth made vows of love for him. They did weep for joy as he for 'sorrow sung''that such a king should play lo-peep and go to the fools among'. Thus the Fool is a protest of the sound commonsense against the foolishness of which Lear is a victim, but a protest pure and full of humour; yet his habitual foolery produces a tragic effect.

In *King Lear* the Fool has the maximum benefit of proverbial wisdom. He is not altogether a fool, but a friend, philosopher and guide of King Lear in the moment of his greatest distress. When Lear is on the verge of madness, Edgar only pretending madness, remarks—'the foul fiend bites my back'. The Fool still comments on the treachery of Lear's daughters by almost an axiomatic statement. 'He's mad that trust in the tameness of wolf, a horse's health, a boy's love or a courtezan's oath.'

'Life is a tale told by an idiot full of sound and fury signifying nothing' - the bitterest discovery that ever Macbeth made. The tale of life is told, the idiot is required no more. In the crisis of the action the tale of Lear's life is told. When it is told the voice of the Fool is heard no more. It vibrates still even after the last tragic blow to Lear. The babbling of the Fool vibrates in our memory as a wild dream before the break of day troubling the active life even after.

All serious dramatists — the classicists in particular — dislike intermingling of tragedy and comedy. Sidney outright condemned it. But Dryden supports the intermingling of tragedy and comedy on the ground of the accepted formula of comic relief.

The Fool in *King Lear* frequently serves as a moral tag and sometimes tries to produce a comic effect upon the audience. His words are most often bitter and ironical. We understand better the difference between the Fool in tragedy and the Fool in comedy. If the Fool in *King Lear* is a fool he is aware of the folly of others too. He asks Kent to take the Fool's cap on his head, because he wants to serve a man like Lear who has no kingdom, no power, no shelter, no resource whatsoever. He speaks in maxims to Lear:

Have more than thou showest,
Speak less than thou knowest,
Lend less than thou owest.

When Lear wants to know why Goneril frowns at him, the Fool answers in a sarcastic tone; 'thou wast a pretty fellow when thou hadst no need to care for frowning; now thou art an O without a figure; I am better than thou art now, I am a fool thou nothing.'

The role of the Fool in *King Lear* is functional. He is by no means a mere appendage to the drama. Rather he moves in lively intercourse with the characters and their passion in the drama. In him fun and frolic are sublimated and idealized into a tragic beauty when his heart is on the breaking point, he never speaks of his own suffering. His anguish is truly the anguish of sympathy. It has been rightly said that but for him the tragedy of Lear would not have been tragic in effect. We cannot but praise the art that makes the Fool an integral part of the scheme of tragedy.

The Fool appears in a complex role in King Lear. Miss Welsford in her very significant work *The Fool* acknowledges Lear's Fool as belonging to a class she calls 'The Sage Fool'. Shakespeare handles Lear's Fool more or less on the line of the Elizabethan and Jacobian tradition of court jester, but he deviates essentially by simply making him approach to the very spirit of tragedy that is Lear's. King Lear's Fool is unique in his role, very distinct from the role of Shakespeare's other fools either in comedy or in tragedy.

Lear's sufferings and redemption in King Lear

Of all the high tragedies of Shakespeare *King Lear* is most serious in its moral purpose. The seriousness is borne out by the introduction of a philosophic fool. All those inversion statements and enigmatical and ironical remarks by the Fool do not at all sound as foolish. They have a bone of serious evocation of truth.

The Fool's inversion utterances are really an essential symptom of wisdom. The Fool read well the true crisis of the King's situation, he saw into the cause of the King's sufferings, and by means of the lashing of his tongue he awakens true sense in the King's mind. It is through suffering that Lear learns wisdom and attains salvation.

Lear's most effective teacher is suffering, a suffering which was due to his folly. Lear was really self-centric right from the beginning of the story. Lear adopted a method of division of his Kingdom which was nothing but a reflection of his mad selfishness. Is it really a sane method to apportion property and kingdom according to the measure of love the three daughters had for him?

It is essentially out of a selfish motive that Lear adopted this method. It was highly anti-Christian in outlook. Sometimes it is thought Lear's ultimate redemption is perfectly the redemption of Christian values.

Lear was sadly wrong in his judgement of Cordelia's heart, as he was wrong in the assessment of the two other daughters' love for him. Lear's failure in judgement is in fact a failure of liberal outlook, he was blind with his own self concentration. Professor James Campbell interprets Lear's conversion as essentially Christian rather than stoical.

Professor John Danby explains Lear's redemption by means of Christian patience which essentially differs from stoic patience, Lear's mistake is mainly due to his impatience which is led to a kind of eccentricity. So the method of division of the kingdom is ultimately a mad method.

No doubt Lear's sufferings reach their climax in the storm scene. All his neglect by his daughters, particularly two, and their cruelty, all were really due to his folly. All these could not essentially alter the frame of his mind, he remained as he was before. Only in the storm scene true sense was dawning on him. The storm scene is the heart of the play. Even in the old Lear play it had a discernible speck. In the old play Leir and Perillius could not be murdered because of a divine intervention in the form of thunder and lightning. Shakespeare transforms this seminal speck into a wild fury of elements, and has made the scene highly dramatic.

The disharmony that has marked the world of men has also disturbed the physical order. The turmoil in the mind of Lear is reflected in the furies of elements. 'The storm is Lear's tutor. Lear's journey towards enlightenment begins from here. He is completely mad, but paradoxically this madness gives him the right measure of reason. Professor Heilman tells us when Lear goes completely mad in the storm he is certainly on the way to true wisdom.

Professor Heilman's most important chapter in this connection is 'Reason in Madness'. Really Lear can speak reason in madness. Lear only lately acquires awareness of the humanity common to himself and the lowest of the low. Lear took the storm as his well deserved punishment. 'Let the great Gods... find out their enemies.' Lear feels now even for a naked man come in the same hovel, he wants to provide some means of comfort to this man who seems to him only 'thing itself' 'unaccommodated man'.

Lear is in the storm scene back to Christian catholicity and love. Earlier Lear thought only of his own interest, his own comfort, his own whim. Now in his madness he feels for others and seriously wants to provide others with comfort. King Lear seems to be Shakespeare's bare attempt at a Christian gospel.

Marlowe : his Doctor Faustus as a tragedy

Marlowe is a sharp contrast with his contemporaries in many things, particularly in his tragic views. As early as 1587 when his first play *Tamburlaine* was completed, Marlowe clearly indicated his difference from others: 'From jigging veins of rhyming mother wits ... to the stately tent of war'. His next play *Doctor Faustus* is yet another step in the development of his tragic view.

Marlowe is a sharp contrast with Thomas Kyd, he is yet altogether a different kind of playwright, far different from Shakespeare. His tragic heroes are not exactly the true model of Aristotelian ideal of tragic hero. Even Doctor Faustus is not realization of that ideal, although he is a great man with some tragic flaw, able to inspire in the audience the double reactions of pity and fear. Marlowe's heroes are fully governed by Renaissance aspiration - a thing which is nowhere to be so completely represented as a tragic flaw as in Marlowe's plays.

Marlowe has clearly suggested what makes tragedy in human life in his masterpiece, *Edward II*. Here is a passage significant well when it comes from the mouth of one of the tragic heroes of Marlowe, young Mortimer:

'Base Fortune, now I see, that in thy wheel
There is a point, to which when men aspire,

They tumble headlong down: that point I touch'd,
And, seeing there was no place to mount up higher,
Why should I grieve at my declining fall?'

The tragedy of Doctor Faustus occurs simply like this; he has reached already the highest point in the scale of fortune and 'there was no place to mount up higher', inevitably the next step is a 'declining fall'.

Faustus is not entirely Marlowe's own creation. The tragic possibility of the character is already suggested in the source material. Already in 1587 a book was published under the title *Faustbuch.* The germ of the play and the tragic ambition, all could be traced in this small book. What Marlowe did exactly is only to make it serve to symbolize a crisis in Renascence aspiration. Here the aspiration is that of knowledge. For knowledge - of course the wrong kind of it - Faustus bartered off his soul. It is a history only of 24 years of that great scholar's life at the end of which the final catastrophe marks the tragic intensity of the hero's irresistible destiny.

Obviously, Marlowe's *Doctor Faustus* is not a regular illustration of Aristotle's conception of tragedy. In this play peripetia and anagnorisis are not exactly as they are in Shakespeare's plays, for example, the climax or say, crisis in the tragedy comes only at the last stage. And that is mainly why the last scene of *Doctor Faustus* is unique in his lyric flights of true passion, unsurpassed even by Shakespeare - a scene of true spiritual crisis where Faustus in spite of his greatest care and concern could not save his soul. Twenty four years of unlimited enjoyment has made it impossible to get the mercy of the Almighty Creator and his Prophet Christ.

Doctor Faustus as a tragedy is a true transcript of what Renascence aspiration might lead to - the highest point of human limitations already reached yet no end of ambition. Marlowe has only tried to adjust it to the already known pattern of tragedy, more or less Aristotelian.

Comic elements in Doctor Faustus

Professor Wilson observes that the play begins and ends magnificently, but this magnificence is scattered in comic and farcical scenes in the middle. It is true that the middle of the play is only a frail link connecting the two lateral scenes of paramount importance. At times they seem to be out of harmony with the central theme. Elizabethan drama allows comic relief even in tragic theme and *Doctor Faustus* is no exception to this rule.

Marlowe's *Doctor Faustus* differs from his other plays in containing a good deal of the clownage or buffoonery which he himself contemptuously disowned in the prologue to *Tamburlaine.* The comic element in the play is directly to be linked up with the Elizabethan convention of clownage scenes even in tragedies.

It is doubted that all the comic scenes in the play were introduced originally by Marlowe. Elizabethan playwrights provided fun for the 'groundings'. The Ist edition of the play, the Quarto of 1604, 11 years after Marlowe's death, contained something that does not tally with the later reproduction of the play in 1616, which was a much enlarged edition. This time some clownage scenes appeared, partly based on the *Faustbuch.* Marlowe's critics believed, these entertaining elements were the work of hack writers.

We have already noted, Marlowe has adopted a curious method of representation in this play - two grand scenes of the beginning as well as at the end are linked up by only a slender thread. The blank in the middle is filled up by closely related scenes or purely comic relief. *Doctor Faustus* with such elements is an exceptional work of Marlowe, his excellence and defects are in one play crudely adjusted.

The play has something to do with a regular clown. But the comic elements are not confined to the roles of the clown in the play. We have got enough of clowning in words, implications and attitude of a large number of characters introduced into the play. Even the Pope himself is very near to a clown; Faustus's two German friends, his servant Wagner, his scholars and some other minor characters appear practically in the role of a clown, only varying in intensity and intention. The meeting between Wagner and the scholars only in the second scene is highly entertaining.

The role of Mephistophilis is only a different variety of provided fun, particularly in the earlier stage of Doctor Faustus' conduct with him.

Scene IV Act I is exceptional in character so far as entertaining element is concerned. It is very difficult to say who is the greater fool, Wagner or the clown himself?

Doctor Faustus was first staged in 1588 a little earlier than Shakespeare's comedies could have been produced. The play has taken note of the earlier stage of the Morality plays; the odd blending of the serious spiritual matter and the very light activities of the devil formed an essential part of the Morality plays. Marlowe seems to have introduced a little of this odd mixture in this particular play. He has introduced the conflict between the good and evil angels as also the seven deadly sins with their riotous devilish dance. These are the elements which whether introduced by Marlowe himself or by a later hack writer are a great source of popular enjoyment.

During the Elizabethan period attempts to provide fun for the groundlings were a regular stage convention with tragedies. Marlowe although not seriously in favour of such provision has no doubt introduced something of that sort in his *Doctor Faustus;* of course later interpolations may have replenished the stock of fun.

Delay motive in Hamlet

Hamlet has always been a problem issue in Shakespeare canon; one of the problems with the critics of Shakespeare is the delay motive of Hamlet as the other is Eliot's charge of artistic failure. *Hamlet* is the play which has raised more storm of criticism than any of the other tragedies of Shakespeare.

Professor Stoll significantly defended Shakespeare against Eliot's charge of artistic failure, and by the way involves the question of Hamlet's procrastination as a side problem. He is of the view, and rightly, that Hamlet's melancholy and procrastination are all of a piece. The play starts with a note of 'heart sickness'; the note is struck by the sentry Fransisco.

The player king holds up the play scene for several minutes for an elaborate disquisition upon the human instability. The play is here and there full of stray references to a sort of 'the native hue of resolution sickled over with the pale cast of thought'. This serves as a symptom of the mind of the hero and the spirit of the whole tragedy. This may be considered as the keynote of the whole play.

Almost all the critics of Shakespeare are sure that the hero is instinct with this special character, Bradley has noted it with special interest. The analysis of the play in his book is quite significant.

Hamlet delays the action unusually long; he offers sometimes his reasons; the ghost of his father appeared sometimes 'to whet the almost blunted purpose'. The ghost appeared to Hamlet in the bedroom scene to remind him once more his purpose of revenge. The whole play is significantly of a nature that explains how unnecessary delay in taking revenge complicates the action. It seems to be the only problem which the hero is sincerely to fight and ultimately Shakespeare himself.

Hamlet is particularly of a character that gives rise to a problem; one side of Hamlet is fighting against the other side. This is really the crux of the problem. Shakespeare perhaps deliberately makes it the subject of his study and the ultimate case of the tragedy. The philosophic mind of the hero is clearly made out in the play, he is a student of philosophy and deeply involved in the dark mysteries of the world.

Only this philosophic bent of mind cannot adequately explain Hamlet's case. Dr Bradley is clear about it. The convulsive oscillation between the two extremes of frenzy and tranquillity is so marked a feature of the hero's character that it cannot be thoroughly explained by a philosophic bent of mind alone. Dr. Bardley has explained it by his theory of 'melancholy'. It is true that this special character ultimately led Hamlet to delay unusually on the pretext of one difficulty and another all through. At one stage he raises a moral question when he seizes his uncle at his prayer.

Hamlet shifts from one stand to another, from one plea to another, particularly to avoid meeting a concrete end and indulges in moral reflections as an alternative course. This is the only reason why he is considered the extreme opposite of Othello who met the end without even a necessary course of reflection on it.

Hamlet is a tragic character with whom delay in action is a tragic flaw. Shakespeare has clearly emphasised the fact almost in every act of the hero. It is not true that the hero is not able to do any concrete thing, although he tries to avoid it he does it as well when something of that nature is directly imposed upon him. He kills when he is unprepared. The last scene is quite an example. He seems to be subjected to paroxysm of passion. This is sometimes explained as a sort of insanity which perhaps very clearly Robert Bridges noted.

The delay in action is therefore a special feature of the hero's character. It is a tragedy that develops out of it. His philosophic mind contributes to it, although it does not cover the whole field. A sort of melancholy in the medical sense as applied by Bradley really intensifies this tendency of directly avoiding concrete fact and meeting it only when he must. Delay is then not a motive but a part of Hamlet's nature.

Hamlet: The play the primary problem, the character only secondary: Eliot's view examined.

In his essay on *Hamlet* Eliot starts with the contention that *Hamlet* the play is the problem rather than the character and that the play is, however, not fair; Eliot seeks to shift the accent from the character to the play. He gives credit to two critics, J.M. Robertson and Stoll, for moving away from the character to the play. According to Eliot, in *Hamlet* Shakespeare does not treat the whole action of the play as demanded by design. On the contrary we perceive that Hamlet is superimposed upon much cruder material which persists even in the final form.

It may be noted that Eliot is not the only critic to take this view of the play. Even Gilbert Murray and Croce endorsed this view. Santayana and Professor Waldock are the two other critics to support this view. Santayana is of the view that cruder materials from the old versions of the play survive in Shakespeare's final handling of it, not having been transmuted and fused by his intention. Hence the incoherence in Hamlet's character. Professor Waldock maintains that Shakespeare's reworking on crude materials has not been properly done. Eliot tends virtually to minimize the importance of the character of Hamlet. The verdict that he finally pronounces on the play is that far from being Shakespeare's masterpiece, *Hamlet* is an artistic failure. Eliot's judgement is unconscionable, if for nothing else, for the fact that it goes counter to the received opinion of about four centuries. The ultimate test of a work of art is its impact on the sensitive minds of not just one generation but all succeeding generations. Surely *Hamlet* has stood that supreme test.

Eliot's view of *Hamlet* as a play that failed rests by his own admission, on the fact that the theme is the feeling of a son towards a guilty mother. But this is by no means the whole truth, which even Eliot admits himself shortly after his reference to Robertson's contention. The feeling of a son towards the guilty mother is not more than a part of the total theme of the play: Hamlet moreover is not just a son. The play is about how things stand in Denmark and about how Hamlet stands in relation to them.

Eliot believes that Shakespeare has failed to achieve in *Hamlet* the 'objective correlative' of his 'antic disposition'. What he means by objective correlative he goes on explaining in a number of phrases like 'exact equivalence' to 'artistic inevitability', 'complete adequacy of the external to the emotion', 'objective equivalence to the subjective feeling' and so on. But all that Eliot is driving at is the close affinity between form and content. Eliot implies that in *Hamlet* the form is not the exact equivalence of the content. But Eliot misconstrues the exact nature of Shakespeare's contents. He argues that Hamlet is overmastered by an emotion which is in excess of facts of his life.

Eliot made his critical survey of the artistic side of *Hamlet* as early as 1920 in his *Sacred Wood*. Since then *Hamlet* has been a subject of close critical debate and Eliot's view was taken up for further elaboration and even some convenient modification by a series of critics. *Hamlet* is a play that has already gained ground in the minds of the generations of Shakespeare's readers and scholars. Eliot's view was replaced by 'the historical' view of Robertson and others, and one of the Bradlites, Charlton, has gone even so far in his *Shakespearean Tragedy* (1944) as to entirely debunk Eliot's view in a language like this: "If *Hamlet* is an artistic failure, then English is a language that I cannot understand". Actually Eliot too made a change of his outlook on *Hamlet*, he himself recognises the mysterious charm of the play, when he describes it as the "Mona Lisa of literature."

Doctor Faustus: a Morality Play

Marlowe is not far ahead of the Mediaeval drama, although he is the earliest successful Elizabethan in the field of tragedy. The first tragedy of the Elizabethan period was *Gorboduc*, acted in 1562. Marlowe's *Doctor Faustus* marks a sharp difference from the first classical tragedy not only with a mark of genius but also in the evolution of the tragic art, staged in 1588.

Gorboduc has of course nothing of the Morality plays, but in *Doctor Faustus* Marlowe seems to be a little closer to the Miracle and Morality tradition of the drama. Artistically *Doctor Faustus* is a little more defective than Marlowe's own masterpiece *Edward II*. The play seems to be a series of detached scenes, in the interstices of such unrelated scenes Marlowe introduced elements very akin to Morality ingredients.

The greatest Mediaeval Morality play is *Everyman*. The play demonstrates best the preoccupation of mind of the playwright, as if serving a serious moral purpose by means of stage performance. The characters who appear on the stage are typified moral principles, more or less brought under two heads, good and evil. *Doctor Faustus* is not exactly calculated to serve a moral purpose. It has no claim to preaching the Bible.

The Mediaeval Morality plays were handmaiden to the Church; originally preaching of the Bible gave rise to a separate species of literature which ultimately took shape as the drama. Marlowe's *Doctor Faustus* however akin to the Morality plays, is not preponderant with the preaching element. Marlowe was against Christianity. Of course he was highly moral as later Shelley was. Marlowe serves a purpose in *Doctor Faustus* which he has not served anywhere with the same acuteness of feeling. The quality of moral and spiritual seriousness in the tragedy of *Doctor Faustus* has brought it closer to the Mediaeval tradition of spiritual seriousness.

Some of the scenes of *Doctor Faustus* are quite characteristic of the Mystery plays of the Mediaeval period, as for example Sc. 1 Act II, a debate between the Good Angel and the Evil Angel. They are as it were debating over the possession of the soul of Doctor Faustus. The role of Mephistophilis in the play as the henchman of Lucifer is quite interesting. Such a character nowhere appears in Marlowe's plays. He is the evil principle adequately represented.

Marlowe introduces an element of moral seriousness in the play. The question is whether the Satanic power that rules the destiny of the protagonist displays Marlowe's own moral seriousness. Although Faustus's character is taken from a German legend and also from earlier books dealing with the legends, the seriousness of purpose that the play betrays is Marlowe's own.

The last scene of *Doctor Faustus* is a scene of spiritual crisis as also the first scene is perfectly in a light trim of seeking easy life of the flesh. The first and the last, these two scenes are so uniquely counterbalanced that the wide gap in between is almost forgotten. These two scenes do excellently establish Marlowe's serious spiritual link with the Mediaeval playwrights. Marlowe is deeply moral without being apparently religious.

Some of the characters in the play are so much typical of moral outlook that they sufficiently revive the air of the morality plays of the earlier period. Such a character is of course the Old Man in the play who serves as a contrast to the pleasure-hunting side of Faustus's character. It is quite evident in Sc. 1 Act V, "Ah, Doctor Faustus, that I might prevail to guide thy steps unto the way of life."

The stage apparatus is so arranged in *Doctor Faustus* that it reminds a regular Mediaeval Morality play in which sin, the earth, the devil and of course the Good Angel of human destiny appear in their respective role. In *Doctor Faustus* we come across Lucifer, Belzebub and Mephistophilis, all representing Hell; the Old Man Faustus's servant and of course his scholars are on the side of heaven. The middle stage is of course clownish, in that role Marlowe has not spared even the Pope. This is quite natural for a playwright like Marlowe who has moral seriousness but who has no respect for the constituted authority of the church.

Marlowe is much satiric about the common ranks of the church, Pope and Cardinal of course included. Faustus is a hero, tragic only in the sense he is deeply moral, although he does not know it. The Mediaeval moral outlook is quite clear in the manner of the conclusion that Marlowe draws in the last stage of the hero's tragic life.

The role of Lady Macbeth in the Play

In the Tragedy of *Macbeth* the role of the hero and the heroine are equally important though the conception of the heroine's role is a little changed here. The hero and the heroine are not in close love relationship: Their conjugal relationship has an exceptional turn, which makes the play exceptional in Shakespeare's canon. The play is called a tragedy of ambition, ambition that is shared by Macbeth and Lady Macbeth.

The sharing of the ambition with the hero is what makes Lady Macbeth's role very significant and highly dramatic. Ambition is in itself very good, but ambition in Macbeth proves to be a tragic flaw, ambition inordinate and misdirected. Dr. Bardley tells us Macbeth was ambitious, a general must have been, but he could not have been misdirected in his ambition, had there not been Lady Macbeth and the witches. The weird sisters and Lady Macbeth were in declared conspiracy against Macbeth, the weird sisters consciously with a plan, and Lady Macbeth unconsciously and completely without knowledge where it would lead.

Lady Macbeth's role is highly psychological and in a way more dramatic than the role of the witches. Goethe called Lady Macbeth 'super witch', perhaps he could see through her complex role in the tragedy of the hero. The witches wanted Macbeth to be destroyed, but Lady Macbeth did not; yet it is she who brought about his downfall and ultimate death. She was no less a temptress than the witches. The witches' role in *Macbeth* is like the role of the ghost in *Hamlet,* but the role of Lady Macbeth in *Macbeth* in the tragedy of the hero has no parallel.

Lady Macbeth detected Macbeth aright, he was full 'the milk of human Kindness', if it is not literally true at least her meaning is not altogether wrong, she wanted him fit for the job. Actually on receipt of her husband's letter in Sc. 5 Act I she is absolutely taken up with the vision of Scotland's throne. She completely identified herself with the ambition for the throne. Her ambition is of a different kind from Macbeth's. He would have it but without any recourse to the evil method. Lady Macbeth must have it no matter whether the path is good or evil, she had better take the shortest route of evil to translate it quicker.

In the murder scene Lady Macbeth shows the unlimited power of evil, it is she who bolsters the drooping strength of evil in her husband, she not only ended by a severe tongue lashing as most of the wives do but actively participated in the bloody act which rarely a woman can if she is not of Clytemnestra's class. Clytemnestra did only an unwifely deed, but Lady Macbeth did what only a wife can, that is the psychological side of her role in Macbeth's tragedy. She must support her husband where he may fail in his purpose. She embraced her husband's ambition, knew only how he could realise it, but lost sight of everything else, even the troubles which may attend it. The basic wifely character in this play takes only a tragic turn. There the tragic blunder psychologically works.

After the murder Lady Macbeth became a little more wily as Macbeth a little more desperate to steady his position. Up to the Banquet scene Lady Macbeth could offer her support to her husband's drooping purpose, but this time by her wiles mainly inherited from the first mother of mankind. But thereafter she retires to her closet and takes no active part in the action, and leaves her husband to fight it alone. This is also basically womanly. She unknowingly and without meaning it at all pushed her husband into the snare beyond her power of control. She must have felt helpless and made herself responsible, as a wife must do, for the sorry mess of the matter. This must have secretly bitten into her soul.

The sleep-walking scene towards the close of the play, exactly in Act V, Sc. I, a sign of total breakdown of nerves, is highly psychological. Shakespeare is a superb artist who does not think it proper to make public the secret desolation of her soul, makes suggestively known the effect of the soul-suffering which has but one ultimate end that does not occur in the play but is only reported by a servant. Lady Macbeth in the sleep-walking scene is so psychologically undemonstrative that Mrs. Siddons had only trying moments of her skill to demonstrate it. She ultimately leaves her husband alone and kills herself only to escape the sorry sight of his troubles she was at the root of.

Dagger Scene: its dramatic significance

In Shakespeare's *Macbeth* some scenes at least consolidate the tragic wonder by their excellence of art and implication in the whole design of the play. Such scenes are Dagger scene, Porter scene, Banquet scene and Sleep-walking scene. Dagger scene is so called for the appearance of a dagger in the air before Macbeth actually murders Duncan. It occurs in Sc. I, Act II, but it does not cover the whole scene, covers only a small part of it.

It is Macbeth's own castle, the king is already there for the night's rest, and must have been deep in sleep. Banquo and Fleance are still not in bed, they meet Macbeth yet not abed but awake.. They finish their short talk about the witches and their prophecy and part. Thereafter Macbeth is alone, not even attended by his servant. The air-drawn dagger appears just then. Macbeth is left alone, not even with lady Macbeth to support him in times of absolute nervelessness. He is to do the deed alone, with his own sword. No doubt a moment of utter crisis of feeling, particularly for a man like him, if one part given to the devil the other given to the divine.

The Dagger scene is a soliloquy sharply contrasted with another equally leading soliloquy in Sc. 7, Act I. Macbeth is full of calculation, tense with a philosophic brooding of mind and practical understanding; the Dagger scene has no occasion for calculation, it is a moment of intensity of total concentration upon the act. The air-drawn dagger, what it is, and to what effect, is the sole subject matter of this very ominous soliloquy.

Macbeth himself has tried to explain it, that is the sane side of his psychology and the other side that eludes his grasp is the subject matter of the critic's discernment. Macbeth sees the blood-stained dagger, horribly dripping blood, explains it doubtfully as the creation of his 'heat-oppressed brain', yet he cannot deny its visible existence. He explains it also as pointing to the actual course he was about to take then.

Whether Macbeth's own explanation is right or wrong there is no doubt Shakespeare is seen quite aware of such a psychological side of the phenomenon. He makes Macbeth a special kind of tragic hero more poetic in vision and sensibility than even Romeo and Hamlet, Romeo more passionate and Hamlet more philosophic, but Macbeth more poetic. To him the actual murder is not the matter, but its anticipation and after effects are. His poetry has no touch of passion, it has the wizardry of the scintillation of the spirit which is more than mere supernaturalism and superstition. When he steps upstairs to finish the job he invokes the dark forces to his aid as poetically as Hamlet descants upon the mystery of life.

The critics have duly taken note of the hallucination theory which Macbeth himself has given rise to, and taken note of the psychological side of the hero's mind. They have more insistently considered the dramatic significance of such a phenomenon. Perhaps Shakespeare has made Macbeth more complex a hero than any other. Even Hamlet can be easily explained but Macbeth cannot be. His tragedy is ultimately due to a tragic flaw, a defect of his otherwise very elegant personality, which is fully exploited by the supernatural forces like the weird sisters. That this defect has a psychological sound basis is thoroughly demonstrated in the dagger scene. Othello is all too passionate to see the devilry of Iago, likewise Macbeth is all too poetic in everything, good and evil, to have a balanced view of his problem, the act he would perform, either of his own or under the powerful inducement of his wife. He cannot have been Richard III in wickedness, for poetic faculty of his mind added enchantment to his evil course. The dagger scene is a concrete symptom of such a quality of the mind.

The spirit of Forgiveness and Freedom in the Tempest

The last stage of Shakespeare's career is marked with a spirit of resignation, here tragedy no longer ends tragically and comedy nowhere persists uninterrupted longer than it should. Everything here gives a life sense, in which everything has its right share.

The last play *The Tempest* is no doubt more so than any of the other plays of this phase. The play has more reason to be so, it was intended to solemnize the betrothal of Elizabeth of Bohemia and presented on Dec. 27, 1612, the betrothal night.

The story is partly derived from Florio's translation of Montaigne, which was published in 1603, but tinged with the colour of the plawright's mind then specially attuned to a happy mood under a practical necessity like that. The story starts with an unpleasant occurrence, the tricky banishment of Prospero, the Duke of Milan by his brother, not just then narrated, and a shipwreck duly depicted in the opening scene.

The whole play thereafter seems to be a scene of conflict though not immediately bloody, undoubtedly not bloodily at long last. Prospero lives on a desolate island with his daughter, himself dispossessed of his dukedom now dispossessing the rightful claimant of the island kingdom, Sycorax's son Caliban. Apparently not a happy transaction whatever the reason might be behind it. Not only that, like a common necromancer he holds a spirit under his absolute control, exactly to use him to torment others, his own men from Milan lately arrived on the island, and the uncomplying deformed devil Caliban there.

Prospero's magic power that controls the spirit world evidently rules the world in the play, perhaps more effectively than in *A Midsummer Night's Dream.* The fairy world and Puck serve quite a different purpose than Prospero's magic and his spirit agent Ariel do. Both magic and Ariel are the driving force of a purely human will, the will of the enchanter in the play and that of the playwright behind it. The spirit world in *A Mid-Summer Night's Dream* is only a part of the fantasy that rules the human world.

Prospero's will asserts itself in everything in the play, over the human and the spirit world, asserts and then willingly relents to a complete resignation, the resignation of the playwright's own mood. So he does not end at all as he began. Himself a victim of injustice and oppression, Prospero knows what it is and knows the value of its opposite qualities, the latter knowledge is the guiding principle of this stage of Shakespeare's writings. Himself a victim of punishment he knows the value of pardon, a victim of subjugation knows the value of freedom.

The change thus in the mind of Prospero brings all the changes in the play, his enemies are made friends and those whom he tormented are released beyond harm's length. Even Caliban whom he has more reason to subjugate, a devil who plotted against his life and more unpardonably against his daughter's honour, is set at liberty in a manner that the devil too had a timely awakening of human sense:

'I will be wise hereafter,
And seek for grace. (5.1.296)

The Folio Editors' Address

The editors of the First Folio were two of Shakespeare's co-actors, John Heminge and Henry Condell, at least they claim them to be so, and there is perhaps no reason to disbelieve them. The Folio Edition of Shakespeare's plays was published long after Shakespeare's death, actually after seven years. They clearly point it out in their Preface. They call them Shakespeare's friends and claim that in the earlier Quarto editions there were distortions of Shakespeare's text, particularly due to surreptitious and stolen elements of his plays and parts.

Evidently they claim for themselves, and not without reason, exact knowledge of Shakespeare's text and its proper numbers. They, of course, confess the work of edition of Shakespeare's plays must have been more authentic had it been supervised 'overseen' by Shakespeare himself. When that is not possible several years after his death people must remain satisfied with the next best arrangement made by the author's friends who, they claim, knew more than anybody else then living. This is really suggested and could have been so effectively expressed in their language.

They mainly avoid any critical jargon and reserve their views although yet they give some warning to readers as to how they can best appreciate Shakespeare. Liking him is understanding him, they mean to say. Without that one can hardly expect to understand Shakespeare, they warn. They have given also their own understanding or appreciation of Shakespeare. He is an 'imitator of Nature' and 'a gentle expresser of it'. His wit cannot lie hid, 'his mind and hand' went together. Their main contribution is also pointed out here, they present the world with the text as it was from Shakespeare's pen, regularizing irregularities of all surreptitious copies.

The Elizabethan Rear Stage

During the Elizabethan period along with the development of the drama there was a corresponding development of the stage craft and the shape of the stage. Dramatic performance was earliest in the Elizabethan period given in the Inns of Court and in the Inn-yard, the guest room being temporarily converted to the tiring room and the open court to the makeshift auditorium.

The earliest model of the constructed Theatre house is the drawing of the Swan Theatre which is the basis of the later renovation of the stage including the Rear stage.

The entire rear stage had its position behind the open front stage jutting out into the yard or pit, the back stage was, however, covered area enclosed three sides by the three storied spectators' gallery. The gallery of course continued even behind the back stage to form the corresponding three-stage tiring room for the actor and their things to be used in the performance. The entire Rear stage was also three storied with even an underground cell to represent in the action a cave or the hell. The entire Rear stage was connected with the back stage by three doors and some possible trap doors. All the psychological scenes could be acted in the Rear stage, so it was really very vital in the performance

J.C. Adams claimed in his attempt at the reconstruction of the Elizabethan stage that the whole back section from roof to floor was the tiring area, and that the inner stage was behind the stage proper and concealed by a curtain for use in discovery and concealment both.

The Swan drawing has no provision for an inner stage, the need of which must have been served by the temporary erection of a booth at the early stage of development of the Elizabethan stagecraft. Thus Rear stage or call it inner stage, was needed for some scenes like Polonius's concealment, Ferdinand's playing chess with Miranda and Romeo's death in the tomb. The developed stagecraft took it into serious account.

Shakespeare's Canon

Only 14 plays of Shakespeare's were regularly in print when he died in 1616. The rest of his plays were first printed in the First Folio under the joint editorship of Shakespeare's two friends, John Haminge and Hery Condell in 1623 except of course *Pericles.* The total number of 36 plays from Shakespeare's pen are called Shakespearean canon.

To ascertain the date of their first appearance on the stage or the actual date of Shakespeare's writing them is an exceedingly difficult task, Scholars have mainly utilised three chief evidences: (i) external, (ii) internal and (iii) style.

The main external sources are Henslowe's *Diary*, Mere's *Palladis Tamia*, *Stationers' Register*, The Master of Revels' accounts and of course some visitors' account in their Note Books. Shakespeare's style and internal evidences of reference in the text to some contemporary events arc thoroughly explored through the ages by experts, more ardently in the late 19th and early 20th century to ascertain thc dates of individual plays. Their success although immense yet one may not accept as final. Still critics accept the first Folio as a more reliable canon of Shakespeare's plays.

From the prompt copy stage of Shakespeare's text to its printed form there has been a complicated passage. In the Address to the Reader by the Folio editors there is a significant allusion to the stolen and surreptitious copies to distort Shakespeare's text. The editors must have referred to Quarto editions. In his *Shakespeare Folios and Quartos* (1909) Malone holds the view that some of the Quarto editions are undoubtedly much better than the Folio texts. So in spite of much progress in the study of Shakespeare's text there remains still scope for further enquiry into the authenticity of Shakespeare's canon.

From Prompt copy to Printed book of Shakespeare's text

From the playhouse copy of Shakespeare's text to its printed form is a long way, no doubt the most complicated way. We know no play manuscript used by a printer during Shakespeare's lifetime has survived. The general history of a play manuscript is, the manuscript of the playwright passed directly to the playhouse, then to the scrutiny and adjustment of the prompter, thereafter to the individual actors in the form of their pieced out roles with cues. Then the play manuscript was sent to the Master of Revels to be censored or licensed. Only after that the manuscript has the prospect of being printed, in Shakespeare's case in so many dubious ways. Manuscripts were copied out by professional copyists, and copy right was not then in vogue. A play could be revised and altered before they reached the printer.

A popular play of Shakespeare's could reach the printer in so many ways when yet it was not meant for publication but exactly for stage performance. Good and Bad Quartos were printed during Shakespeare's lifetime, yet most of them could not have been more authentic than the First Folio which was published seven years after Shakespeare's death. The Folio editors pointed out in their Address to the readers that earlier editions were 'stolen' or 'surreptitious'. Even if a copy is stolen, however, immoral the act is the copy can be unaltered and original, but surreptitious copy cannot claim that authenticity. Two theories are current as to how printers got Shakespeare's plays for printing, the shorthand theory and minor actor's theory. Through shorthand notes of a running play they got the play as much as they could, or sometimes they got it through bribing a minor actor who could give his part intact and what he could remember of other actors' parts. These two channels are responsible for Bad Quartos.

The publisher could however buy the playhouse copy with some possible alterations for stage performance. Evidence is still lacking to show that Shakespeare himself supervised printing any of his plays, they came to the printing stage by mainly indirect means during his lifetime, which made the task difficult for later explorers of his text. Even detection of Shakespeare's handwriting was made not all too easy.

The Drawing of the Swan Theatre

The shape and pattern of the Elizabethan Stage are not clearly known, only attempt has been made to have an idea of from different sources, mainly three, of which the Swan drawing is the most outstanding. This is the earliest shape and lay-out of a theatre house, from the crude drawing of which other theatre houses are supposed to have been constructed.

A single contemporary sketch of the Elizabethan stage survives. A Dutchman named Johannes de Witt visited London about 1596 and made a sketch of the Swan Theatre. The sketch was copied by his friend Arend Von Buchel. The draughtsmanship is crude, yet it is sure it gives an idea of the contemporary stage. It had no rear stage. A platform open to the sky came jutting out into the open yard which could be occupied by the spectators during performance. Three-tier galleries surrounded the stage from three sides and each must have been continued to form the tiring room for the actors behind the stage. Behind the open stage forming the front there was the main stage covered and with an upper stage just above it. The main stage had only two doors opening inside to offer some interior view of acting. The two doors left a blank space in-between. The central door was lacking. The top was provided with two windows and a side door.

Palladis Tamia

Shakespeare had long been neglected by his contemporaries, uncertainty about the date of publication and composition of Shakespeare's individual plays is mainly due to that. The exact date of their writing could hardly have been ascertained, external evidences could help us only to know before which particular date which play must have been written. One of such external evidences is a young student's accounts in his book *Palladis Tamia* by name.

Francis Meres wrote this book in 1598 almost in a diary form to note down his appreciation of books, sometimes short comparative accounts of books, sometimes, short comparative studies of poets, as a chapter in it may suggest 'A Comparative Discourse of our English Poets with the

Greek, Latin and Italian poets'. That is mainly why he calls the book 'Similitudes'. Among the contemporary poets Shakespeare must have been his favourite one. He praised him as one of the eight by whom 'the English tongue is mighty enriched, and gorgeously invested in rare ornaments and resplendent habiliments'.

He brought Shakespeare into the limelight of European importance at that early stage:

> 'As the soul of Euphorbus was thought to live in Pythagoras: so the sweet witty soul of Ovid lives in the mellifluous and honey tongued Shakespeare, witness his Venus and Adonis, his Lucerne, his sugared sonnets among his private friends etc....'

'As Plautus and Seneca are accounted the best for comedy and Tragedy among the Latins: so Shakespeare among the English is the most excellent in both kinds for the stage...'

Thereafter he makes mention of 6 comedies and 6 tragedies of Shakespeare's early stage, of them one *Love Labour Won* must have been lost. Before the book went to the Press all these plays at least were written and performed, one can say.

Henslowe's Diary

One of the chief sources of external evidence of Shakespeare's plays is Henslowe's diary. In 1904 the W.W. Greg edited *Diary and Paper* of Phillip Henslowe appeared and changed the direction of Shakespeare studies considerably as did the R.B. MaKerrow edited *Thomas Nashe* in the same year.

Henslowe was the owner of several London Theatres: The Rose, the Fortune and others. For a period of ten years, from 1592 to 1602, he kept an exact account in a large ledger of his dealings with various companies that played at his theatres. It is the most valuable of all records of Elizabethan stage history. For the next 24 years the first Elizabethan tragic actor Edward Alleyn who married Henslowe's stepdaughter worked with him in partnership.

After Henslowe's death in 1616 the papers passed into Alleyn's possession. As well as the Diary they included contracts with actors, letters from dramatists, the agreement with the builder for building the Fortune Theatre, and many other documents which are invaluable.

The Diary was first edited and published in 1845 by John Payne Collier, who of course later invented some Elizabethan documents in his enthusiasm, it is Greg who did the shifting work, and clear it of all Collier additions.

The Stationers' Register

During the Elizabethan period copyright was not strictly observed. This gave rise to some publishing problems for contemporary authors. Most of Shakespeare's early Quarto problems sprang out of this uncertainty. As a solution to this problem the Stationers' Company was incorporated by a royal chapter in 1557. No one, not a member of this company, could print anything in the kingdom for sale unless empowered by a special order of the Crown.

The Company had a Register called Stationers' Register in which the members had to enter any book desired to print at a fee of 4d and 6d. Some of Shakespeare's plays were entered in it for publication, so it serves as a valuable document for the study of Shakespeare's canon. The Company's control waned in the 17th century, so in 1709 by an Act of Parliament the sole right to print was protected.

Shakespeare's plays from their copy book to the printed form passed through endless irregularities, the Company's Register offers valuable information of some of them at least.

The Master of the Revels

The Master of the Revels is an officer appointed to superintend masques and entertainments at court. He is first mentioned in the reign of Henry VII. The first permanent Master of the Revels was Sir Thomas Cowarden appointed in 1545.

In the Elizabethan period the Master of the Revels attained greater importance as one of the very valid sources of information as to the printing trade and performance of plays, particularly the plays of Shakespeare. The subject is fully explored in Peter Cunningham's Revels Document (1842). In 1607 the authority for licensing plays was vested in the Master of the Revels. It was the licenser's duty to see that no play was acted which was politically dangerous and offensive to home Government or to the ambassadors of friendly countries; from 1606 on the duty included also to eliminate profane oaths and irreverent use of God's name in books. Hence the substitution of 'heaven' in the First Folio for 'God' of the earlier texts.

Quartos (Good and Bad)

The two words Folio and Quarto refer to the size of the book, Folio a single sheet folded once, and Quarto a single sheet folded twice, the first a format of two leaves, the second of four. Before the Folio text of Shakespeare's plays all his plays were printed in Quarto format, 14 were published in Shakespeare's lifetime.

Quarto texts were good or bad so far as Shakespeare's plays were concerned, the quality denomination was based on how the copy was prepared for printing. The authenticity of the text was doubtful in Bad Quartos because they were printed from pirated and patched up copies. The Good Quartos were believed to have been printed from playhouse copies duly purchased from them. Although Good Quartos were in print during Shakespeare's lifetime, they were not got directly from Shakespeare nor the printing matter was supervised by him.

Bad Quartos had then a special history. The printers got the plays sometimes from a pirate minor actor or from shorthand notes of a running play, either way the copy must have been defective in everything, spelling, punctuation, and introduction of conjectural elements, so two removes from Shakespeare's texts. There were four such Bad Quartos. *Henry V. Romeo and Juliet, The Merry Wives of Windsor* and *Hamlet*.

The First Quarto and its successors had no division into acts and scenes and stage directions fewer in numbers and vague. The First Folio was an obvious improvement in all these over the Quarto text.

Sir Thomas More

Except for six signatures and the words 'By me' no definite autograph of Shakespeare survives. In 1916 Sir Edward Maunde Thompson with his special knowledge of paleography made a startling discovery of what he said was Shakespeare's handwriting, a monograph of the same name. The manuscript is in the British Museum and is known as the *The Book of Sir Thomas More* – a chronicle play showing scenes in life and death of More. The MS is in seven different handwritings, and was never printed. Most of the play is in the handwriting of Antony

Munday, the rest is in other hands labelled as Hand A, B, C, D, E. Of these Hand E is Thomas Dekker's and Hand C is in the Playhouse Reiewer's of The Rose Theatre. Thirteen leaves of the MS are written in a main hand which Professor Greg calls Hand S. The seven leaves of Additions only are by five others. Hand D is attributed to Shakespeare covering only three leaves of 147 lines, the problem is argued at length in *Shakespeare's Hand in the Play of Sir Thomas More* (1923) ed. by A.W. Pollard, in which the contributors are Greg, E.M. Thompson, J.D. Wilson, R.W. Chambers and Pollard himself.

The play is by itself not important at all, it was never staged in the Elizabethan period; it gains in importance only because it offers clues to Shakespeare's hand and to further textual studies of Shakespeare canon. Hand D in it offers some very close parallelism to Shakepeare's minim letters where confusion occurred in readings as they have done in Good Quartos which are believed to have been printed from Shakespeare's autograph.

The crowd scenes in these pages are also close parallel to such scenes in other Shakespeare plays, for example Julius Caesar, the sentiment and outlook are also the same. Dover Wilson supports the view by a more thorough enquiry into the spelling and misprint in the Folio and Quarto editions of Shakespeare plays which explain possible cases in Hand D in the *More* manuscript.

Holinshed's Chronicles

Holinshed's *Chronicles* of England, Scotland and Ireland were published in 1578 and contained inexhaustible material to satisfy the feverish nationalism of London citizens, Shakespeare made use of the materials in his English Histories, two Tragedies and a Romance. The *Chronicle* is the counterpart of Plutarch's *Lives*. But Holinshed supplied only the dry bones to which Shakespeare gave flesh and blood.

Shakespeare is nature's child, has his powerful imagination which he used even in the context of history. The language, characterization and some of the characters themselves are Shakespeare's own; he found no material for the sub-plot of Henry IV in Holinshed and little for Hotspur. It is not altogether wrong to say that Shakespeare fell upon Holinshed only when he felt bored and found no inspiration to invent. Of the English plays Richard II is the closest.

Plutarch's Lives

Plutarch's *Lives* was translated by Sir Thomas North not from original Latin but from Amyot's French version and was published in England in 1579. Shakespeare must have been acquainted with it in his youth. Like Holinshed Plutarch is Shakespeare's source for Greek and Roman histories, but the difference between them is very great, Holinshed supplied Shakespeare only bare skeleton and the drama was his own, Plutarch supplied him drama too.

North's Plutarch was a collection of heroic portraits with an immediate appeal to the men of Shakespeare's age. Shakespeare accepts from him hits for his style and pattern of his plot. There are a good number of examples where Shakespeare has done it. Caeser's life in Plutarch's pages is in places close parallel to Shakespeare's play. *Coriolanus* and *Antony and Cleopatra* have so many common passages from North's translation for Shakespeare to form his plot and learn his style. Shakespeare's adaptation from *Life of Antony* is to the point, for example he started right from the most dramatic rendering of North – 'the last and extreme mischief of all (to wit the love of Cleopatra) lighted on him'. Shakespeare utilizes often the dramatic possibilities rather than the plain line of history, in which Plutarch helped him more than Holinshed.

Hamlet: First Quarto

Hamlet is one of the four recognised Bad Quartos, printed first in that format in 1603, in a manner generally all the others were. Elizabethan printing trade was much flexible and irregular, book trade was then infested with pirates and edition of books was often a patched up matter. Hamlet was subjected to all these corruptions.

The *Hamlet* of 1603 was a surreptitious edition as the first Folio editors stamp in their address all earlier editions, it was therefore replaced by an improved version Shakespeare's fellow-actors claimed as genuine copy. This is the second Quarto of 1604. The Hamlet copy of 1603 disappeared from view until a copy was discovered in 1823 by Sir H.E. Bunbury of Burton, bound with other Quartos.

As early as 1880 in his preface to the facsimile of the 1603 *Hamlet* Dr. Furnivall had pointed out that the accuracy of the speeches of Marcellus and Voltemar suggested the use of 'some parts bought or got from actors', this supports the minor actor theory of Shakespeare's texts.

The First Quarto text of *Hamlet* when compared with the text of subsequent editions appears in many places short and cryptic, as for example the fencing bout towards the close of the play, the middling sized passage given to the king is completely absent in the first Quarto. The king there uses in no case more than a short cryptic sentence and speaks of 'foils' conspicuous by its omission in the subsequent editions.

John Manningham's Diary

John Manningham was a barrister of Middle Temple, and a contemporary of Shakespeare. He kept a Diary in which some of Shakespeare's plays were referred to as he saw them staged. Two of such plays are very important, *Richard III* and *Twelfth Night*. Shakespeare's plays were much talked about among his contemporaries, but hardly anything of Shakespeare's own reactions are in our possession. In this Manningham's Diary has a significant role to play. At least one concrete anecdote survives, the only anecdote, Manningham had noted in his Diary.

The anecdote relates to *Richard III* recorded in 1602 in Manningham's Diary. The story shows Shakespeare's sense of humour. Burbage played Richard III and a citizen was so much impressed by it that she invited Burbage to her place that night by the name of the Richard, which Shakespeare overheard and went to her before Burbage and was entertained, when it was announced that Richard III was at the door. Shakespeare made a lively humour of the case by saying William the Conqueror was before Richard III.

To ascertain the date of *Twelfth Night* Manningham's Diary is very helpful. The latest date is fixed by an entry dated 2 February 1602 in Manningham's Diary. He writes in his Diary they had a play called *Twelfth Night* at their feast, the play being compared to *Comedy of Errors* and two other Italian and Latin plays; the central comic point, the steward led to believe his lady in love with him, is also clearly pointed out in the Diary. The account seems to suggest the play's Inns of court history.

Edmund Malone

Malone belongs to the later half of the 18th century and the first half of the 19th and makes significant contributions to the studies of Shakespeare canon. Since Malone it is an accepted fact that Shakespeare was for some time a 'play dresser', and served his apprenticeship as such.

Malone's epoch-making work, *Attempt to ascertain the order in which the plays attributed to Shakespeare were written*, was published in 1778. The title of the book is self-explanatory. At the beginning of his *Attempt* Malone sums up the position of the already achieved scholarship. Malone's annotations in any book from his library are profuse and almost always relevant. His copy of Capell in ten volumes in the British Museum, re-collated throughout, with copious remarks, is a landmark of the year 1781. In 1780 he published a Supplementary two vol. to Steevens, containing the *Poems*, the doubtful plays from Folio 1664, a first sketch of his pioneer *Historical account of the rise and progress of the English stage, and numerous annotations.*

In 1790 he issued his edition in ten vols., with revisions of his chronology and stage history and vastly increased illustrative material. He and Steevens are the chief builders of Variorum editions. Malone-Boswell in 21 vols. in 1821 is the Third Variorum, and in these are summarized and incorporated the body of the 18th century scholarship.

The 18th century is a landmark in Shakespeare scholarship and to it Malone's contribution is immense. Malone can be named with so many other of his time, but no one perhaps opened up new horizon of Shakespeare criticism so eminently as he did. He extensively explored Henslowe's papers and Meres's too.

Eighteenth Century Criticism of Shakespeare

The 18th century criticism of Shakespeare is rather an evolution of Shakespeare's genius by the side of the classical masterpieces of drama. Shakespeare's success as a dramatist is very often taken up with the success of the Greek and Latin dramatists, and sometimes with the success of Homer as a perfect delineater of life.

In fact Theobald is the first editor of Shakespeare's plays (1734) with an adequate knowledge of Elizabethan literature. Beside him we have other important critics of Shakespeare, critics like Rowe, Pope and Johnson, in this period. Addison and Steele do of course casually estimate Shakespeare, more or less as a writer of true human nature.

The weighing of faults and beauties was the favourite exercise of the 18th century critics. They mainly devote their energy in a close study of Shakespeare's excellence by the side of the classical pattern.

Pope is thoroughly a classicist. He estimated Shakespeare's success, as in his *Epistle* to Augustus, with Racine and Corneille and saw 'fluent Shakespeare scarcely effaced a line'.

The same note is carried on further in his Preface to the Edition of Shakespeare's work of 1725. Pope could however isolate Shakespeare from the classical hallmarks of success; he takes Homer to judge how far Shakespeare was successful in the delineation of Nature. 'Homer himself drew not his art so immediately from the fountains of Nature.' He took Shakespeare to be an original author, as original as Homer. What imperfections Pope detected in Shakespeare's times were mainly due to his absolute preoccupation with the classical standard. Pope however thought quite rightly that Shakespeare must not be judged, because he cannot be, by 'Aristotle's rules'.

Nicholas Rowe in his Preface to Shakespeare saw Shakespeare as a genius who deviates from the classical pattern, and he is better so as no author was earlier. To him 'this Author's genius do's nowhere so much appear, as where he gives his imagination an entire loose'. Whether it is comedy or tragedy Rowe found in Shakespeare's plays the same type of high regard for imagination and fancy that lift mankind a little above 'the limits of the visible world.'

Addison and Steele only scrappily discussed Shakespeare in their *Spectator* Articles. Addison detects how Shakespeare's critics were more or less misled in the judgement of Shakespeare's qualities by the classical standard. His view is very clearly stated in No. 592 of 1714. 'Our critics do not seem sensitive that there is more beauty in the works of a great genius who is ignorant of the rules of art, than in those of a little genius who knows and observes them.'

The greatest critics of the period is of course Dr. Johnson. In his Preface to Shakespeare he tends to summarize faults and beauties as some of his predecessors have done. Johnson's Preface is yet acknowledged as the culmination of Shakespearean criticism of the previous hundred years. Again Dr.Johnson weighs Shakespeare's depth by means of his classical outlook; but he does one thing that none of the neo-classical critics of Shakespeare has done; Johnson clearly defines where Shakespeare has far surpassed the classical attainment, and knows where he has done. "Shakespeare's excellence is not the fiction of a tale but the representation of life."

Johnson has further defined what sort of life Shakespeare has delineated and how. He tells us Shakespeare's plays are not in the rigid sense either tragedies or comedies. Exactly what they are no one has expressed it better than Johnson. "They are composition of a distinct kind, exhibiting the real state of sublunary nature, which partakes of good and evil, joy and sorrow mingled with endless variety of proportion and innumerable modes of combinations."

Dr. Johnson has however listed some of Shakespeare's defects but he has already understood more than anybody that Shakespeare's genius requires a different standard of judgement than the already accepted principle of criticism. In that Johnson is the beginning of the still faint suggestion of Romantic criticism. His remarks on Falstaff and Polonius can be regarded as the true beginning of the Romantic criticism.

The Romantic trend of criticism is still more clearly detected in the isolated criticism of Shakespeare by Maurice Morgann (1777) in his Essay on Falstaff. Even Dr. Bradley gave high praise to the treatment of Falstaff carrying it a step further. Morgann heralds a period of Shakespeare criticism to which he does not yet belong but highlights the prospect of taking Shakespeare's characters as living.

The 18th century criticism of Shakespeare differs from the earlier period mainly in the sense that it takes Shakespeare as a true genius who should be taken with the Classical masters but who cannot all be explained by their principles. It differs again from the next period of Shakespeare criticism mainly in that Shakespeare cannot be taken altogether out of the already set principles of drama although his is a world just unique in itself.

Maurice Morgann: Precursor of Romantic criticism

Maurice Morgann wrote his essay on Falstaff in 1977, just in vindication of courage against the charge of cowardice of this delightful character. But ultimately he scaled beyond the set limit of this preoccupation. It covers not only the secret of this character in two of Shakespeare's historical plays but also the essence of Shakespeare's genius that makes him still unsurpassing in his own field. The true character and style of Morgann's approaching to Shakespeare is properly speaking a deviation from the 18th century neo-classical stand on the subject.

The 18th Century approach from Dryden to Dr. Johnson via Pope, was rational and more or less objective; neither their evaluation of Shakespeare's plays takes into serious consideration Shakespeare the man nor is it based upon the subjective predilection of the critic's mind. Morgann is a departure from this line of criticism. Morgann's estimate of Falstaff rolls out of his very dislike of the general notion of Falstaff's cowardice, and is all the way greased in his personal passion, although still not further away from the 18th century standard of judgement.

Morgann has still a tendency of rationalizing prescription in judgement as in his inquiry into the difference between 'Impression' and 'Understanding' which one is to take proper note of for a right assessment of the character of Falstaff. But thereafter Morgann breaks away from the 18th century prescriptive method, and evolves rather an emotive personalised principle which seeks to veer round to the pivotal point of enquiry. It is very difficult to segregate John Falstaff from the critic's love and sympathy for him, sometimes his respect. Really speaking Falstaff is a pampered fool in Morgann's love and sympathy as Wamba was not in Cedric's house. Falstaff is regarded simply nursed up by Shakespeare himself. By the very impression of the character one is led to think him quite distinct from the other two similar characters, Parolles and Bobadil.

Morgann does not end by lending his own mind and feeling to the Fool of Shakespeare, he finds a similar contribution of Shakespeare's own to the right proportion of Falstaff's personality. Morgann has duly crossed the border of prescription into the Romantic evaluation of the creator's role in his very creation, his personality behind everything he creates; his remark here is—'For what is Falstaff, what Lear, what Hamlet, what Othello, but different modifications of Shakespeare's thought?'

The creator in a different form in his creation concept is a Romantic conception of art, essentially subjective, though yet not completely free from the restraint of the thought element. To this new element of Shakespeare criticism can be added another purely Romantic element of judgement of an individual character, not merely in the context of the work in which he is given a lease of life, but as a living person the critic's imagination may conceive him, living his life as we all do, although it is known that the life that he lives is given by the author. Morgann is sure of that power of Shakespeare which makes us forget that he is his (Shakespeare's) creation.

Morgann has not yet proceeded up to Bradley to share the sorrow of the broken heart he has simply attributed to it in his 'Rejection of Falstaff' essay, but surely he has taken the first step towards that end. Falstaff is an embodiment of wit and humour Shakespeare supplied him with. He is completely identified with it, his courage or weakness, folly or wisdom, honesty or falsity, anything else is a part of that element of humour, Morgann is sure.

Morgann's estimate of Shakespeare as a whole is one step ahead of the 18th century tradition of criticism, 'True poesy is magic not nature'. The 18th century Nature concept of poetic imitation is left behind here for a Romantic concept of the magic power of poetry. Shakespeare possessed this power more than anybody else, and with that power he cannot be brought down upon his knees to surrender to Aristotle, Morgann tells us. Morgann is rightly on his way to the Romantic critics like Hazlitt, Lamb and Coleridge, and further up to Bradley so far as his treatment of Falstaff is concerned.

Romantic Criticism of Shakespeare

The Romantic criticism of Shakespeare is a luminous chapter in Shakespeare studies. It should better be estimated just beside the 18th century development of Shakespeare criticism. From Dryden to Dr. Johnson via Pope is a quick sweep of more or less rational approach to Shakespeare. But the Romantic criticism clearly marks out a different kind of approach best estimated in the context of the Romantic ideals.

In a sense the Romantic criticism of Shakespeare started with Maurice Morgann. Maurice Morgann's single essay on Falstaff was written in 1777. It was really a sharp deviation from the 18th century method, best noted in an observation like this: "Falstaff is the word only, Shakespeare is the theme."

Morgann unconsciously struck the Romantic note which took the varied shapes in the hands of the great Romantic critics like Lamb, Hazlitt and Coleridge. These three great critics of Shakespeare brought about a great change in the very judgement of Shakespeare's art and idea.

Lamb in his Magazine article on the tragedy of Shakespeare takes up only one issue of Shakespeare's art, *viz.*, stageability of Shakespeare's plays. Lamb is quite clear about his idea that Shakespeare's plays are not meant for stage performance, no stage machinery can maintain the lofty ideals of Shakespeare's poetry; it is a travesty of fact that Garrick "bade them breathe anew", "the world sunk in death that Shakespeare drew".

Evidently Lamb pointed out the excellence of Shakespeare's plays as mainly the work of a master poet. The excellent quality of which is sure to be lost in the stage performance. Hazlitt's *Characters of Shakespeare's Plays* published only a few years after Lamb's Essay is really just in the same tradition of the critic's personal view of Shakespeare's excellence and attainments. All the Romantic critics are possessed with a joy of a discovery. They thought that they understood Shakespeare as he had never been understood before.

The plays of Shakespeare are regarded as embodiments of real life. The characters are treated as fellow beings and the business of critical estimate of Shakespeare's plays was primarily with the world that Shakespeare created.

Hazlitt estimated the character of Shakespeare not at all in the perspective of the social background against which Shakespeare placed them. Every hero of Shakespeare's tragedies got a new birth in the mind of the critic; even the plays as a whole assumed a new form as perhaps none contemplated them to be in Shakespeare's writings. Ultimately the total Shakespeare is given his due when placed in the company of the great poets of English literature, Shakespeare regarded "as the poet of Nature," Spenser "as the poet of romance" and Milton "as the poet of morality". Hazlitt treated Shakespeare as mainly a poet.

Contribution of Coleridge to Shakespeare's studies is very great. He is already imbued with the Romantic colour of mind, and in his powerful imagination gave Shakespeare a new colour which made Shakespeare appear as he had never appeared before. Already Coleridge delivered a series of lectures on Shakespeare; but his most important course was not delivered till 1818.

In his *Biographia Literaria* Coleridge estimated Shakespeare as mainly a poet, a poet of *Venus and Adonis* and *The Rape of Lucracia.* Even while estimating Shakespeare's plays Coleridge estimated Shakespeare more as a poet than as a dramatist.

Colerdge approached Shakespeare with a philosophic mind when philosophy was considerably influenced by his poetic imagination. Practically Coleridge's estimate of Shakespeare is characterized by a grand synthesis between these two apparently distinct qualities of his mind. Coleridge's is therefore, a highly balanced approach to Shakespeare which is best seen in an observation like this: "The judgement of Shakespeare is commensurate with his genius... reveals itself in his judgement as in its most exalted form."

Coleridge never keeps Shakespeare's art completely isolated from his abiding sympathy for life at large. "Shakespeare himself a nature humanised, a genial understanding directing self-consciously a power and an implicit wisdom deeper even than our consciousness."

Coleridge is the climax of the Romantic trend of criticism in Shakespeare studies. He is essentially Romantic in all his judgement but nowhere the judgement has severed the healthy link, the philosophic enquiry into the cause of things, while judging every individual mind and art in the world Shakespeare has created.

Victorian Criticism of Shakespeare

All the Romantic critics of Shakespeare made their subjects of the great playwright either in one way or in another in their mind highly coloured by their own temperament although sometimes very close to the truth of Shakespeare's genius. The best of the whole lot was Coleridge. The Victorian criticism of Shakespeare is a long way from this individualistic approach and a little closer to systemization of rational principles.

It is better to start Victorian criticism of Shakespeare with Carlyle. In 1840 Carlyle delivered a course of lectures in which he claimed that "Shakespeare is the chief of all poets hitherto known. "He further adds, "There rises a kind of universal psalm out of this Shakespeare, not unfair to make itself heard among the still more sacred psalms."

Mrs. Cowden Clarke was a faithful follower of Carlyle. Her *Complete Concordance to Shakespeare* deals with the girlhood of Shakespeare's heroines along with other things. It is only a Victorian plunge into sentimental bardolatry and the beginning of the emotional treatment of the characters as if they were real people.

Some Victorian critics took the clue from Coleridge, as eminently Bradley did. But they fail to maintain the 'organic whole' concept of Coleridge, rather they were separating the man from his work. Some of them were simply carried by their uncritical hyperboles into a sort of chimera. Some European critics like Gervinus, Goethe and Schlegel endeavoured to systematize the chaos. They treat each Shakespearean play as a unified whole, the unity maintained by a ruling idea.

In a way 18th century rationalism was revived in the Victorian period for a new approach to Shakespeare's plays. There was then a spurt of critical survey of individual Shakespearean plays which of coure avoided all over-philosophical interpretation of Shakespeare themes. The critics took up different questions of Shakespeare's plots, characters and themes for an overall estimate of each play. This of course leads to an even thorough exposition of Shakespeare's texts in the 20th century.

Professor Dowden made a significant contribution to Shakespeare's criticism. His book *Shakespeare: His Mind and Art* was published in 1875. It is a sensitive and sympathetic treatment of all Shakespeare's plays of course adopting a new principle of division of Shakespeare's plays, which was later a subject of criticism among the critics. It is still acknowledged as a standard critical work on Shakespeare.

Fleay discovered a new scientific method of applying material tests to Shakespeare's plays. The process was further carried on by J.M. Robertson.

Swinburne claimed in his study of Shakespeare in 1880 that Henry IV and Henry V alone established him as the greatest playwriter of the world. He is also idolatrous in approach.

The next significant critic is Moulton. His book *Shakespeare as a Dramatic Artist* (1885) is a scientific study in which he attempted to build up a theory of drama from Shakespeare's practice. In another book *The Moral System of Shakespeare* Moulton tried to detect a systematic evolution of a principle of morals in Shakespeare's plays.

The late Victorian scene of Shakespeare criticism is of course crowded with some great figures, figures like Bradley and Water Pater. Bradley in particular considered as the climax of the gradual progress of Shakespeare's criticism in the Victorian period. He must be recognised as the link between the Victorian and the modern approach to Shakespeare. Walter Pater wrote his Measure for Measure article and wrote His Essays on Shakespeare's English History which are accepted as a landmark in the history of Victorian criticism of Shakespeare. It is the best since Arnold himself fougt shy of the subject. Bradley of course has little to say about the aspect of Shakespeare's genius handled by Pater. Pater, Bradley and Dowden a little earlier are perhaps the cream of the Victorian criticism of Shakespeare.

CHAPTER V

METAPHYSICAL POETS

John Donne: St. Lucy's Day: A critical appreciation

John Donne is the leader of the Metaphysical group of poets. Almost in every poem, whether it is a devotional poem or a love poem, he maintains his metaphysical character, both in idea and style. *A Nocturnal Upon St. Lucy's Day* is really a love poem only in a metaphysical garment, quite representative of Donne's genius.

The poem does not begin as a love poem, there lies perhaps one of the essential characteristics of the metaphysical conceit. The poem in its first two stanzas explores the atmospheric background of the land. It is the St. Lucy's Day "The sunne is spent," the light of the sun is a little mellow, "The world's whole sap is sunke".

Just in this background of slump of energy and spirit the poet studies what it is to be loved. From here one is to know that the subject matter is love. The poet asks people, particularly those who are lovers, to follow the changes in him as a man in love. A change will come surely with the coming of the spring. It was for the poet lover a completely different world. It is the dead poet brought to new life by the alchemy of love—"In whom love wrought new Alchemy".

At this stage of the poem a thorough disquisition on the process of creation is introduced but not completed, although it has only a very frail link with the subject matter in hand. The lover knows, the whole creation was out of 'nothingness'. He wants to say that he came to be almost everything covetable in life out of mere nothing that he was. The lover's idea is "I am re-begot/Of absence, darkness, death".

It is then quite clear that the poet is metaphysical in outlook and in the use of images. He is full of metaphysical conceits to define his own paltry case.

The next stage of development in the life of love is marked well again by means of metaphysical analogies, in the rest of the poem. The poet makes a sharp contrast between his own life of love and the general trend of life outside. Other people draw their good from so many other things of life, soul, form, spirit, etc.; but the lover poet has all his good only from love, paradoxically from all 'that's nothing'.

The poet defines how the two lovers came to unite and how they felt because of their separation from each other. He conceives, they shed fears and their tears create a flood in which "Drowned the whole world, us two". Strangely enough sweetness and misery which are the result of all love can be so prodigiously queer as in this case—the two lovers only 'two chaoses' when they shifted their care to anything else.

A simple withdrawal of affection comes to a dead end, and the bodies are simply left without souls, and left a lifeless lump 'carcasses'. With all these analogies the lover wants to strike deep at the root of all the bliss and languishment of love they two underwent.

The poem is a representative love poem deep in the metaphysical tradition in which seriousness of love, even sincerity of passion, is made a fit object of personal conceits duly expressed by means of apparently odd terms of science and discoveries of new learning. The excellence of the poem lies in the sincerity of passion and the perfection of a style better explained by Dryden's epithet 'affectation of metaphysics' as a form of conceits.

THE EXTASIE: A critical appreciation

Wherever he is, Donne is always conceitous; whether it is love or religion, the same trend, the same habit of mind betrays itself. The trend is psychologically rendered in a term first adopted to explain it by Dryden. The term 'metaphysical' has a special connotation when applied to Donne and his followers of the 17th century. 'Extasie' is a poem that fully represents Donne as Metaphysical poet of the tradition noted above.

Love is the subject matter of the poem, but the subject is not so important as its style of execution. Yet the theme cannot be altogether ignored, it has its unique quality, its individuality of conception which is neither explained by Platonic concept of love, nor by the Biblical theory of a higher passion for the ultimate Cause of the Creation.

It is clear Donne has a personal feeling about love, much derived out of his own experiences. Ecstasy is no doubt the outward expression of love, love that is between two persons, here of course between a man and a woman. Donne's idea is not essentially philosophic, neither borrowed from any other source all through. Love is a matter of a mysterious revelation, a concern of two souls as he feels.

Donne eventually links up love with the principle of a close relationship between body and soul. Donne ignores neither. When it is all body it is too gross, again when it is all soul it is apparently of no earthly value, it is ultimately both. It is no concern of one side alone, it links up both, yet transmutes two into one, although yet it is not Biblical concept of oneness.

Now it is the stylistic uniqueness that proves more effective and makes the idea even clearer. The poet's conceits are all, the images and allusions are all from the knowledge of science, but the use of them makes all the difference. The poet applies his knowledge, the knowledge apparently very odd, a little unrelated, but in his application it builds up a private myth of his passion.

The souls of the two part company with the bodies and in-between their existence the souls unite and form into a unit, a proof how love can make that transmutation possible. Then of course they return to the bodies so that the body cannot be ignored. Human body that induces love is love itself. The very existence is love. Donne's 'Extasie' is a clear evidence of his excellence and originality.

AFFLICTION: A critical appreciation

George Herbert as a Metaphysical poet follows Donne in his rendering of life and faith, but temperamentally he is quite different from his master. The first striking difference is that in him love and faith are not of separate existence, they are blended in his soul: the second difference is that his allusions and imageries are although studied, not so strangely conceitous as in Donne's poems.

'Affliction' is a representative poem of Herbert. The poem opens as a love poem, or it could be interpreted as such. The poet's heart is enticed, to whom until you go to the second stanza of the poem you cannot form your idea about it. The enticement is in terms of material temptation as though in a lady's boudoir. This is no doubt in the Metaphysical tradition of presentment.

The poet ultimately leads to his unwavering faith and unconditional love for God. The poet is nearly Puritanical in his attitude, he does not require any pleasure when he has served the King of all pleasures. Affliction may be on as vast a scale as in the life of Job, but his faith is even more monolithic in the face of greavest of doubt than it was Job's . The poet is sure no pleasure can be as enthralling as the pleasure of God's love. God showered upon us joys of all kinds, but we turned them to sorrow:

> 'I was entangled in the world of strife,
> Before I had the power to change my life.'

The poet gives a new explanation of sorrow and affliction in his life. He does not know any complaint of his soul in affliction, 'I should too happy be in my unhappiness'. Love has its sorrows too, sorrows there are sure source of joy. This is indeed the strength of his love for God.

Herbert surpasses even Job's faith in God, Job sometimes whished he were not born, he knew how to complain, but Herbert's love knows no such complaint, it is too deep and too firm for such a wavering. Love is without any string, unconditional. 'In weakness' he 'must be stout'.

The last few lines of the poem are the most conceitous and the best of Metaphysical ideas. The poet leaves all directness of statement only to prove his strength of faith, expressions are as oblique as they can be and his faith is a redoubled confirmation by the negativity of his negatives as here:

> '..though I am clean forgot,
> Let me not love thee, if I love thee not'.

CANONIZATION: a representative poem of Donne

Donne is basically a love poet who turns to his human beloved, as Herbert turns to his God, with the same passion. All his personal conceits, either borrowed or private invention, drape his love gaudy for himself. He has neither any outside ideal of love like Shelley's nor the purity of impassioned soul of Wordsworth, nor any philosophy of Browning's ideal. He loves like himself, the passion is charged with his personal conceits.

'Canonization' is a poem that has only a thin screen of divinity, as the title suggests, but it goes all secular and even mundane, essentially to do with the material plane, often the body. The poet begins the poem with a vague undefined address, which is again a part of his Metaphysical apparatus. It is immaterial whom he addresses to present his case and when he has already gone so deep in love.

He cares little for any reason or argument forbidding love, he knows Church prohibition of love, bodily love; he too belonged to the Church, but he is not ready to listen to anything against love, he is all in love, 'for God's sake hold your tongue let me love ... '. He offers his own argument, love is innocent, it has no harm for anybody. 'Who is injured by my love?'

Love is a part of human nature, if one is to care for it. Donne of course does not care even for that support, he is all too personal for that. In the third stanza it is really a peremptory personal vindication—'Call us... we are made such by love.' The vindication is all through Metaphysical conceits, odd expletives. The lovers' sighs can drown ships, the tears can overflow grounds. The Phoenix is even a symbol of love as its own ultimate source.

Donne is even ready to embrace death by love, because love is life eternal, lovers are canonized in undying verses as in the Italian sonnets and in their Elizabethan counterparts. Donne's personal reactions in love has a true character, in love alone one finds peace though it begins with rage, two become one though they begin with sharp difference of their own.

Donne paints a love that remains a passion, and remains content in that state. He does not spiritualize it, because that means a remote quality far beyond the reach of the earth, on earth it is no less solemn.

CHAPTER VI

EIGHTEENTH CENTURY SATIRE

Absalom and Achitophel: Characters–Achitophel & Zimri

Dryden has a unique role in the religio-political controversy of his age. All his satires, particularly *Absalom and Achitophel*, are out of the great interest in the controversy itself. There lies his essential difference from the two other great satirists of the age, mainly Pope.

Absalom and Achitophel is the unique creation of Dryden, a creation that involves the myth of the Bible as well as the realities of his age. The satire is epic in structure and has a permanent value which only a political lampoon can hardly expect to have. The occasion of the satire is clearly known to all. It was in the year of a great political event when Shaftsbury was arrested on charge of subornation of high treason for conspiring for the death of the King and 'subversion of the Government' and awaited his trial at the Old Bailey, November 1681.

Undoubtedly Shaftsbury is the most important character in the satire. He appears under the Biblical character of Achitophel. Dryden's treatment of the character is not of course exactly on the line of the Old Testament. The character at best differs from the Old Testament history, but Dryden closely follows the spirit of the Bible account, and the real history of Shaftsbury comes very close to the history of the Bible.

Shaftsbury as painted by Dryden is a popular political leader, who in spite of his great influence is a wrong-headed devil. The main assault of Dryden's powerful language is primarily against the controversial role of the character. Achitophel championed the cause of Absalom against his father David, in the Bible he was almost bullied by Achitophel to even an unthought on sinful act of 'going into the concubines of his father.' Shaftsbury is not painted as devilish as that in Dryden's picture, but to achie 'e his own end he proves to be even more crafty in political manoeuvre.

Shaftsbury is a public figure who not only harms public interest by his secret ambition for power but at the same time by a surely distorted manners and motives of his own. He utilizes the political instability, particularly in the form of the problem of succession to the throne, championing the cause of Monmouth against the Duke of York. Of course he had neither love for Monmouth nor any hatred for the principle against which he fought. His motive was purely personal, at least Dryden paints him so:

> But wild ambition loves to slide, not stand,
> And Fortune's ice prefers to Virtue's land,
> Achitophel, grown weary to possess
> A lawful fame and lazy happiness,
> Disdained the golden fruit to gather free
> And lent the crowd his arm to shake the tree.

Dryden himself was a Tonny so his attack against Shaftsbury was almost a personal attack, although his bitterness of feeling is not of the order of Pope. He had already shuffled it in the mythical grandeur of the Bible. Dryden's picture always has a realistic broadside steeped only in the idealistic panorama of the Jewish history. Shaftsbury in the midst of the Roman mob-like unthinking countrymen is gathering his political fruit free by simply exploiting their innocence and utilizing the contemporary political instability. He is the most crafty among the crooked politicians of his age. Dryden's scorn for all his resources as a political leader is perhaps the strongest. 'Of these the false Achitophel was first/ A name to all succeeding ages curst.'

In spite of Dryden's hatred for such a political leader clearly pronounced the picture that he paints of Shaftsbury, although very close to the real picture, has the seminal principle that at once raises the picture to the level of general truth, the truth about motive-hunting misdirected political figure with enough power but with complete absence of integrity and honesty of purpose. Such a picture Shaftsbury undoubtedly is, a unique creation of Dryden although very close to the real picture and the original of the character.

Absalom and Achitophel: Zimri

Dryden's *Absalom and Achitophel* is no doubt a political satire steeped in the mythological allusions of the Old Testament. The beauty of the satire lies in Dryden's complete mastery over the two worlds, the history of the Jewish people as narrated in the Bible during the reign of

David and the contemporary history of England. All the characters in *Absalom and Achitophel* have doubled implications, with an inevitable impact upon the heightening of effect.

No doubt Achitophel is the character first in importance, but Dryden calls Zimri most interesting and regards him 'worth the whole poem'. It is however easy to see why Dryden considers Zimri so interesting as a character. Like Achitophel Zimri is a real character in history brought under the mask of a mythical character of the same name. Zimri is the second Duke of Bukingham, George Villiers, who was the son of the favourite of Charles I.

Dryden's picture of Zimri, the mythical name given to the Duke, is not all a distortion of fact. He was a profligate and unsteady in all his political career and was given to folly until he died in 1687. Even Pope has painted the picture of this character 'in his Moral Essays'. Buckingham appears also in others' writings of the age; but Dryden's model was only any of his contemporaries' picture of the character. Dryden carefully took note of the real character and furnished it with the literary hints taken from two classical models. Horace's portrait of Tigellis and Juvenal's Greek parasite.

Dryden in his 'Essays on Satire' makes the memorable remark on this very character. Dryden's idea is the uniqueness of portrait as a character although it is only second in importance to Achitophel. Buckingham is in quality and character sharply distinct from Shaftsbury. Buckingham could in no way serve in the leading role as Shaftsbury has done. Shaftsbury fully utilized the political muddle in his age to serve his own political ambition. Buckingham could not serve any such purpose, because his was all too unsteady for a consistent purpose. Dryden makes the character as curiously oscillating as perhaps he was not in life.

Dryden's portrait of Buckingham is curiously the consummation of inconsistency. Shaftsbury made use of the political situation of his age, the uncertainty in succession, as also some leading factional characters of which Zimri's name comes first. Dryden depicts him at once a curious type of political indecision inherent in the very constitution of the man:

> A man so various that he seemed to be
> Not one, but all mankind's epitome.

The individuality of the character is only to be noted in the excess of inconsistency in all affairs of political importance. Dryden's idea is that the character is swayed by his personal constitutional peculiarity. All his principle or better the lack of it, is governed by his personal predilections and dispositions. Dryden brings it out in this passage:

Swift in opinions, always in the wrong,
Was everything by starts and nothing long.

Dryden penetrates deep into his personal character, because he takes it as a guiding factor, personality overruling his principle. He was undoubtedly all too bad in his private life; Dryden's portrait makes him a sad womanizer. Dryden tells us:

Then all for women, painting, rhyming, drinking,
Besides ten thousand freaks that died in thinking.

Buckingham's character in *Absalom and Achitophel* is no less satiric than the character of Shaftsbury. Shaftsbury is still on a higher plane of political game, and Buckingham is on a lower plane, always in the mesh of his personal idiosyncrasies even for his political acts and decisions. He is a character always in the extreme. Dryden's word is 'over-violent or over-civil'. Everyman to him was either 'God or Devil'.

His another art for political influence was to use money as an instrument, 'squandering wealth was his peculiar art' but wealth regularly deceived him. He was 'beggared by fools whom still he found too late'. His habit was to form parties which he ultimately failed to lead.

Thus the portrait of Zimri deviates a little more from the account of the Bible than the character of Achitophel. In painting Buckingham Dryden perhaps outpaced the limitations of the Bible and was essentially carried by the spirit of satire.

The subject of Mac Flecknoe: The historical background

Dryden as a satirist is deeply involved in the contemporary religious and political controversy. *Absalom and Achitophel* is an occasional poem with of course some timeless qualities of its poetry and art adopted by the poet. *Mac Flecknoe* is a personal satire deriving its force from some political controversy. The history of its origin is quite interesting.

Dryden could not influence the Grand Jury by the timely publication of *Absalom and Achitophel*, Shaftsbury was released from the Tower. The Whigs were in jubilation. So Dryden wrote *The Medal* as if the jubilant Whigs required one. This was replied by a satire entitled *The Medal of John Bayes* by Shadwell. This inspired Dryden to write *Mac Flecknoe* in October 1682.

In the poem Shadwell is personally the target of attack, almost an undisguised attack. In *Absalom and Achitophel* the target of attack is mainly Shaftsbury, but he is disguised under the mask of a Biblical myth, but Shadwell is directly named in the poem, the mask is not mythical, but only under an Irish name Flecknoe, Richard Flecknoe's son as he is supposed. Richard Flecknoe is a historical name. Richard Flecknoe was a Roman Catholic priest, also an industrious scribbler for upwards of half a century. Mac Flecknoe is supposed to be the descendant of this Richard Flecknoe, a true repository of dullness.

Dryden's satire of Shadwell is mostly unjust, he is anything but dull, he had what Dryden lacked, a deep vein of humour, more successful as comic poet than Dryden, always lively; yet Dryden makes him a butt of ridicule and attributes to him all those disqualifications of art and literary creations most of them undeserved. The poem is a good study of literary values, if only viewed positively. The effect is only negatively satiric.

Whether personally by name or under the mask of Mac Flecknoe Shadwell is brought into the values of literary creations only to show or claim complete blank. The 18th century values of 'nature', 'sense' and 'wit' are thoroughly explored, and the greatest demerit of a piece of art its dullness. Shadwell is lampooned sharply by means of a literary discourse in which he simply misfits. The worried father laments his son's incapacities and teaches him his native qualities. Dryden makes fun of both and attains the highest point of satire by playing the trump card at the right moment. The satire is severe here where his father teaches,

'Success let other teach, learn thou from me
Pangs without birth and fruitless industry.'

Mac Flecknoe: Dryden's quality of satire

Of the three major satirists of the last 17th and early 18th century of English literature, Dryden is one, but sharply contrasted with the other two, Pope and Swift. Dryden belongs to an earlier period. He is more involved in contemporary politics than the other two. Only *Mac Flecknoe* is an exception in which Dryden is a little closer to Pope, personal and undisguised in his attack like Pope.

As in his other major satires Dryden takes court of history in *Mac Flecknoe*, but does not hide history behind allegory or myth, in *Absalom and Achitophel* behind Biblical myth. In *Mac Flecknoe* history is only hidden behind another history, the history of an Irish poet. Compared to *Absalom and Achitophel* it is of lower artistic excellence, the allegory is not at all of the same grandeur with that of *Absalom and Achitophel.* It does not lead to another very interesting world, it remains just where it is. The shaft hits direct the target.

Dryden's excellence as a satirist in his poem is his style of evocation, he has fully exploited enmity to the best service of poetry. The lucidity of his verse which was better appreciation in his age makes satire enjoyable to others, all except his subject; not only that, Dryden's treatment of his subject attaches a literary issue, in its indirect exposition, mainly the first quality of liveliness in literature. Shadwell lacked this quality - 'Mature in dullness from his tender years'. All other attendant qualities like 'wit', 'sense' and unaffected true nature Shadwell is said to have lacked.

Another lively style of satire is, Shadwell is presented as by his own father as commonly unruly sons are discussed by their fathers among his friends, again as taught by them a lesson for true conduct. This letter part of the father Flecknoe is more enjoyable than anything else:

> 'Nor let false friends seduce thy mind to fame
> By arrogating Jonson's hostile name;

Mac Flecknoe can be regarded as an excellent study of the best qualities of the 17th and 18th century poetry, the qualities Shadwell totally lacked, 'sense', 'nature' and 'wit'. Flecknoe's advice to his son in disguise Shadwell is again from a perfect knowledge of true artistic sense which falls flat upon his dull son, satire lies in this failure. This is one side of his satire, the other side of his incapacities he leaves to his son not only to inherit but also to augment. This is the other side of the satire.

The nursery arrangement and coronation scene in the poem are most entertaining and there Dryden lifts satire to the level of humour, true enjoyment lies there and an otherwise scathing satire uses the feathery end of the shafts for itching pleasantries.

Absalom and Achitophel: Its Biblical setting

Dryden's *Absalom and Achitophel* is a satire, but a satire of a special kind. The tradition of satire in the late 17th century England was really a classical tradition to which Dryden belonged. The plan of the poem is not perhaps original. The idea of casting satire in the epic mould was suggested no doubt by the 4th satire of Juvenal. Horace and Lucan undoubtedly supplied models for the elaborate portraits, especially Lucan's description of the political condition of Rome did.

Absalom and Achitophel is a political satire cast in the mould of the Biblical myth. The uniqueness of Dryden's satire is in the close link between the old Testament myth and the contemporary political imbroglio of England. Dryden has adopted the allegory of the Jewish history to explain better the political condition of England.

The analogy between the Jewish history in the reign of David and the condition of England around 1681 is highly interesting. In the analogy David is Charles II, Absalom is Monmouth and Achitophel Shaftsbury. They are close parallels as characters, and the history is more or less similar. Dryden has utilized the parallelism quite effectively.

Dryden of course has predecessors in the use of Biblical material for literary overtones. A Roman Catholic poet for example had in 1679 paraphrased the scriptural story of Naboth's vineyard applying it to the condemnation of Lord Stratford. Again a small prose tract was published in Dublin in 1680 entitled *Absalom's Conspiracy*. So Dryden may have taken note of such attempts one or two years before his own poem.

Dryden took the story from the Old Testament history of King Saul in the Book of Samuel. The story corresponds with the story of the problem of succession in the late 17th century of England. In Samuel I Chapter 13 Saul is held *persona non grata* for his obvious transgression. Samuel simply told Saul, he had not kept the Commandments of the Lord, the result was he would be replaced by David. In Samual Book II David, already on the throne of the Israelites faced a problem similar to the problem of succession in England during Dryden's time. In this part of the Bible Absalom, the illegitimate son by one of David's concubines, for some time in exile, is led by a tricky political leader, Achitophel by name, as the only claimant to the throne of Israel.

Monmouth in English History was likewise a natural son of Charles II. He was similarly persuaded by Shaftsbury to claim the throne of England in the absence of a regular successor. His claim was set off against the claim of the King's brother, Duke of York. The whole problem of succession in England was intrigued not only by the political partisanism of the people but also by the religious,conflicts in the higher echelon of the Church.

Dryden has clearly understood the close parallelism between the Bible story and the history of his own times. In some cases at least Dryden has not all too closely followed the old Testament myths. He has not of course followed literally the ultimate end of Absalom in the Bible story, nor even the altogether sweet relationship between David and Absalom only embittered by the tricky manoeuvre of Achitophel, nor even that very sad and ugly suggestion made by Achitophel to Absalom to go into one of his father's concubines.

Dryden in his use of the Old Testament background of life has clearly taken note of the problem of succession and the very tricky role of a statesman. His portrait of the tricky statesman is the crux of the satire, his scorn is for the leader of the people and for the people themselves. The Jewish people are easily led as the Londoners of his time. They are easily befooled by people like Shaftsbury who simply added fuel to the fire of political fury. He has no doubt a kind of respect for the royal born Monmouth however illegitimate he might be. In the choice of the Bible story Dryden has duly satisfied his Tory outlook.

Absalom and Achitophel is a satire that closely utilizes a mythical background of life for the heightening of effect of real history. Although the plan is allegorical with its two planes of implication the ultimate effect is a strong account of a chapter of history, in which Dryden himself took great interest and acted his role in his own style.

Comparative study of Dryden and Pope as satirists

Dryden and Pope belong to the same tradition and the same age, Dryden a little early and Pope a little late, Dryden late 17th and Pope early 18th century of English literature. Dryden's *Absalom and Achitophel* and *Mac Flecknoe* are the cream of his satires and adequate representation of his genius. Likewise Pope's *Satires and Epistles* is full of cardinal qualities of his satires. But the two are of two different qualities of genius. They write satires because satire was then the convention of literary creation, particularly inspired by religious and political controversies of the age.

Dryden was instigated by a political controversy, perhaps the most intriguing controversy of succession to the throne, in *Absalom and Achitophel*. There was of course no such political or any other controversy to incite Pope to write his *Satires and Epistles*; it was written by Pope for form's sake, the title is there very suggestive, *Satires and Epistles Horace Imitated*. But the imitation of Horace, although very close, is not indispensable for appreciation of Pope's quality of satire. The first striking difference between Pope's *Satires and Epistles* and Dryden's *Absalom and Achitophel* is the mythical apparatus which Dryden adopts and adds to the poem's literary excellence and its very interest. Pope has no such interest to claim here.

Dryden's *Absalom and Achitophel* is comparable to Pope's *Rape of the Lock*, in its mock heroic structure and artistic excellence. Dryden's *Mac Flecknoe* is a little closer to Pope's *Satires and Epistles* in the severity of its personal and the fury of direct attack. Pope garbs the contemporary minor poets in the mask of classical names, some of them drawn from Horace. Dryden of course has no such significant literary mask in *Mac Flecknoe* except one from Irish history. Only his attack is less soothed than in *Absalom and Achitophel* and more humoured than in the pages of *Satires and Epistles*. Here is a passage from Pope's *Satires and Epistles* where even humour is all too cutting than direct hit of a Satire:

Poor Cornus sees his frantic wife elope,
And curses wit, and poetry, and Pope.

Pope exaggerates his importance less politely than Dryden in his *Mac Flecknoe*. Of course in both the poems there is an attempt, indirect no doubt; Pope in his attack of Grub Street and Drury Lane poetasters depicts the wild craze for literary ambition in his age which no doubt hauled down the status of poetry to the low level of rhyming couplets. Dryden of course holds Shadwell to ridicule by naming his faults and exaggerated servility of imitation of other's affectations, thereby exploring the whole field of literary conventions in all indirectness. Shadwell is a blank, a pure humbug of a poet.

Pope is almost always unrelieved, the strain of his attack upon the minor poets, mostly uncatholic and uncharitable, if not absolutely undeserved, is seldom made light by wit or humour. If there be any spark of geniality or artistic gracefulness of expression or any beauty of imagery or allusion - there are some no doubt - they betray the artist Pope is, but not really the noble mercy or the tolerant attitude which one may expect of a great man. There he differs from Dr. Johnson. Dryden's *Mac Flecknoe* and other satires, especially *Absalom and Achitophel*, are full of literary grace, artistically more relieved than Pope's satires. Dryden gains in lucidity and grace and Pope in strength of his attack. Pope hits at the right place, because he knows he must not spare or miss his enemy and Dryden makes the shaft even a well-dressed instrument of beauty. Each is rightly in his own sphere an incomparable master.

Pope's style of Satire

Pope is better distinguished between two other satirists of his age, Dryden who precedes him and Swift who is his exact contemporary. Pope's *Satires and Epistles* came out in 1734, and Swift's *Gulliver's Travels* in 1726 and Dryden's *Absalom and Achitophel* in 1681. Pope among them has a virility of attack more severe than any of the rest. He fully imbibes the 18th century convention and leads it to a great extent.

Pope has pointed out the greatest quality of his satires in the advertisement of the poem - 'truth and sentiment', sentiment is purely personal, and truth is not universal as one may have thought. In *Satires and Epistles* Pope has no universal truth as Swift's *Gulliver's Travels* may justify its author's claim. The theme of Pope's satires is scurrilous attack upon his enemies and his life so far as a satiric exposition may include. His envious opponents paint him so as to lower his position to those who do not know him. Pope introduces himself in the form of classical Epistles addressed to a friend, that too in classical dialectic form.

In the Prologue part of the Poem Pope sweeps over a wide area of his time, naming almost all his unworthy enemies, some concealed behind classical names and style imitated from Horace in particular. Pope's own history in this part is true, particularly his claims, 'I lisped in numbers, for numbers came'. This natural genius of rhyming perfection which counted much in those days never left him, rather attained the high water mark of excellence in his satires. Although his satires were severe and scathing they attained the grace of excellent poetry, poetry practically out of trash, as an example here out of many such:

'Pains, reading, study are their just pretence,
And all they want is spirit, taste, and sense.'

Arbuthnot and Pope are supposed to argue their points in the Prologue, finally Pope offers his reason to hurt his enemies, his sincerity and seriousness may be disproportionate to the target of his attack, the people, their status, and attainments. There pope's catholicity is to be questioned, and there he offers a sharp contrast to Dr. Johnson. His *Dunciad* by its very title and content bears it out, as *Satires and Epistles* also does. Of course that is the moral and ethical side of his personality, which seldom disturbs his art that remains a finished form, worthy to be classed with the classical master's achievement.

Pope in his satires reveals a good sense of wit which was in those days a worthy substitute for modern humour. Wit has often soothed the gash of the sharp cutting weapons though they do not get blunt thereby, rather proved the fighter's skilful swordsmanship. Only in *The Rape of the Lock* Pope unconsciously attains the geniality of humour both in purpose and stylistic effect, in *Satires and Epistles* his geniality does not scale beyond wit, sense he has embraced all through and his excellence in this province is that he can attain the effect of good sense out of apparent nonsense, a good example is here:

'Arthur, whose giddy son neglects the laws,
Imputes to me and my damn'd works the cause:'

Pope's attack is clear and direct, all the defects of the poetasters are so meticulously woven in the warp and woof of poetry that it lends a character to his style. None of the satirists of this period, neither Dryden nor Swift could do this. Pope is a master artist of his craft, perhaps none has this complete hold on rhyme as Pope has.

Gulliver's Travels: Irony and satirical effect

Gulliver's Travels is one of the best satires even known in English literature, but the method adopted by Swift is far different from that of the other two great satirists of his age, Dryden (a little earlier) and Pope. The difference is not only as between prose and verse, which is accidental, but also between the presentation of truth and the strength of their animosity. So Pope's and Dryden's is satire proper, the method too, and Swift's is satire in effect while the method is irony.

Irony in *Gulliver's Travels* is a cover to present the truth in which there is no party to be hurt and none to inflict it. Truth is always, so irony is only the method of serving the dish. *Gulliver's Travels* seems to be the modern version of the Mediaeval *Mandeville's Travels*, the only difference is its ironical style of presentation with a satiric effect. Gulliver himself is carried through several lands, mainly four, to be ridiculed in all those odd companies. The usual size and sentiment and all those common human habits of a model Englishman to represent the whole of the European culture are in sharp contrast with the unusually small size of the Lilliputians, the extremely monstrous size and height of Brobding nagians, the inconceivably tricky people of a flying island, and grotesque simplicity of the horse population of the land of Houyhnhnms.

It is a sheer irony of a standard specimen of European culture to be ridiculed by all those sub-standard savage types of those wonderlands. The author brings it to a satiric effect, the pride of place of the European races in particular and the whole of mankind in general is open to ridicule everywhere outside their own fortification. The intensity of his passion in the bitterness of the banter betrays Swift almost as a misanthrope. Gulliver is more than once called upon to make a public demonstration of his nakedness, twice in the land of Houyhnhnms, once to exceeding wonder of his master, then again tempting a female Yahoo while bathing in a steam. In the land of the Lilliputians he was to extinguish the fire in the queen's closet by discharging urine upon the flame when he could thought of no other easy means.

Towards the close of Gulliver's travel in the land of Houyhnhnms the author under the mask of the hero makes the satiric strain of his fictitious story clear. Better a passage from this part be quoted:

> ...But instead of proposal for conquering that magnanimous nation, I rather wish they were in a capacity or disposition to send a sufficient number of their inhabitants for civilizing Europe; by teaching us the first principles of honour, justice, truth, temperance, public spirit, fortitude, chastity, friendship, benevolence, and fidelity...(pp. 314-5).

Here the author's role of a corrective jester is quite evident. The British ambition of conquering a newly discovered land by the navigators as in the Renascence period and always thereafter is an unacceptable proposition to the author. The ambition is not only unethical in terms of human values, the values he has preached, but at the same time sure to be brought to a sad end for the nation. The author has clearly stated what might be the ultimate result of the First Minister of State's proposal for invasion of the otherwise innocent Houyhnhnms, he has clearly defined it in this part.

The beauty of this book is not its oddities, its accounts of the wonderlands, in which attempt, though he far exceeds Mandeville's attempt, or its exploring the novel method of fictional writing—which paved the way for the rise of a new species in English literature—but a conscious attempt at balancing positive human values against all those monstrous inhuman fluids of human civilization, particularly in its stronghold of the British regime.

The political acumen that Gulliver met with in different lands of his visit is in sharp contrast with the British wisdom in as many various ways as there are lands; the author satirizes both their odd humour of political and other social wisdom and also the systems in his land; both of them conflict with his own sense of values, although they are not here reduced to explicit principles. That's why his method is ironical in which no extra responsibility of a clear statement of truth emburdens the author's wisdom. With all cultures and civilizations he considers his people the European version of Yahoo as the philosophic superior horse race of his wonderland termed him one, and ousted him from the land of reason for fear of contamination of the Yahoo qualities, as the Lilliputian contrived to cause his death in a slow enfeebling process best known to them for another kind of fear and envy. In the author's view the British race for all their boast of civilization is but a hated Yahoo race for lack of essential human qualities.

The Rape of the Lock: Supernatural machinery

Alexander Pope finished his *The Rape of the Lock* in 1712, then he did not seriously think of the supernatural machinery. Two years later Pope introduced it in the very structure of the poem, and got it dressed up in the regular shape of an epic. The pattern is heroic but the ultimate effect absolutely unheroic which definitely makes the poem mock heroic to all intents and purposes.

Pope himself gives his idea of the word machinery in the very dedicatory letter addressed to Arabella Fermor. He defines the term machinery as invented by the critics to 'signify that part which the deities, angels, or demons are made to act in a poem'. Pope however was quite clear as what purpose this machinery would serve in a poem like *The Rape of the Lock*, the machines would be governed by "the Rosiucrucian doctrine of spirit".

Pope in the same letter discusses his source of the Rosicrucian doctrine; his source is a French book called *Le Come de Gabolis*. The Rosiucrucian allows four elements to be inhabited by four different kinds of spirits - Sylphs, Gnomes, Nymphs, and Scamanders. Pope in his supernatural machinery allows all the four to appear, but only two act their elaborate roles in his mock heroic epic. Sylphs and Gnomes appear, particularly Sylphs, and Umbrical a Gnome is introduced only in Canto IV.

The Poem is essentially mock heroic in character. The spirits are involved in the very structure of the poem in obedience to the epic tradition of their elaborate use. Pope of course differs from the epic poets in this ultimate effect, the effect of this use. Pope is in fact a satirist. The epic grandeur that he develops in the poem ultimately serves his satiric end. The supernatural machinery has also a satiric cast.

In his use of the spirits Pope again differs from Shakespeare. The supernatural elements introduced in Shakespeare's plays is by contrast highly dramatic in effect, as in *The Tempest* and *A Midsummer Night's Dream* in particular. Ariel also appears in Pope's poem, but it is not Prospero's Ariel, nor the use that Prospero made there. In Pope's Ariel is only a 'watchful sprite'.

Sylphs are in abundance in *The Rape of the Lock*, and they serve as an invisible army gathering round the beau and the belle in order to protect the highly entertained delicacy of their appearance. They gathered in the boudoir of Arabella in order to enjoy the fun of the elaborate beautification of the lady's body. It is also essentially of satiric undertone.

In Pope's use of all these invisible spirits there is a systematic adjustment of their roles to the expected effect of the whole mock heroic atmosphere. There is an elaborate heroic arrangement in the poem itself brought ultimately to serve a totally unheroic end. All the spirits who appear with all seriousness of their roles in the protection of their beauty, in the nursing of their delicacy and also in the hope of sharing the human activities *par excellence*, do ultimately disperse as quickly as they gather together. Such a plan serves well the true purpose of the poem, the purpose that lends itself to the tone of the poem.

Pope names of course Homer, he has perhaps the epic structure of the Iliad and Odyssey in mind. But he knows quite well that his Bellinda does never wreck the towers of Troy as Helen does. His awareness of his limitations as the poet of his mock heroic poem is quite clear, even in the particular use of phantoms and spirits as here.

CHAPTER VII

MILTON

Lycidas: the early stage of Milton's poetic excellence

L'Allegro and *Il Penseroso* are *en bloc* an improvement upon the *Nativity Ode*, and *Lycidas* upon *L'Allegro* and *Il Penseroso*. All these poems represent Milton's early stage of attainment. Around 1632 Milton was deep in Nature sentiment, and in two of his poems of this period he studied only the implication of the two contrasted moods, mirth and melancholy. The next improved stage is marked by *Lycidas*, mirth or melancholy whatever it is, it must not end in itself. Milton leads ultimately to something higher than either of them. *Lycidas* is philosophically that achievement.

Lycidas is not a mere loss, not a simple lamentation either, it is a realization of something far above that. The shepherds mourn the loss of their friend, a fellow shepherd, Milton mourns his friend's death, but it is not an elegy like that of Gray who laments likewise his friend's death, West's death, and laments the loss of values, merits in general. Milton does not do it at all. He scales beyond misery to attain a sort of Hebraic faith of final redemption. It is hardly to be isolated from the *Nativity* Ode and the divine melancholy and creative gaiety of the other two poems.

Lycidas is pronounced more as the evidence of artistic maturity of the poet's early stage than as the maturity of its thought content. The poet is on his way to originality with his successful use of classical learning, his deepest appreciation of the Greek art and innovations. The wise and unique application of pastoralism in the elegy is quite in harmony with Milton's original sentiment. The Greek myths in use are not mere apparel, they result in the excellence of the poet's mood. The loss is to be lamented, but it must not make one forget God's mercy and the majesty of the moral order.

Milton does not care for originality for originality's sake, but for the convenient use of one's acquisition. Milton stresses more on the second line of interest in this period, and his early stage is not a mere effort but excellence in another form. The only immaturity of Milton's art is his more exhaustive and more elaborate allusion and imageries, although none of them misplaced and wide of the mark.

This period is duly in the poet's Horton predilection, obviously steeped in nature sensibility, the poem is as it were in a dressed up world of Greek myths filled with the freshness of the English countryside. The pictures could have been an odd mixture in a less expert hand, in Milton's artistic sense, although only in its early stage, they are shaped, into a perfect unity of effect. The Sicilian Muse here calls the Vales and bids them hither cast

'Their Bells and Flowers of a thousand hues.
Ye valleys low where the milde whispers use
Of shades and wanton winds and gushing brooks,
On whose fresh lap swart star sparely looks,
Throw hither all your quaint enameld eyes...

Lycidas: The quality of its elegiac note

Milton is not normally a poet of lamentation, 'On His Blindness' has proved it, he is like a later poet Browning could easily avoid writing anything of melancholy strain. Milton's elegy is of the same note with Browning's 'Prospice, although when pastoral cloak is superimposed. Pastoralism is Milton's artistic side, a reflection of his classical learning and the relic of his Horton life, which element has made an inroad into the fabric of his epic.

Lycidas is only an occasional poem, one of the 20 elegies written on the death of a Cambridge friend Edward King. The elegy becomes quite Miltonic, distinct from the early melancholic note of English poetry, the very tone of Christianity and Pagan lucklessness alike, it is like his 'On His Blindness' an occasion of sad lot inspiring faith instead of doubt. It is ultimately like Browning's 'Prespice' a justification of the decrees of God.

In Greek vest it is a sincere lamentation that inspires hope and offers consolation which is ultimately Miltonic. Milton's art and artistry of expression are so pre-eminently elegant that normally the question of sincerity of the poet's sentiment is raised. King seems not to be very intimate with Milton, even Dr. Masson has not cited any close link between them in his voluminous study of the poet's life. Yet the poem does not bear evidence of Milton's absolute indifference or insincerity, *Lycidas* is not less sincere than Shelley's *Adonais*. What could have been in a less expert had a glaring defect is no doubt an extra grace here. Its semi-mythic and all-pastoral association only add grace to the sentiment.

In *Lycidas* Milton has done well to adopt a pastoral apparel to make good his lack of intimacy with the subject of the elegy, the Greek tradition has easily led him to the universal recompense of individual loss. He could have fallen back upon the Christian idea, but that would not perhaps make the poem all so artistic a success as it is. Milton's Horton life must have led him to the Chithaeron scene of Shepherdom. Even in an elegy like this Milton's personality is easily detectable.

In some way Milton foreshadows *In Memoriam* quality of lamentation, a long poem of lamentation written over 17 years through cannot be all a personal elegy, it tends to a philosophic poem in Tennyson's hands, so does mourning note turn ultimately to Miltonic faith in *Lycidas*. He bids them

'Weep no more, woeful shepherds weep no more,
For Lycidas your sorrow is not dead,
Sunk though he be beneath the watery floore,
And yet the day star in the Ocean bed,
And yet anon repairs his drooping head,
And tricks his beams, and with new spangled Ore
Flames in the forehead of the morning sky:'

He justifies as he would do in *Paradise Lost* later the ways of God to man, God's eternal care even after death. Lycidas is not lost, he sinks here but rises elsewhere.

Paradise Lost: The character of Satan

Milton's *Paradise Lost* is an epic of twelve books in which we have got the evolution of the character of Satan and his relationship with the Almighty Creator and his human creation. In the first ten the evolution is consistent, but in the last two books, which were added later to the first block of ten, the serpent called Satan is replaced by Man.

Satan in the original chapter of the Bible, Genesis 2, is simply a principle of evil, a serpent in shape and wickedness of motive. Milton of course did not take his subject simply from the Bible, he has taken note of some of the earlier works dealing with the subject and dealing mainly with the role of Satan. *Adam's Exul* is a Latin tragedy which was published in 1601. *Paradise* of course was of far earlier date. In the Middle Ages *Adamo* deals with the subject. Although the play was written in French and by a Norman it was performed not in France but in England. The subject is the fall of Adam and Eve by means of the machinations of Satan.

Milton took the main characters of his epic particularly from this Mediaeval drama, but the character of Satan shows a development which far exceeds its treatment in the earlier European and English version of the subject. Even in the epic itself Satan shows a consistent evolution. Satan appears in the first Book of *Paradise Lost*. There he is simply a seminal principle of evil rising against the power of God with all the strength of body and spirit. Critics sometimes feel tempted to consider Satan as the hero of the first two Books of the epic. Satan is so powerfully set against Man, even against God that the first and second Books of the epic attain perfection of art mainly because of the creation of the character of Satan as it actually is.

In the third Book Satan is only a remote threat and not at all a living force as he is in the earlier two Books and as he will again be in Book IV. In the first two Books Satan's character is a monument of towering energy; but in the fourth Book Satan is undoubtedly an object of bitter psychological conflict. Satan is here not an emblem of energy and strength. Milton perhaps appreciated more vital human courage and strength of body and mind than integrity of character. So far as Satan is concerned Milton did not minimize the importance of a strength of character in whatever form it is, even though it might not be ethically acceptable and spiritually sound. All these he has done in his earlier two Books. He is neither like Marlowe's Faustus nor like original Faust of the German episode. He is evil but the evil has yet a noble purpose to serve. He opposes the great power of good and attains greatness by the very opposition.

In the fourth Book Milton's concept of human strength, although it is evil, undergoes a complete change. Satan's picture in the fourth Book is a picture of psychological conflict and not at all a picture of great power. In the fourth Book Satan is highly dramatic with an internal conflict. The conflict arose from a close scrutiny of not spiritual validity so much as a contrast between the earlier and the present position of the character itself. Here Satan is more or less like Marlowe's Mephistophilis who laments his role as an agent of evil.

Marlowe's Mephistophilis knows hell is where he is; and Milton's Satan in the fourth book knows it clearly that he is a figure of lost brilliance. He compares his past position of divine power and divine brillian̂ce that passed the brightness of the sun. Now at the sight of the glory of the sun he recalls the depth of degradation he has already reached. And out of the comparison between his present state and the brightness of the sun arises his envy and his deep remorse:

O sun, to tell thee how I hate thy beams,
That brings to my remembrance from what State I fell.

In the later part of the epic Satan gradually yields place to either God or his noblest of creation man. But in the earlier Books particularly the first two, Satan assumes more importance than either God or man. In the fourth in particular Satan is a character that must have been the indirect reflection of the Puritanical predilection of Milton. Satan is here in a crisis of self-reproach arising out of transgression and revolt against God. All the positive values of life of faith offer a sharp contrast to all those negative desperate impulses to which Satan fell a ready victim. Sometimes Satan seems to be a close parallel representation of Milton's own personality as also a side of the political controversy that was raging in Milton's contemporary England.

Paradise Lost as an Epic

Milton is very often placed in the company of Homer and Virgil, and of course more or less correctly. Milton remains undying and unforgettable for his two epic poems, particularly *Paradise Lost*. Homer and Virgil are in their own place as epic poets, and Milton although in the same tradition has ultimately maintained his individuality.

Aristotle has defined Epic in his *Poetics* as a serious objective type of composition on a vast scale, often involving the whole history of a nation. Milton had of course the same idea when he started writing an epic poem as early as 1639. Milton had his life's ambition to write a national epic, but he had to spend long years to settle upon the theme of his epic.

At least three stages of Milton's attempt towards the writing of this long cherished epic are to be noted. Up to 1640 Milton more or less considered Arthurian cycle as his possible subject. In the second period, from 1640 to 1642, there was a change of subject and there was no mention of King Arthur as his possible choice. Milton wrote some verses of *Paradise Lost*, dealing with obviously a different subject. After 1642 up till 1658 we have no knowledge of Milton's progress in the writing of the poems. He was perhaps too deeply involved in contemporary politics. In the third period Milton took it up, and by Aubry's testimony the poem was completed in 1663. Of course *Paradise Lost* was in printed form not before 1667.

It is clearly seen that Milton took long years to write these poems, and in the choice of subject he clearly marked a departure from Homer and Virgil. Homer's and Virgil's were national epics, although Homer a little more legendary and more mythical than Virgil. Milton's *Paradise Lost* cannot in that sense be regarded either a national epic or absolutely mythical, at least in the Homeric sense.

Milton based his epic upon the story of the Bible. The story is in itself a myth to which Milton has added something of his own predisposition. Ultimately Milton's epic maintains a different form and a different subject not originally covered by the Greek and Roman traditions of epic.

Milton mainly utilised the story of the first parents of mankind as narrated in Chapter 2 of Genesis. It is really the story of the fall of man. There Milton is objective and highly general in outlook, handling the common fate of mankind. But Milton's objectivity is not undisturbed as it is in Homer's *Iliad* or in Virgil's *Aeneid.* Milton is very often subjective in the interpolation of his own sentiments, and often in the admixture of the political history of his time.

As an epic *Paradise Lost* is no doubt vast in compass, a work of as many as 12 Books, of the size of the *Iliad.* An epic is not only vast in compass, not only objective in outlook, but at the same time heroic in treatment. All the major epics of the world, either in the East or in the West, are heroic poems. The *Mahabharata* and the *Ramayana* of India are as heroic as the two epics of Homer. But in Milton's *Paradise Lost* we are not at all certain about the hero of the story. In the first two books Satan seems to be the hero, although he is evil incarnate. In the rest of the epic it is not clear whether God or Man appears in the role of the hero. This is of course to be regarded as a special quality of Milton's epic and not as glaring defect.

Milton's *Paradise Lost* is an epic with the clear stamp of Milton 's own originality and the smack of his own genius. Milton adopts all the epic devices and all the major stylistic innovations of an epic, and there he is rightly in Homer's and Virgil's tradition. But in spite of that Milton's *Paradise Lost* is unique in its own curious shape, with its own special subject and with its mixed qualities, *Paradise Lost* is in English literature what Homer's *Iliad* is in ancient Greek literature.

Paradise Lost has a special place in English literature, quite distinct from that of the Homeric epics and their counterparts in India. It is not a heroic epic; no warring hero evokes any heroic spirit. What it does is the awakening of spiritual awareness out of the proper exposition of a myth of the Bible. Nothing can be more unheroic than Satan's slyly stealing into the garden of Eden in Book IV with a spiritual conflict within himself, although it exactly reveals the spirit of this Miltonic epic, the need of Man's standing guard against the cunning assault of the agent of evil,

> To whom with stern regard thus Gabriel speak.
> Why hast thou Satan broke the bounds prescrib'd
> To thy transgression and disturbed the charge
> Of others, who approve not to transgress
> By thy example...

Paradise Lost: Diction and imagery

Milton differs from the ancient epic poets of Greece and Rome, no doubt from the two great epic poets of the East; but he follows more or less the epic style of Homer and Virgil. *Paradise Lost* is not a national epic as the *Iliad, Odyssey* and the *Aeneid* are. Yet the method of treatment in it is almost the same.

Paradise Lost is full of epic similes which compare those of *Iliad* and fall short of the extended stories of the *Mahabharata* as similes. Milton seems to have led his readers through the grove of the ancient myths of the East and the West to reach his never experienced truths of a world far beyond human scrutiny very often. One example from Book IV make the point clear. It is Satan's purposely slowed journey to that humanly inexperienced point of Eden duly attracted to the rich silvan view of its outer wall of verdure and in a sweet swoon of an intoxicating smell thereof as it were compared to the mythological story of Asmodeus's love for Sara and unwilling withdrawal from her presence into Egypt.

Milton's originality lies in his thoroughly explored abundance of historical names in the vast area of myths. No one in English literature is so thorough in his knowledge of the Middle East as he is in this epic. In that Milton is only second to the poet of the *Mahabharata*. His use of geographical and historical names of the scene of action of the first parents of mankind and its surrounding areas is very striking and an extra charm to the poet's flights of fancy. Even in Book IV the names are too many.

Milton knows his subject in *Paradise Lost* is highly spiritual, in Book IV the contrast between God's angels and the minions of Evil, greatest of them Satan, on that issue of their claim on Man and Eden where he lives. All Milton's idioms and coinages heighten the conflict and underscore the spiritual implication. Milton's diction is attuned to this special nature of his subject. Satan's cunning encroachment into this Eden is described by means of a common larceny:

> 'Leaps over the fence with ease into the fold.
> 'as a thief bent to unhoard the cash
> Of som rich Burgher'.

Satan 'clomb this first grand thief into God's fold'.

Not only by means of simile but also by Satan's own curious turn of phrases or sentence pattern in self accusation as one here from Book IV 'which way I fly is Hell; my self am Hell;', his role is eventually depicted.

Satan's self-pity from an obvious contrast between his fallen state and the glorious brilliance of the sun he meets upon his journey to that blissful world with an evil motive is another very effective Miltonic device to denounce transgression.

Milton's sincere appreciation of natural beauty and the grace of human form gives an additional flavour to his theme and style. He has described the God and Son conclave in Book III, the grandeur of Satanic revolt in Book I, and the true beauty of nature and human form in Book IV; all these heighten the majesty of his epic style. Milton depicts first the superabundant vigour and verve in nature, which is not simply a close reflection of the Horton background of natural plenitude. To this Milton's close scrutiny of the naked comeliness of Adam and Eve in their pristine innocence is a happy contrast.

Milton's idioms and imageries in the description of the blissful innocence of their nakedness are so lavish yet so restrained that they point to the disciplined appreciation of beauty and grace in 'with native honour clad in naked majesty' in relation to Adam 'Yielded with coy submission, modest pride,' 'sweet reluctant amorous delay' in relation to Eve; as again in the concealed parts of the female body, called 'mysterious parts', 'there was not guilty shame, dishonest shame.'

The juxtaposition of the two Trees as in Book IV is originally a Bible story, but Miltons's imageries and idioms help bring out the meaning of the myth. In the whole of the epic Milton is essentially an interpreter of the theme of the Bible, to which work his own experience in life lends an extra force only. The whole passage in this part of Book IV is replete with Miltonic purity and charged with the power of his reason, both which striking at the right point of Biblical wisdom.

In spite of a great mind working in every choice and in every word in *Paradise Lost* Milton remains finally a great poet by his original unique use of imagery and diction and by his use of a verse form which sets free his power of vision, depth of feeling and his insight into truth.

CHAPTER VIII

EARLY NOVELS : FIELDING

Tom Jones : A comic epic in prose

Henry Fielding is a contemporary of Richardson who officially introduced a new genre in literature, later called the novel. But Fielding is the opposite pole of the art lately introduced by Richardson. Fielding started his career with the parody of Richardson's first novel *Pamela* in as many as two works, *Shamela* in 1741 and *Joseph Andrews* a little later. Fielding wrote exactly consciously, 'a comic poem in prose' still later. It is Fielding who for the first time declared his war against sentiment and clearly defined his area which is 'human nature'. The introductory first Chapter of *Tom Jones* is clearly Fielding's stipulation how he would write his novel, 'the provision, then, which we have here made is no other than Human nature'.

Tom Jones is no doubt Fielding's masterpiece, published in 1749. Here Fielding covers as vast an area as would justify his claim of epic compass for it. The earlier works only attempted it but did not achieve as successfully as *Tom Jones* has done.

Fielding's claim of epic vastness of his picture particularly in *Tom Jones*, is a significant claim, that makes the next stage of development of the novel in English literature. In *Tom Jones* Fielding never tried to exploit any sentiment, nor explored anything of that sort, Christian or otherwise, ethical or moral. His compass is as extended as the whole history of the nation, just developing in every detail particularly of the countryside. It is rather a thorough history of the 18th century life of England as no history would be able to bring out. In this sense Fielding's *Tom Jones* could be compared to Thackeray's *Vanity Fair*. The only difference with that 19th century masterpiece is the difference of the author's outlook. Thackeray is satiric while Fielding is comic in spirit.

Tom Jones is an epic, and a comic epic duly to be defined as a study of life of a period in all its aspects but avoiding ultimately as by Jane Austen the 'lasting pain' that life may suffer. *Tom Jones* is however a study of human nature as Fielding claims it for himself–in a vast number of men and women drawn from different corners of life, giving everyone his or her due completely withholding any undesirable and undue encroachment of sentiment or moral view or philosophical idea.

Tom Jones the hero is set against a completely different type Blifil, Allworthy and Squire Western are of a different group completely new in character and implication; again Sophia, Lady Bellaston and Molly Seagrim are all women but everyone a sharp contrast to each of the rest, all in her own place and with her own nature. Fielding has covered the whole of the countryside, every place with its clearly defined peculiarity and gathered all the threads in the cosmopolitan city of London, where a lady like Bellaston rules the upper class. Fielding of course ignores no farcical element, neither in character nor in situation, as in characters like Thwackum and Squire and in situation like Tom Jones's encounter with Mrs. Water.

Fielding has covered a ground which none of his contemporaries has attempted, neither Richardson nor Laurence Sterne, nor even Goldsmith of Smollett. His *Tome Jones* has the Odyssian compass of the whole truth as defined by a modern novelist Aldous Huxley in his essay 'Tragedy and the Whole Truth' in *Music at Night* (1960). Huxley's study points out the epic vastness of Fielding's treatment in the novel not simply owing to a wider canvas of life, but ultimately to an all-embracing attitude to life, in which Fielding has upheld the whole truth of life without exception and without discrimination between the opposite forces playing in it, neither between good and evil nor between Christian and Pagan, nor even between the comic and the tragic. Fieldings portrait of life in the novel covers everything pleasant and unpleasant and gives an impression of life itself, which is no less a truth than any philosophic concept of it.

Fielding has a special place in the 18th century evolution of the novel. His *Tom Jones* is an adequate representation of its author and his special character as a writer. Fielding is an emancipated spirit who completely identifies himself with the pleasure of life without any misconception of life either as good or bad or as pleasant or unpleasant, but with a sense of life pure and simple.

Fielding's Moral Vision of Life

Fielding came hard upon Richardson who gave English literature the first novel in 1740. Pamela really stirred Fielding to write *Shamela* in 1741 and then *Joseph Andrews* a year after or so, both as parody of

Richardson's style and outlook. Fielding did not like at all to take a sentimental view of life, either religious or otherwise. His choice of subject is mainly to illustrate 'human nature' with a thoroughly liberal view of life and relationship.

Fielding's vision is quite adequately reflected in his masterpiece *Tom Jones*, published in 1749. The novel is a class by itself with the broadness of outlook and compass that can be of an epic. It is a prose epic with a different kind of form than that Richardson or Sterne adopted. He does not adopt Richardson's letter form nor Sterne's conceits. His is a simple narrative style, the fit vehicle for a comprehensive view of Hanovarian England. *Tom Jones* is rightly to be called an 18th century social history more authentic than history itself. Fielding has widened the area of life and made a choice of a suitable form in *Tom Jones*.

So far as the volume of the novel is concerned *Clarissa Harlowè* is more voluminous than *Tom Jones*, if *Pamela* is not exactly, but *Clarissa* has not the national compass as *Tom Jones*, nor the wider concern of life than merely a sentimental view of a narrow convert's. Fielding's objection is to the narrowness of Richardson. He is again contrasted with a later novelist of the same period, Sterne whose *Tristram Shandy* (1767) is really a non-committal rare display of freakishness of the mind. Fielding takes a liberal view of life. Even his study of society of contemporary England is totally unbiased and uncoloured.

The choice of the hero is a deviation from the epic tradition, although Fielding claims his novel in one of his prefatory commentaries to be epic in canvas. Jones is a foundling grown to maturity with as much folly as genuine good qualities. Allworthy is the presiding deity of the world of this novel so to speak and Jones is reared up heroic after the pattern he conceived, to which Blifil offers a sharp contrast. Both Jones and Blifil represent Allworthy's, that is Fielding's, positive and negative sides of moral vision. There Fielding is a sharp contrast to Richardson.

From birth to burial Tom Jones is not a moral picture, neither the heroine Sophia who does not enter any such question at all. Tom is a contrast to Charles Grandison and Sophia to Pamela. Pamela and Charles are Richardson's constricted moral pictures. Tom and Sophia scale beyond the narrow limit of their society. One may be tempted to compare Tom to Shakespeare's Falstaff and Sophia to Ophelia, but Tom and Sophia are not like them; Tom shares Falstaff's vitality but not his clowning, Fielding has introduced other clowns and need not incorporate clownish element in the hero's character; and Sophia is all too lively a woman for the dull innocence of Ophelia.

The only countable sin in Fielding's world is hypocrisy, its ready symbol in *Tom Jones* is Blifil. Fielding can very well accommodate other lapses as he has done in many characters of the novel, in the hero most. All Jones's wild oats, even sex offences, have been treated sympathetically and adjusted in his life as the excess of energy and vitality which requires only a timely accommodation and right channelling. Fielding has done it with many young men and women in this novel, as with Molly Seagrim, Mrs. Waters and Tom.

In his vision Fielding makes no sharp difference between tragedy and comedy, he takes no such partial view of life, he knows life is a bottomless sack in which everything, whether it is pleasant or unpleasant, has ultimately to pass through and leave it yet empty. Perhaps Aldous Huxley has detected it in his view of Tragedy and the Whole Truth, and rightly cited the *Odyssey* and *Tom Jones* as the examples of the whole truth. Fielding's moral vision is as wide as the whole truth of Huxley's opinion. It is a world where the true sinner is Blifil, hypocritically constricted, and no other, not even Lady Bellaston and Molly's mother who was brought to the bed of her first child only a week after her marriage.

Fielding's art of characterization in Tom Jones

Fielding starts his career by parodying Richardson's Pamela in 1741 and then again repeating it in a work *Joseph Andrews* in 1742. He projects his view of nature against Richardson's sentiment. His studies of character open a line of human nature closely enquired into in all his novels, particularly *Tom Jones* his masterpiece.

Tom Jones was published in 1749. In the study of life Fielding involved 'truth and human nature itself' in this novel as Walter Scott observed. Fielding's main purpose is to present his 'fair field full of folk', rather a modern parallel to Langland's *Pears Plowman.* This really offers Fielding the outline of his character studies. He does not however penetrate deep into the psychology of all those people he paints; but all his portraits are interesting characters on the canvas of the entire age. *Tom Jones* is a work of epic compass. It is often called a 'comic epic poem in prose'.

Fielding is often compared to his contemporary Smollett, both interested in realistic study of life, Fielding of course is a little more serious than Smollett. *Tom Jones* as a whole is a grand comedy, representing the whole view of life, 'the whole truth' of Aldous Huxley's view. All the characters in this book represent almost a string of pilgrims, so to speak, of Chaucer's *Canterbury Tales*. It is a vast world of people drawn from different spheres and interests of life of the contemporary 18th century England.

Sometimes the characters fall under some specific groups and types, often sharply contrasted, as are the two main characters Tom and Blifil. Both these characters are the two extreme poles of moral implication. Blifil is a symbol of moral hypocrisy and Tom Jones an emblem of moral openness, even though it means inclusion of some common vices of humanity.

Allworthy is perhaps the representation of Fielding himself with the same profession and the same outlook on life. In his study of character, Fielding never takes the sentimental view of his great contemporary Richardson, he follows the line of free development of human nature in which good and evil are held in balanced equipoise. Here Fielding takes a rational view of humanity. Even the hero of the novel is not fashioned after a flawless model. He is the representation of the natural growth of an enormous fund of energy to a happy human destiny. Allworthy just beside him is not only guardian but also his presiding deity to form his destiny.

Fielding's greatest creation in this novel is Squire Western who could have been another Tom Jones if only he could be a little younger than he. He is the father of the heroine, but with the same enormous energy that guides him sometimes wrong but ultimately brings him to a fair end of human balance. Allworthy and Western are really of two different trends of characters, one a little more explosive yet of a more positive frankness of expression and understanding. Squire Western just in his tyrannical role of a father reveals another unique quality of authority that ultimately softens as readily as it stiffened earlier. He upholds the briskness of youth although he has nearly passed that stage.

Sophia Western, the heroine of this novel sharply differs from Richardson's heroines like Pamela and Clarissa, mainly in her free accommodation of vices and virtues in her womanly grace. Her adjustment to Tom Jones is perhaps an impossible feat in any of

Richardson's novels. Sophia is again a distinct character from Fielding's later heroine Amelia. Sophia has perhaps greater charm of a human boisterousness and Amelia only a greater pious sobriety that brings her closer to Richardson's Pamela. Sophia is more lovable than Amelia, because she is more human even with her girlish immaturity and imperfection than the other. Hazlitt describes her as a 'pretty simple tone' which perhaps she is not. Her imperfections are also painted with 'extraordinary tenderness' upto the last.

The book of course centres on Sophia and Tom, but the events of their life are dramatically enacted against a background of life full of varied interests. Fielding neatly paints this world with unique penetration into every field of activity. He draws minor characters with perfect understanding as none of his contemporaries perhaps did, at least Richardson did not. Fielding often looks to Swift as well as Cervantes, particularly in his studies of minor characters. In *Tom Jones* there is a vast number of characters who are farcical representing a sort of Jonsonian humour, for example Thwackum and Square, Lady Bellaston and Molly Seagrim are another pair. They represent what in Ben Jonson could have been a kind of fad not always of sound moral principle, rather often just its opposite. In a way Fielding foreshadows D.H. Lawrence in his view of man as a 'good animal, true to his animal instincts'.

Tom Jones is not only Fielding's masterpiece but at the same time a great novel in the English language in which almost the entire 18th century life in the countryside has been painted with perfect thoroughness of understanding of every interest as perhaps Chaucer has done in his Prologue to the *Canterbury Tales* of his own age. The principle of his study is again similar to the study adopted by Chaucer earlier and adopted again in his own age by Smollett and later adopted by Dickens. Although he differs from Dickens his study of character has essentially a Dickensian quality, apparent distinction between and among his characters without being deeply psychological.

Tom Jones: An account of human nature

Fielding opposed Richardson and his sentimental novel, and served the provision of 'human nature' instead. He started with parodying Richardson's themes and ended by depicting the natural habits and thoughts and impulses of men and women in society without taking a sentimental view of life. What Goldsmith does in drama Fielding does even with greater interest in fiction, an easy passage from sentiment to nature.

Nature in Fielding's novels is cut to the 18th century size and sense. It differs from the Romantic sense of the terms. The 18th century nature is realistic and not idealistic as in the Romantic movement, traced inside man and outside in his manners and activities, and not outside human scope as mainly in the Romantic concept. *Tom Jones* is externally an account of Hanovarian England both in city and the countryside, as thorough as nowhere in history, but internally it is testament of the truth of human nature. All the characters are disclosing their nature and thereby the nature of life in society, in every home and in every individual.

Tom Jones's hero is a gift of nature, enters the fabric of the story so, a foundling of untraced human origin. The hero is to the last a record of unfettered natural growth, with all his dirt and filth and glowing gems, in the final stage dirt and filth washed away leaving the gems in their native glow. So he leaves behind Molly Seagrim and Mrs. Waters, those ugly evidences of dirt and ends with a happy match with Sophia. Blifil beside him is a distortion of nature, he has only the artificiality of pretended culture, a sharp contrast to Tom's unassumed moral growth of nature as from the follies and frivolities of adolescence to the sanity of youth, all through demonstrating the natural endowments of life and energy which Blifil lacked.

All the other characters, except only Blifil, have the same gift of nature, even Mr. Allworthy is not an exception. Squire Western bears testimony to Allworthy's College day's follies: 'I remember Allworthy at college..many a wench have we two had together. As arrant a whore master as any within five miles...' (Vol. I, Book IV, Chapter X). There are varieties of weaknesses and follies that life may hold. *Tom Jones* seems to be an exhaustive account of human follies, an obvious part of life, as Fielding must have noted in his age.

The whole of the 18th century society of England, both in the rural and the urban areas, was before Fielding and he has thoroughly explored it to detect the flash of the whole truth of life and nature, and that is mainly why nothing in *Tom Jones* ended tragically except unnatural pretension as in Blifil. Justice as it is in the pages of *Tom Jones* is tolerant and quite within the scope of human nature, because the judge himself is not beyond human follies, as also not and cannot be absolutely without human excellences.

Molly and her mother practically sail in the same boat, although the mother teaches the young girl a good lesson. The girl's charge against such lesson is quite characteristic : 'You yourself was brought to bed of sister there within a week after you was married (*Ibid.*, Chap. IX).

Black George's family is in one way, Mr. Partridge's in another, a close study of nature that persists in every corner of even highly organised society, the 18th century's only less so, perhaps to offer Fielding an extra advantages over the modern writers. The quarrel over the maid in the family, the wife's suspicion and gossip in the neighbourhood - all are testimony to how life behaves in less organised flexibility of the countryside. The London scene with Lady Bellaston is another very sharply contrasted picture in which in a different way the realistic account of life of the highly organised polished society is offered.

Fielding is not Hardy, neither in mood nor in the habit of background painting, he paints human nature in every bit of daily contact and conflict, avoiding Hardyan tragic consequence, seeing something far above such gloom in life, its whole truth. This is Fielding's nature best depicted in *Tom Jones*.

CHAPTER IX

ROMANTIC POETS

Wordsworth : The Prelude Book I: Pantheism: Sensibility fostered by beauty and fear

The Prelude is a highly ambitious plan ultimately cut down to the size of his genius; what was proposed to be a philosophic poem finally became autobiographical, and in it philosophy is confined to what retrogressive analysis of his personal experience in close contact with Nature transpires. 'Sensibility fostered by beauty and fear' is his private experience, and pantheism is only its reduced principle of philosophy.

In the whole of the poem 28 years of his experience of growth and reactions of his mind is introspectively explored, exploration not always lively, rather often dull; but in the introductory Book I the poet's vigour of the mind exorcises dullness, while his philosophy and the outline of his plan stand out clear. Wordsworth's love for nature is a well-known Romantic element, but his pantheistic view of Nature is a distinct quality of his poetry, as seen in *The Prelude*. This view stirs his sensibility.

In Book I of *The Prelude* Nature seems to be not only living but also omnipresent; Nature is everywhere and living in every bit; Wordsworth's pantheism is a new religion of Nature that replaces God. Nature is 'law and impulse' to Lucy, but in *The Prelude* she is 'beauty and fear'—beauty inspires and fear restrains. Wordsworth has personal experience of a power in Nature awakening his power of mind 'I grew up fostered by beauty and fear'.

Wordsworth's Hawkshead experience of the open valley and free movements in the mountain slopes gave him a foretaste of Nature's self-sufficience and her free education for man. *The Prelude* gives an idea of Nature, not the less in Book I, as the inspiring source of the poet's intense feeling and far-extending power of imagination. Wordsworth has given an account of what could have been the possible themes of his proposed work in this Book, but he ultimately breaks off from all those alternatives and falls upon Nature to guide his pen.

He looks upon nature as a restraining and inspiring source and felt often the living presence of shapes in nature for punishment for his sins and encouragement for his good deeds, in Book I mainly through fear and appreciation of beauty. The poet's stealing a boat and a caged bird incurred Nature's wrath, and he saw horrible forms when awake and when asleep to teach him a lesson.

Wordsworth defines in this part of the poem, 'there is a dark inscrutable workmanship that reconciles discordant elements, makes them cling together in one society.' This presence of an inscrutable power in Nature, is in him the creative principle. Wordsworth believes Nature in man is not alien to Nature outside. Wordsworth's pantheism stems out of that affinity.

The Prelude in its poetic excellence is not a great poem, but it is undoubtedly the truest testament of his faith. He makes a new faith of Nature's power and Man's wholesome development under her influence. In Book I again Wordsworth quotes from his experience:

'Wisdom and Spirit of the universe!
Thou Soul that art eternity of thought
That givest to forms and images a breath...'

The Prelude is not a poem like *Immortality Ode* or *Tintern Abbey,* although in them too Wordsworth's pantheistic ideas are widespread; the poem is a distinct achievement in the inquiry into the poet's own soul and its close relationship with the Spirit in Nature. How it can the poet is clear here:

The scenes which were witness of that joy
Remained in their substantial lineaments
Depicted on tho brain, and to the eye
Were visible, a daily sight; and thus
By the impressive discipline of fear,
By pleasure and repeated happiness,
....
Were fastened to the affections.

The Prelude : a record of the growth and development of Wordsworth's mind

Of all the autobiographical poems of the Romantic movement Wordsworth's *The Prelude* is perhaps closest to the poet's own life and attitude. The poem was started and originally planned as a philosophic poem at the suggestion of Coleridge. But in the actual composition Wordsworth not only changed its title but also changed the entire subject matter and the principles of composition. It no longer remained a philosophical poem but shaped itself exactly as an autobiographical record of Wordsworth's growth and development as a poet.

When the poem was started Wordsworth was only twenty-eight and he started it quite in earnest with a complete shift from Coleridge's own expectation of him. So when the poem was complete Coleridge was shocked to see that it was just the opposite view of nature and man's relation to it—quite opposite to his own.

Wordsworth took at least 35 years to give the poem its final shape to be published under a changed title suggested by Mrs. Wordsworth after her husband's death. The title is really suggestive. It is an autobiography of a poet, but not as it has been with Byron. It has a special quality, the introspective inquiry into the development of the mind and feeling of the poet at the earlier stage of his life.

Wordsworth took essentially the opposite view with regard to the relationship between man and nature—opposite to the view of Coleridge: Coleridge expected Wordsworth to prove in this very philosophic poem (as he originally thought it to be) that the senses were development of the mind and spirit, but Wordsworth was content with the view that the mind was formed by the senses.

This diverging line of approach is very significant so far as the present poem is concerned. *The Prelude* practically establishes this view by means of particular instances of Wordsworth's experience in the yet unformed mind of his adolescence. Wordsworth develops just like his Lucy, a child of Nature, developing under the direct influence of Nature.

In the introductory part of the first Book of the poem Wordsworth records how he 'escaped/ From the vast city, where I long had pined/ A discontented sojourner.' This gives clearly an idea how Wordsworth felt about artificial city life and how felt himself completely free in the atmosphere of the country side.

Wordsworth must have been then a child of ten only—'Ere I had told ten birth days', when he moved among the mountains, valleys and forests; he was merely a school boy and moved on freely in the midst of Nature, 'Fair seed time had my soul, and I grew up/Fostered alike by beauty and fear.'

Wordsworth obviously was not yet a poet, but he gathered already or was beginning to gather, the inspiration from Nature which would ultimately form his mind and feeling of a future poet - 'poetic numbers came/Spontaneously to clothe in priestly robe/A renovated spirit singled out.'

The Prelude as it is ultimately settled as the biography of Wordsworth's creative self at the early stage is a record, perhaps the most authentic record, of Wordsworth's attitude to Nature. Wordsworth looked upon Nature as not only living but also as the final source of 'law and impulse' for at least a creative mind like his own. In the poem Wordsworth records his early truancy, sometimes stealing birds from other's snares, sometimes stealing a boat and at times wheeling around upon winter show - every time feeling from the very inmost soul a guiding impulse from behind the visible shapes of Nature.

Thus Wordsworth in his adolescence put absolutely his very unformed mind and feeling in the direct care of Nature. He formed himself simply as a child of Nature, the future poet unconsciously shaped fit for his job. *The Prelude* being a record of such a development of Wordsworth's mind and feeling essentially differs from Byron's *Don Juan* and *Childe Harold.*

Wordsworth's views on the language of poetry

Wordsworth in his Preface to the second edition of Lyrical Ballads (1800) sets forth his whole programme of literary creation, particularly the principle he should adopt in his poetry. The first striking deviation from the 18th century convention of poetry is the selection of his subject, and then the choice of his language.

In Wordsworth's plan of poetry both the subject and the pattern of expression are well calculated strikingly new. He tells us in the Preface, 'the principal objects in these poems were to choose incidents and situations from common life...' With regard to the language he should use in such poems Wordsworth makes also a clear statement 'to relate or describe them...in a selection of language really used by men and at the same time to throw over them a certain colouring of imagination...'

Wordsworth deals with rustic life, at least he proposed to do it in the Preface, and the language he should use would be also the language of common people; he does not absolutely discard 'a certain colouring of imagination'; he gives in this regard his reasons 'whereby ordinary things should be presented to the mind in an unusual aspect.' He tells us further in such a selection of language he could better trace 'the primary laws of our nature'.

Wordsworth does not end here as regards his idea of language in poetry. He further elaborates the reason for such a selection of language. He tells us 'humble and rustic life was generally chosen because in that condition the essential passions of the heart find a better soil in which they can attain their maturity, are less under restraint, and speak a plainer and more emphatic language.'

Wordsworth in his support to such a selection of language from ordinary rustic life cites some examples. His subject matter is clearly stated, and the true purpose of his poetry is also thoroughly explained. He defines poetry as 'the spontaneous overflow of powerful feelings.' What purpose the colouring of imagination would serve Wordsworth has also defined clearly, he makes no essential difference between the language of prose and the language of poetry. The only difference is metric arrangement of the selection of language from common life.

Wordsworth tells us if the selection can be made from the language really spoken by men 'with true taste and feeling', it will really mark distinction far greater than would at first be imagined. What Wordsworth means by this application of taste and feeling has also been clarified, it is only to avoid 'the vulgarity and meanness of ordinary life.' The next striking distinction would be metre, and if metre be superadded, Wordsworth tells us 'a dissimilitude will be produced altogether sufficient for the gratification of a rational mind.'

The flaws of Wordsworth's theory of language, a language really spoken by ordinary people, free from unnecessary diction, a language of spontaneous feeling and natural emotion and passion, have immediately been detected by Wordsworth's own friend Coleridge. Coleridge of course pointed out his disagreement with Wordsworth in his *Biographia Literaria,* Chap XVII in the year 1817. Perhaps no greater success was there in the whole of the critical efforts for a true understanding of Wordsworth's theory anywhere. Wordsworth was right almost in everything but Coleridge disagrees with him particularly on the question of language of real life, a language which actually constitutes the natural conversation of men under the influence of natural feeling. Coleridge makes an elaborate criticism of what Wordsworth means by the word real.

Coleridge entertains a different view of verse composition, he tells us 'I adopt with full faith the principle of Aristotle', that 'poetry is essentially ideal', 'that it avoids and excludes all áccidents.' He tells us referring to some of the best poems of Wordsworth himself e.g., *Michael*, *Ruth* etc., that even Wordsworth does not use the language of real men and women. The greatest concern in poetry is not realism, rather it is the 'generic' attributes and the common character of a class and not of an individual.

Coleridge's criticism of Wordsworth does not invalidate Wordsworth's theory of language because under the influence of Wordsworth Coleridge himself, too attained natural simplicity of language. What Wordsworth primarily proposed is to adopt a natural language of spontaneous feeling and to avoid all artificiality of diction which must have stood in the way of natural expression in the whole of the 18th century poetry of England.

Byron: Don Juan as satire

Byron is perhaps the single example of satiric undertone in the whole of the Romantic poetry; he is not without justice regarded as one more of the 18th century tradition than of the 19th. Even in his personal estimate of English poets he is more favourable to the 18th century pets than to his contemporaries. He carries on in particular the tradition of Pope and Dryden in the Romantic movement.

Don Juan is perhaps a special case of Byron's calculated satire, Nature in outlook and strong in effect. The poem bears the stamp of Byron's own personality than any of his earlier poems. It is in this poem that he underlines the view 'Every poet his own Aristotle.' He also underscores the trend in his own language:

Thou shalt believe in Milton, Dryden, Pope;
Thou shalt not set up Wordsworth, Coleridge, Southey.

In his account of his contemporaries Byron is more like Pope than like any of his contemporary poets, highly scornful to the achievement of his three great contemporaries.

Don Juan was written towards the close of Byron's life and could not really finish the poem, although he wanted to execute his plan of a grand epic in 24 cantos. He tells his publishers in some of his letters that he made the choice of his hero to execute a satiric purpose. He would send his hero 'on a long series of ventures' in different countries of Europe 'so as to show the different ridicules of the society in each of those countries.'

Obviously *Don Juan* is satire on abuses of the present states of society.' Although under the name of the hero Byron himself appears, yet the poem is a close study of irregularities and abuses of society not only one Byron personally lived, but also those he understood better than any of his comrades.

Byron of course differs from the tradition of the Spanish hero because he is essentially romantic in outlook and because in everything he writes he specially reaps up his own personality. There lies perhaps the essence of Pope's influence, Pope was personal in his satiric attack more than any of his 18th century contemporaries. But in one point at least Byron differs from Pope, as in *Don Juan*, he never spares himself and his own family from satiric attack. Byron under the title of the hero discloses the very satiric relationship between his parents which lays an inevitable impact upon his own stinted development. This portion at least attains the liveliness of humour although the attack is essentially satiric:

> But oh! ye lords of ladies intellectual,
> Inform us truly, have they not hen-peck'd you all?

The account that is given of Dona Indez and Don Jose is primarily the account of Byron's own parents, and all those exploits in different lands of Don Juan are essentially attributed to Byron himself. He is like Goldsmith's Traveller, but the only difference is Goldsmith's Traveller is an impartial observer, while Byron's observation is tinged with a scorn that lends itself to his expressive pattern.

Byron idealised his hero, marking a clear deviation from the proverbial Don Juan, gave him a little of his own scorn, a strength of his own language, so as to execute a purpose which he himself could not do so effectively. Here is again Byron's individuality, and his independence from the old 18th century tradition of satire. He did not make Don Juan a libertine as he originally was in the Spanish legend, he makes him a sincere lover, and gave him his own personal beauty and idealised him into an epic hero more to be loved than to be held in scorn.

His bitterness of feeling is to be noted when he is back to England, his own country and his own people, particularly his contemporaries. He explores the entire literary field of England in the European context and saw them scornfully lagging far behind in achievement. His attack against Wordsworth is perhaps the bitterest. "A dowsy frowsy poem, called the Excursion, written in a manner which is my aversion."

Don Juan is only epic in frame but satiric in execution, perfectly of Byron's own tradition, in which he stands fully revealed. He has taken the best of the 18th century tradition and adjusted into the romantic values of his own age, yet brought it to a shape and sound thought specially to be made his own—a satire that bears the essential Byronic stamp.

Shelley: Adonais, its title

Adonais is one of the leading elegies of English literature. Shelley mourns the death of John Keats under the mask of a mythical hero, Adonis. Shelley is at once in the tradition of pastoral elegy which was initiated by John Milton as early as 1634.

Keats died in 1821 and close after his death Shelley started writing this poem of lamentation. Shelley took the classical model, and took particular note of the pastoral elegy that *Lycidas* was, good exemplar for Shelley to follow. Shelley of course was more indebted to the Latin authors and the Greek poets particularly Bion and Moschus.

Shelley borrowed the title no doubt from Bion of the 2nd century B.C. Bion's '*Fragment of the Elegy of the Death of Adonis*' perhaps inspired Shelley to write this poem on the death of Keats under the same title.

What prompted Shelley to change the spelling of the Greek name is not clearly known. It is obvious that Shelley has introduced some changes in the very myth of Venus and Adonis. The first change that strikes us is the overall change of that erotic character of the myth which Shelley has totally shelved. Venus does not at all occur in Shelley's poem, in her place Shelley has put Urania.

Shelley has completely differed from Shakespeare in his use of the Greek myth. Shakespeare continued the same story of love under the title *Venus and Adonis.* Shakespeare is more or less in the unaltered Greek tradition; but Shelley only took the Greek form but deviated from the Greek interpretation in the story.

In Shelley's treatment Urania appears in the role of the mother who simply took back the already tired soul of John Keats. Perhaps Shelley took note of Urania, Muse of Astronomy and Venus Urania, goddess of heavenly love and also the Venus Genetrix Lucratius invokes, and made a healthy change out of all these basic originals for a character that can serve well his purpose.

Shelley altered the name of the hero from Adonis to Adonais. The change may have been due to greater musical suitability, of course the change has already provoked a good deal of discussion. The Adonis legend of Greek tradition is only taken to make a contemporary case of literary misfire more suitable in elaboration and interpretation. Here John Keats is Adonais who is killed by the proverbial boar, in Keats's case the reviewer of the Quarterly.

Shelley makes John Keats a shepherd among all other shepherds of his time. His death was caused by the bitter criticism of the Quarterly critic; Shelley believed the savage review of *Endymion* had ultimately killed John Keats. He also regarded the critic as a boar.

The title is of course highly significant, because Shelley carefully utilised the killing of the legendary hero to explain the untimely early death of Keats caused by the severe criticism of the critics. Keats died of consumption in his 24th year, but Shelley takes it simply as a death caused by the cruel attack of the critic who did not know how fatal it could be to a sensitive poet like Keats.

In English literature pastoral elegy is not rare, already Milton has written it, afterwards Arnold has attempted at least two major poems in the same tradition; but Shelley's *Adonais* seems to be even more effective as it has stood closer to the classical pattern and to the original Greek myth although he has deviated much from the treatment of the same myth by Shakespeare. The title as has been selected by Shelley has served him well particularly when it has interpreted the case of Keats's death so appropriately as no other could have done.

Wordsworth on the poetic process

Wordsworth offers his idea on poetic process mainly in his Preface to the second edition of *Lyrical Ballads* (1800). Of course Wordsworth has written an appendix to it, and another Preface in the year 1815, all these taken together would give an idea what Wordsworth actually meant by his own process of verse composition.

In at least two places in the Preface to the second edition Wordsworth points out what poetry exactly is- "Poetry is spontaneous overflow of powerful feelings." To this however Wordsworth has added how the overflow of powerful feelings takes its origin. - 'It takes its origin from emotion recollected in tranquility.' In this connection Wordsworth is very clear about what he tries to mean by all these stipulations.

Wordsworth offers his own interpretation of the final source of powerful feelings. He notes that emotion is not all for verse composition, there he differs from Shelley; creative emotion is not the emotion excited by the direct experience of things, it is a product of a later contemplation of the original experience, only recollected in tranquility - "an emotion, kindred to that which was before the subject of contemplation is gradually produced."

Wordsworth in his original Preface—Preface to *Lyrical Ballads*—clearly pointed out what should be the choice of his subject and how the language would be formed for an adequate expression. He made the choice of 'humble rustic life'—a life closer to Nature. The language should of course be the language of passion—passions of the heart that find a better soil in the unsophisticated life of Nature.

Obviously Wordsworth was misunderstood by later critics, as for example, in the 20th century Wordsworth was adversely interpreted, specially under the anti-romantic reaction. They mainly ignored Wordsworth's own interpretation. In this connection, T.S. Eliot is to be mentioned. Eliot does not carefully consider Wordsworth's own principle. Wordsworth does not say, poetry is an emotion, recollected in tranquility but only says that it takes its origin in such emotion. The fact is Wordsworth based his theory upon his own experience and therefore the principle adopted by him may not cover the whole field of poetic composition. Some critics at least pointed it out in their interpretation of Wordsworth's theory.

Wordsworth's poetic process as it was adopted by him allows obviously a gap, long or short, between the first experience of the poet and the actual composition out of such experience. Wordsworth seems to suggest this process of recollection in tranquility in the last passage of the poem *The Daffodils*: "In vacant and in pensive mood/ They Flash upon that inward eye/Which is the bliss of solitude." Again Wordsworth comes to this in his two *Yarrow* poems.

Wordsworth has however pointed it out even in his Preface. Wordsworth has recognised even in his powerful feelings and impulses a ruling, consciously or unconsciously adopted, thought element—"Our continued influxes of feeling are modified and directed by our thoughts."

Wordsworth is very clear about the choice of his subject, the source of emotion and passion and the language which is to be adopted for an adequate communication of the poet's ideas and feelings Wordsworth simply broke away from the 18th century convention with an added importance of the element of nature not only outside man in the visible universe but also in the invisible world inside him.

Keats: Why the second Hyperion a vision

Keats's *Hyperion* and *The Fall of Hyperion* have a history behind their composition and the very scheme of their form. *Hyperion* is an ambitious poem, the poem, was sought to have been of epic compass, its composition coincided with the very sad experience of a brother's death spasm for a long period. Some of the gloom of his personal experience must have percolated into the almost picturesque sorrow of the Titans.

The Fall of Hyperion is altogether of a different plan and scheme, it takes the form of a dream, a vision, and in the poet's revision the whole myth is left behind. The whole background is changed, with the change of the poet's personal experience. Unlike the Homeric epic Milton could not hush up the spasm of his soul in *Paradise Lost*, so also Keats could not in *Hyperion*, but Tom is no more, he died in December and Keats took up the revision of the poem under the changed mental predilection in the second half of 1819.

The Fall is comparable to Coleridge's *Christabel* II, the continuation of *Christabel* I, a step towards the world of realities from an altogether different world. Here the hero is the poet himself, here the sorrow is not mythical and monolythic, it is the philosophy of real life. Keats has already detected his sagging energy, he could not complete the epic, when he started revising it he saw his whole outlook changed, felt also the silent steps of a new philosophy which finally broke into bits his epic framework. The Giant drove his truent soul out of the garden.

The Induction part of the poem, more than 300 lines, is of more interest than the rest, because here the reflection of the poet's changed mind is in sharp contrast with the earlier *Hyperion* poem. Apollo's meeting with Mnemosyne, the goddess of Memory, contrasts sharply with the poet's meeting with Moneta, the goddess of Counsel, in the second *Hyperion* poem; the god of poetry replaced by the poet himself and memory replaced by wisdom is a great change, the poet is determined to be guided by wisdom or good counsel rather than by memory or past experience. The very quality of sorrow is also changed, it is instinct with the spirit of wisdom.

The poet is converted to wisdom with his sorrow and he now detects his folly of being confined to memory. He sees from his experience of grief and loss a new prospect of wisdom out of it. He makes out a new meaning of sorrow, the creative source of all poetry as in the Indian conception, Sloka out of Soka, the true implication of Bedana (pain):

"Then saw I a wan face,
Now pin'd by human sorrows, but bright blanch'd
By an immortal sickness which kills not;
It works a constant change, which happy death
Can put no end; deathwards progressing
To no death was that visage;"

In the earlier *Hyperion* Apollo shed tears for Mnemosyne and Mnemosyne not only felt for him but knew what was that grief up to, to the creation of poetry—

"Thou hast dreamed of me; and awaking up
Didst find a lyre all golden by the side,
Whose strings touched by thy fingers, all the vast,
Unwearied ears of the whole Universe
Listen'd in pain and pleasure at the birth
Of such new tuneful wonder."

But in the later the poet throws up his disguise in the mythical mask and finds the goddess of Counsel in a mourning state 'and by her voice I knew she shed long-treasured tears', Moneta said: "This temple, sad and lone,/ Is all spared from the thunder of a war...is Saturn's."

Evidently it is no ordinary grief, it has no concern with earthly troubles or pain; it is the very nature of wisdom or counsel, she tells the poet:"My power which is to me still a curse/Shall be to thee a wonder." The poet now knows how to make the best use of pain and grief, with his brother's death he is a changed man, he is no longer in the *Hyperion* trim, he has already scaled beyond for a revision of his earlier idea of grief.

CHAPTER X

THE VICTORIAN NOVEL

Hardy's Tess *versus* Society

Hardy took the real life of Wessex as the background of all his great novels, *Tess* is not an exception. The only individuality that the novel may claim in the whole canon of Hardy's work is that society here surpasses all other novels in its extreme form of cruelty. Hardy of course does not make this cruelty the subject matter of his novel here, he takes it only as an inseparable part of his theme which is destiny.

Tess was estimated casually by Hardy himself as a work that justifies the gloomy view of *King Lear* in this extract:

"As flies to wanton boys are we to the gods;
They kill us for their sport."

It is the act of destiny that the tragedy occurs in the novel, of course it is not essentially of the Greek view of fate. In Greek tragedy fate can be healthy independent of the forces of society, but in Hardy's novels, particularly in *Tess* destiny is inseparable from the human background of life.

In other earlier novels, particularly *The Return of the Native, Far from the Madding Crowd* Hardy avoids the tragic death of the heroine. In the *Tess of the D'Urbervilles* the heroine not only dies but also her death was caused in the process of a justice which can hardly be accommodated to our sense of moral propriety.

The Mayor of Casterbridge is also a story of sufferings and ultimate death of the hero, but Tess's death in the present novel is so undeserved that the novel can be not only termed as an example of bitter irony but also as the final blow of fate. The society in which Tess was born and brought up plays its role in the tragedy of her life just in the manner it has caused a good deal of sufferings in the life of Jude in the next novel.

Apparently Tess is a young lady made a ready victim of gross injustice of the society. There were many vices in the society of the Tess's time, one form to be noted in Alec D'Urberville, another in Angel Clare, yet another in Farmer Groby. All those vices really made a hell of Tess's life. Tess was placed particularly between two young men—Alec and Clare—both of whom could equally claim her as their wife when Tess was particularly of none of them. The result was Tess's ultimately committing a murder, she was driven to murder one to flee with the other. The situation was not saved, she was tried for murder when she was going to attain the highest bliss of her life in the embrace of her husband, the husband whom she took with deepest of affection and love then.

Tess's life in the novel is led to such a crisis as could not be easily overcome in a human way; for example whom she will call husband—the man by whom she was forced to get a child, or the man whom she ultimately married? In a physical sense Alec was her husband, she referred to it in the story; in the social sense Angel was her husband whom she accepted, rather tried to accept, with the whole support of her heart. In the long run Tess could live with neither of them, and was flung to the fore winds as a trash and as a criminal deserving death.

Hardy has used enough of irony in the earlier novel, *The Mayor of Casterbridge*, irony has not deepened into a sense of destiny in that novel as it has done in *Tess*. Tess has gone through all sorts of ironical situations, chance and accidents frequently disturbed her world, and occasionally crossed her in all possible comfortable achievements. She was definitely crossed when she was almost near the end of happiness, a happy life of love with Clare her husband, when destiny shaped it otherwise. She was arrested, thrown into prison and was ultimately hanged for committing murder. The law court considered only the murder of a person without caring to take into account the sins and crimes the person had committed and the society indulged to the utter helplessness of a young lady. The court of justice is also a sham instrument of torment of the society. Ultimately the impression is one that has been emphasised by Hardy himself towards the close of the novel. "Justice was done, and the President of the Immortals, in Aeschylean Phrase had ended his sport with Tess."

The subtitle of the novel 'a Pure Woman' clearly indicates that Hardy has deep sympathy for this heroine and her tragedy was definitely caused by the interaction of the forces of society and destiny. There is no doubt the heroine herself is not a tragic character in the Shakespearean sense, she has no tragic flaw, her quality is supremely beyond the scope of the ordinary machinations of the world, her tragedy occurs only because she is personally all within that scope.

Tess a pure woman

Of all the novels of Hardy *Tess of the D' Urbervilles* is perhaps purely concerned with love ultimately ending in the tragedy of it. Love is a major subject of Hardy's novels, but the nature of love in this particular novel has given it a special character.

Tess of the D' Urbervilles is not an ordinary tragedy that Hardy paints here. The heroine comes out as a pure woman even though she is crushed under the wheels of destiny, the wheels of the contemporary machinery of law. Hardy of course did not unnecessarily add a sub-title – 'A Pure Woman' to this novel.

Hardy's reason is to be noted not in any particular place of his story itself. Tess is a heroine who cannot be compared with the other heroines of Hardy's tragic novels. She is neither like Bathsheba nor like Eustacia, nor even like Elizabeth, and not at all like Sue. The contrast between Tess and Sue is a significant fact when they belong to the same period of Hardy's writing.

Tess is a simple woman, even more simple than Thomasin, but Sue is a complex character. Both Eustacia and Sue are to be considered in the vanguard of modern women. Tess is essentially a simple woman, with a purity of life as simple as the simplicity of her true nature.

Tess cannot at all be held responsible for the tragedy of her life; even the last death blow to Alec is not so much a purposeful offence as it is an act of helpless reprisal. Tess has to suffer all through her life mainly because she was pure and at the same time simple. If in her place another heroine of Hardy's novels could be put, particularly Sue, tragedy could be averted.

Tess is a pure woman but her purity is not the purity of Pamela. Richardson's Pamela is a character symbolizing Christian piety and chastity: but Tess is a character symbolizing love, love that can closely be accompanied with the purity of heart.

All that happened in that novel was controlled by forces simply beyond the power of Tess. When Tess was ravished by Alec it was an act for which Tess has no responsibility. It is an injury of a strong young man upon a weak and helpless girl who was in no way armed with any protective measure.

Tess's tragedy was at least partly due to her simplicity and purity. She did not know that she was born into a complex world where frank confession had no value. Her eagerness to confess all that happened to her earlier before her marriage with Angel Clare and even after had a trail of tragic complexity of her situation. It was a mistake which she willingly committed because her purity of heart demanded it.

Perhaps no other heroine in Hardy's tragic novels could have been so morally bullied into so easily agreeing to take Alec as her husband when Clare could not accept her and did not respond immediately to her earnest appeal. At last Eustacia and Sue could not be so betrayed into such a false step. But Tess did all that because she had a different set of moral values.

After the murder of Alec all that Tess did was simply dictated by her true love which at least temporarily forgot all the danger that was then hedging her in. She forgot only because she was angelically simple and took no notice of what course law might take. The last phase of Tess's life in the story is a life of primal simplicity, a simplicity that we lost since the day of our first parents committing a sin of transgression. Tess is a tragedy of simplicity and purity which is misplaced in a world of the crises of complexity.

Hardy values human civilization only to a limited extent beyond which civilization is no doubt a state of wild savagery. He has demonstrated it in some of his major novels, but no more effectively than in *Tess of the d' Urbervilles.*

Hardy: His Tess interpreted in the light of the comment made in the last part of the conclusion Chap.

All the novels of Hardy are tragic in their ultimate impression except only one in the early stage of his writing, but none so deeply as *Tess of the D'Urbervilles. Jude the Obscure* is equally grim, perhaps a little grimmer, but a sense of waste and at the same time the great prospect of love so grievously lost is nowhere in Hardy so touching as in this novel.

The last few lines of the novel rightly sum up the final impression of the story. It is a personally undeserved tragedy, Tess is not at all a modern woman of Sue's order, her simplicity and grace are miserably exploited by the world, to this the divine machine only lent a hand to complete the destruction of a 'pure woman'. Hardy has nowhere painted love so pathetically tender, yet so cruelly crushed under the wheel of destiny. The heroine is least responsible for her destruction. Things so happened that the story leaves one the final impression of a secret complicity of destiny with the human agencies of the daily acquaintance.

Tess is born into a depleted great family, the still roaring opulence of one branch of the family comes to the direct death blow to the sinking part. Their contact is complicated by the secret hand of destiny in the plot, as for example Tess raped by Alec d'Urberville in a helpless state, things thereafter take an adverse turn as far as the helpless girl is concerned. A child is born and dead before marriage, and the marriage a little after at Talbothays with Angel Clare is also a cursed marriage, brought to a sad end on their honeymoon. Tess parted from Clare with a heavy heart, and the parting gave rise to a new chapter in her life, kept open to the possible intruders even when she was serving at the Flintcombe Ash farm. The intruder is once more Alec d'Urberville.

Tess is for some time a victim of these two persons' different degrees of irresponsibility. Tess has nothing but simplicity and the natural predilection for a loving husband, to one she was regularly married and to another she was forced by circumstances a victim of direct physical contact at one stage a and befooled seduced woman at another. Clare whom she frantically traced and sounded by letters for restoration and recovery of her position as wife in the face of direct seduction from Alec, but to no effect. Destiny played a trick there, to which human agencies only lent a hand. Clare's family on the one hand and Tess's family on the other gave cold shoulder to each one's search for the other. Tess was on the breaking point of her patience and in the long absence of Clare she submitted to the temptation held out to her by Alec.

Up to this human agency worked, but thereafter all the play of destiny or the unseen Ordainer of the fate of man. Tess's letter fell into Clare's hand unusually late, the receipt of it a little earlier could have saved the situation. Alec took Tess to a southern pension where Clare reached only too late, met only a changed Tess. But within a few moments she changed further to leave behind the dead body of Alec to be near the rediscovered Clare her married husband.

A scene of sincere love and happiness opened with, however, the Democle's sword hanging overhead. Tess forgot it altogether, but Clare remembered, yet loved. The trial of Tess under the human law held her guilty of murder and had her hanged. The hanging was noted from a distance by the two most concerned people, Tess's husband and younger sister.

The last part of the concluding chapter of the novel sums up the final impression of Tess's absolute helplessness in life, as if everything for the helplessness is contrived by both man and God, man rather under the direction of God who would not perhaps have Tess a blooming sapling.

Hardy's Moral Vision: The Mayor of Casterbridge

It is very difficult to say why Hardy has taken a gloomy view of life, particularly in his novels, but it is quite evident that he takes. Of his tales only one has a comfortable ending, the world of *Under the Greenwood Tree* is really healthy; but all other novels are grim tragedies, particularly his mature works are. *The Mayor of Casterbridge* is one of such great works, compared to the other two later novels simple in construction easy to detect the gathering darkness.

Hardy takes essentially a non-Christian attitude to life all through, he has no firm faith in the existence of God, he notes only a moral order that rules the Universe, there he is merely a 'meliorist' as he calls himself. Pessimist is a wrong word for him although the greatest temptation one may feel to call him so. He does not see darkness everywhere, he feels it is wrong not to see darkness where there is no light. Even in his *The Mayor of Casterbridge* Henchard saw brighter days, he rose to the Mayoral position from his hay trusser profession, so did Farfrae in life. The tragedy happens because Susan had yet a flicker of Victorian morality, she came back to her married husband from her unmarried partner. Behind the tragedy there is a persistent irony, first the irony of an auction sale of a wife.

The novel is an example of the frequent use of irony, almost every turn of the situation in the action is ironical, irony lends to a tragic waste. For Hardy it is a part of the truth that life presents. The only curious thing about Hardy is that, lack of Christian faith has left him (his heroes) a bark without a port, Henchard too got no God to fall back upon. Fanfrae rose without any God to guide him so also fell Henchard without any support from any God. It is a Godless world, without any Christian consolation to sustain the drooping spirit. Henchard died like Shakespeare's Timon. Died with no Christian hope.

Hardy's God is replaced by chance or a Pagan god of unaccounted mischief. Man only fights an unequal fight against it. So in Hardy's world human role is very substantial. Man falls, but not without fighting against it to the end. Henchard fought, so did Tess and Jude, but Henchard first a master of irony, then a slave, while Tess and Jude in their own way remained a victim of a situation and fought like a slave or victim. So in these two later novels Hardy made an impression of destiny, in the earlier only a sense of irony.

Hardy is not really Grecian in his concept of destiny, he only seems to be a little closer to the Greek concept, but not exactly that. Obviously Henchard's world is not essentially a Greek world, it is a Godless world, more to be seen in relation to Lucetta, who never felt herself under any power of divine inevitability. More than any other novels Hardy's *The Mayor of Casterbridge* seems to be more dominated by human agency, even the hero's tragedy is caused more by his folly than by any moral force. The two other mature novels differ from the Greek drama in a still more curious way.

Hardy seems to be clear about a moral order enacting its own law no matter how grievous a damage it might cause to what and whom, and no matter whether there is a God to preside over it or not. Hardy is not like the Greeks after any such God, nor ready to adjust his created world to His supremacy. *The Mayor of Casterbridge* is a world where no such God rules, neither there is any Grecian Oracle to communicate to him the sufferings of the earth born. Man is left alone to fight his own battle, either to victory or to demand defeat.

The Mayor of Casterbridge: Donald Farfrae's role

The Mayor of Casterbridge has its plot entirely built upon irony to which the main contributors were three outside characters. Farfrae, Newson and Lucetta. Henchard fell as he rose, in his fall these three characters acted their roles, mainly Farfrae did.

Farfrae was manager to the corn-factor, during his service Henchard's trade prospered; he left Henchard and there was a slump in his prosperity, of course that was not the only reason. Thereafter there were repeated ironical turns in the situation for Henchard, in some of the outstanding Farfrae was involved. One very remarkable was the triangular love-affair with Lucetta, Henchard lost her to Farfrae. In another conflict of love and affection too Farfrae won. It is his taking

Elizabeth to wife in the face of Henchard's opposition to it. Henchard tried to keep Elizabeth to himself finally as his only object of affection to save him from the haunting loneliness of his life.

In the story Farfrae and Henchard are the opposite poles, as if the positive and negative poles of the same scheme, very rare in Hardy's other tales. So Farfrae's role in this respect is very significant. Farfrae represents light and Henchard darkness in the plot. Farfrae gained what Henchard lost - his business, his Mayoral position. Farfrae got a stable station in life not after gloomy days of sufferings, as did Henchard in this novel once more to be deprived of it and as did Farmer Oak and Diggory Venn in two other earlier novels; he had only a steady rise.

This difference from Hardy's other plots betrays, Hardy is not absolutely blind to the existence of light, that is why his claim to his 'meliorist' status is not unfounded. His Farfrae is a sharp contrast to the character of Henchard, the hero of the novel. Henchard fell not simply by the trick of destiny, such a trick is also a part of the truth in Henchard's world but that is not the only thing to take into account, Henchard fell mainly by his character, thc character that could not adjust or utilise Fate's trick. Farfrae is a character that can use it and adjust it and therefore he rises.

Farfrae is a healthy character, he combines in him acumen, energy and lively human feelings, which let him ride over danger and difficulties and sail a smooth course fully utilising what destiny gave him. He could retain in him a healthy friendly love and sympathy in the last hour of Henchard's life and even after.

The Mayor of Casterbridge : Use of chance and accident: Plot construction

Hardy's thought is well-executed in his plot almost in every novel, his masterpieces most. *The Mayor of Casterbridge* is particularly to be noted because of Hardy's greater insistence on irony of fate in the hero's life. Hardy believed man has often to fight an unequal battle against an indifferent moral order, heedless to individual destiny to serve an unknown universal purpose. The design of his plot is brought to bear upon this belief.

The Mayor of Casterbridge is an exceptional novel only in this that the story's design is all too apparent as it is not in the other two masterpieces of Hardy's later tales. Irony is a little more punctuated in this novel. The story starts with a masterly stroke of irony, with the auction sale of a married wife at a fair to an unknown person. Susan, Henchard's wife, went with her new owner with her breast baby to an unknown destination.

The next remarkable turn in the story is still more subtly ironical. Nearly 21 years later Susan fled her home accompanied by her daughter to search after her married husband, for she felt acutely the moral pinch of a distinction between a married husband and an unmarried partner of life, all even more trickily hastened by a false information of Newson's death. She got her husband then at the peak of his glory, a corn merchant with brisk business and in his Mayoral position at Casterbridge. Destiny played a good trick to make him rise from the position of a hay-trusser to the position of a Mayor.

It is again an irony that Michael's wife deceived him well by thrusting upon him the child of Newson who bought her at an auction bid. A woman who behaved so innocently became a little crafty, and this turned into an irony in Henchard's life, particularly owing to the wrong information of Newson's being drowned at sea proving so and his coming into the picture to act his father's role twice over. How it came to be the story has taken into proper account.

The entire plot illustrates a sea-saw movement with the hero, Henchard rose and then fell, he became Mayor from a hay-trusser position, then became hay-trusser again. Between Donald Farfrae and Henchard destiny played an ironical trick. What Henchard lost graced Farfrae as the favoured child of fortune. Farfrae came as a servant but became master and the Mayor of the city at last. More than that Henchard lost Lucetta to Farfrae as a lover and lost Elizabeth Jane to Newson as father and then finally to Farfrae. Henchard lost as father and Farfrae gained as husband.

This story of loss and gain is so grimly Hardyan that it ultimately brought the hero down to the desolate and forsaken state of Timon, the only difference is he could not avoid yet another blow at the hand of Elizabeth at her wedding and had at least one faithful servant to stand by him at his death, a servant not his own, but owned by his enemy. Hardy has yet tried to add some streak of pure humanity to a grim tragedy like willful self-immolation which Shakespeare has not.

Hard Times: A study of fact and fancy : Utilitarian Philosophy

In his study of The Great Tradition Dr. Leavis makes a special case of *Hard Times* in the work of Dickens. Dr. Leavis is really correct in his approach to Dickens, particularly this novel in which Dickens has dealt with a serious subject. What that subject is Leavis has not immediately pointed out, although he is very clear about the seriousness of it.

Dickens is generally accepted as a writer more didactic in his approach than anybody in his own age. The same trend is more emphatic in the present novel. It is to be considered as a 'melodrama' of facts and modern science. Even in his treatment of the subject matter Dickens says righteous indignation cannot condescend to humour nor even to pathos, although humour and pathos are almost inseparable in nearly all Dickens's novels. In *Hard Times* Dickens satirically views the contemporary emphasis on science and materialistic evaluation of life.

Dickens appreciated liberalism, which must have been the lesson of two great Revolutions, French and American. He understood equality and fraternity, but not the other, liberty, although his contemporaries emphasized only the last one. During his age he saw a vast attempt at scientific and philosophical revaluation of life. He saw scientists and philosophers like Spencer, Bentham, Bright and Mill. He saw also an enormous progress in the organization of the Church. Dickens could appreciate none of them, rather he saw a kind of craze for science which distorted all human values.

Hard Times is a novel in which Dickens takes an ironical view of the craze for science and Mathematics as the only way to human prosperity. In *A Tale of Two Cities* Dickens gives what he understands by revolution, a revolution like the French Revolution; in *Hard Times* a little earlier he gives what he understands by the industrial revolution and the revolution of science.

The novel exactly begins with facts, "Now, what I want is facts." The scene is laid in the industrial town called 'Coke Town'. The action is mainly concentrated upon the two families, the Gradgrinds and the Boundarbies, both upholders of enormous progress of science and materialism. One an industrialist, the other a great financier, both joining hands for a civilization essentially based upon facts, upon science which is nothing but facts. They are the wrong interpreters of Adam Smith and Malthus.

The real crisis of facts is, however, to be noted in Mr. Gradgrind's school where he propounded only the hard realities of life, excepted everything but facts and calculations. He is a man always "with a rule and a pair of scales and the multiplication table." The contrast between the two young scholars of the school, Cecilia Jupe and Bitzer, is what Dickens brings to a finish, to a crisis indeed. Cecilia is a failure and Bitzer a success in the test of facts at school; both ways the school is a massacre of innocents, Dickens's words 'murdering the innocents.'

The teacher of this school M'Choakumchild is so elaborately described in Chap. Two of this novel that the story leaves no doubt about what it is after. The very sound of the name suggests that the master would choke all the emotional possibilities in the children under his care. He is one of the trained 140 school masters, trained for the success of the new system of education, which takes care of only such things as have no role of fancy and emotion. The plan includes subjects like orthography, etymology, syntax and biography, astronomy, geography, algebra and vocal music etc.

The plan of education leads ultimately to a dead end, the master is rather 'over done'. Dickens's own remark is 'If he had only learnt a little less, how infinitely better he might have taught much more'. Quite ironic! Fancy is regarded only a robber lurking within; the sole purpose of this education is satirically to kill it outright or at least to 'maim him and distort him'.

All the Gradgrind children, born and brought up in their 'matter of fact home' called significantly Stone Lodge, were curious, products of this attempted civilization. The youngest child Thomas is a distortion in one sense Bitzer a distortion in another; both ironically meet towards the close of the story where Bitzer brought up in the Gradgrind philosophy proved ultimately a threat to one of the Gradgrind children, Thomas.

Bitzer rejected ironically Mr. Gradgrind's human appeal in the form "you were many years at my school". Bitzer's reply was in the language of facts, "My schooling was paid for, it was a bargain".

The marriage between the eldest Gradgrind child Louisa and Josia Bounderby is a marriage that sufficiently proves the failure of facts. It is an odd match, although both the families inculcated the same principle, the materialistic value of life, that is the value of facts. It is the fact that fails here in the whole course of the story. It is purely due to the denial of the essential realities of life left out awfully in their mad insistence upon facts.

The utilitarian philosophy which gained ground in Dickens's time is a philosophy that went wrong in the insane utilization of all those principles in practical life. Dickens only made it the subject matter of his novel and exposed its essential folly.

Hardy's tragic vision/philosophy of life as in the *Tess of the d'Urbervilles*

Hardy deals with life in his novels in such a way that he can be regarded as the remote replica of the Greek view of life; of course Hardy is only the modern version of the Greek conception of destiny. All Hardy's novels are tragic except only one, *Under the Greenwood Tree.* Of all those high tragedies of human destiny three are particularly very important in Hardyan canon - *The Mayor of Casterbridge, Tess of the d' Urbervilles* and *Jude the Obscure.*

Tess of the d' Urbervilles was published in 1891, that was the period of Hardy's highest achievement. *Tess* represents Hardyan view of life as has been nowhere so clearly done. *Jude the Obscure* is only a little more grim than *Tess.*

Hardy never believed in Christianity, so he had no idea of the grace that we are expecting every moment at the hands of God. Hardy's view of the Universe is nearly a Pagan view, more close to the pre-Christian Greek view. He took it to be 'a huge impersonal mechanism' that the Universe is moved by some mysterious power completely indifferent to human agencies.

This view, although more or less the Greek view of fate, is made out of the modern complexity of human life, in almost all the great novels of Hardy, particularly the last two, Hardy is therefore far removed from Greek conceptualism. Hardy had a concrete picture of life before him, which the Greek tragedians forgot to take into account.

Tess is a tragedy of character, but the tragedy is not out of the Greek view of 'destiny an inscrutable force'; the tragedy of the heroine is destined as it is ultimately made out in Hardy's story, but it is a destiny that evolved out of the heedless operation of the forces practically human in shape. Hardy's conception in *Tess* is 'man is working to one end, destiny to another'. But there is obviously a human force.

Alec d'Ureberville and Angel Clare are the two dominant figures who in particular represented two specific levels of society between which Tess was crushed. Love in Tess's life came to be regarded as a human element, a problem in itself, especially in relation to love in these two male characters. Hardy very often treated love not only as a problem issue in his novels but often as an instrument of destiny. Such it was in *Tess of the d'Urbervilles*. His theme is 'mankind's predicament in the Universe'. *Tess* is the perfect example of it.

Hardy of course kept in mind Shakespeare's *King Lear* when he wrote *Tess*. He quoted in his Preface a passage from *King Lear*:

As flies to wanton boys are we to the gods;
They kill us for their sport.

Obviously Hardy posed himself as essentially Aeschylian as Shakespeare was a little in his *King Lear*. So far as the tragedy of Tess is concerned the heroine fell a ready victim to forces quite wanton and completely heedless of the cruelties involved in their very operation and impact. The forces were human and social in Hardy's case which were not in the case of the Greek Master. The court procedure with regard to Tess is a significant departure from the Greek concept of destiny, but which is the essence of Hardy's view of life, ultimately pessimistic and inescapable in effect.

Hard Times: Dickens's pattern of symbolism

Dickens is commonly known as a great writer who is at the same time a great 'entertainer'. but *Hard Times* is an exception to this view, and Dr. Leavis has rightly taken it so. Dickens is not at all an entertainer in this book, he is all serious, and has thoroughly expounded a subject that he has nowhere done. Naturally in his use of images and symbols he has been a little more particular.

Hard Times was published in 1854, rather in the heyday of philosophical dispute of a particular type. In this period utilitarian philosophy and materialistic outlook got the better of all human sentiments. Cosmic systemizers like Spencer, great social philosophers like Bentham, practical politicians like Bright and political economists like Mill dominated the period. Dickens took all of them into fair account, but he knew something more that they perfectly ignored in their recognition of values.

Dickens is highly satiric particularly in this novel, and his satire is effectively expressed in symbols and images. Even the title of the novel is essentially symbolic, a sort of misprise as Dickens has taken it.

Dickens is not a symbolist in the 20th century sense, but he has symbols to hit hard the core of his idea. All that he paints in the novel is symbolically a critical world, the outlook on it is sharply scathing. Dickens does not appreciate at all the utilitarian outlook and the total disregard of moral and emotional side of life in the too rigid emphasis on mathematical computation of life's essence. Dickens has made his characters serve as symbols all taken from the material achievement of his contemporary age. Character like Gradgrind, Bounderby, Sparcit and even a school master of the name M'Choakumchild are all symbols of the hard realities of the period, both in the inflection of the sound and in the implication of the sense of their names. Particularly Gradgrind and M'Choakumchild are symbols of hard heartedness that Mathematical outlook has mainly introduced. The name of the very school master suggests that all the children under him are likely to be choked in all their impulses and emotions.

Bounderby and Gradgrind are the people who dominate the material world where everything to be Mathematically understood and solved. They are the true citizens of a town called Coketown, a town symbolising the essence of industrial civilization with all evils in the wake. The Lodge, the Bank he had for his residence is symbolically named Stone Lodge. With all these Dickens tries to hold up his clear view of heartlessness of the industrial civilization and so called progress of science in his age. In such an age human passions and tender feelings are so damnably discouraged that the younger generations feel themselves confined in a prison-house.

Charles Dickens has written a novel on the French Revolution. There his symbols are highly critical of the revolution itself as he is of the symbols of industrial age and scientific progress. In this novel O'Sleary's circus is a symbol of a true caricature of Bounderby's mathematical outlook. Gradgrind and Bounderby make this caricature possible. The horserider of the circus shows up the ultimate consequence in a pathetic waste of human values, which we have noted almost in everything in the novel, particularly in the horse-rider's own daughter Sissy's destiny. There must have been so many Sissies in the world whom Dickens could not but take in earnest for a story of tragic waste.

Hard Times as a novel is highly satiric in its ultimate impression, and satire is made out by means of so many images and symbols Dickens has used all through, in the selection of the title and the names of the characters, in the choice of the background of life and ultimately in the mere waste of their apparently sincere effort in a direction that ultimately reaches a point of no return. Dickens is highly moral in almost all his novels and always in a vein of humour in his exposition of life, but in this novel all these change their colour to a degree that he has nowhere attempted as in the present novel. His seriousness of purpose is symbolitically presented to make it highly effective.

A Tale of Two Cities: The Revolution

Dickens is hardly comparable to Scott who has a perfect fidelity to fact, he is better comparable to a modern novelist, Conrad, in this regard. Both Conrad and Dickens have written historical novels, painting in their characteristic way a picture of revolution, Dickens the French Revolution mainly and Conrad the Russian Revolution specially in his *Under Western Eyes*. In spite of their basic unity Dickens and Conrad differ in their portrayal of Revolution because they belong to two essentially different kinds of genius.

Revolution in *A Tale of Two Cities* is a widely known history, but the Russian Revolution is history duly coloured by Conrad's own personal experience of Russian autocracy. His Razumov is his close representation. Conrad is more occupied with the revolutionary activities outside Russia, but Dickens with the destructive progress of Revolution in France in a way that it seems more thorough. The Revolution theme in Dickens's pages is more thoroughly explored than in Conrad's pages. The taking of the Bastille recalls Scott's breaking of the Midlothian prison.

Dickens's portrait of the French Revolution is not like Carlyle's, Carlyle is a historian and Dickens is not. Dickens presents the revolution in its historical spirit only, not history. His study of the cause of the revolution and its consequence is individualistic, in close harmony with his private feelings and personal predilection basically human and moral. The cause of the Revolution is extreme form of tyranny and oppression to many like Gaspard and Madame Defarge before marriage. Dickens's picture of the Revolution is another form of tyranny no less cruel than the autocratic rule.

Dickens has painted both the aspects of Revolution as Conrad has not done in his novels, particularly *Under Western Eyes*. Dickens does it more effectively by spectacular excess both ways which in a way make good its blank of psychological depth. The excess of Revolution is more demonstrative in the Foulan killing, if not in the taking of the Bastille, as also in the heartless cruelties of vengeance of Madame Defarge, not sparing even the man (Dr. Manette) who really suffered endless cruelties of the autocratic rule for the sake of her family. Madame Defarge becomes even more demonstrably blood thirsty than Lady Macbeth. In her vengeance she joined hands with the forces of ingratitude.

The cruelties inflicted, or rather sought to be inflicted, upon Doctor Manette's daughter, her married life, are more than Dickens with his keen moral sense can stand. So the story ended in a poetic justice. Madame Defarge is killed by her own secretly stored bullet under her breast garment. In *A Tale of Two Cities* the lasting values are not revolution and vengeance, revolution is rather the darkest form of oppression. Dr. Manette, Lucie and Darney form a trio of human values that replace all other fleeting vagaries of revolution. Dickens does not propound Rousseau's ethics of equality, fraternity and liberty; his values are love, fidelity and integrity, to which revolution may often present a contrast.

Hard Times: a realistic novel

Hard Times is a controversial novel which marks Dickens's maturity of art and attitude. Even Dr. Leavis has considered it as the only serious novel of Dickens and included it in his *Great Tradition.* Shaw praises the novel significantly as bearing the stamp of Dickens's prophetic predilection of mind. The novel is more than any other in Dickensian canon an approach to the realistic rigmarole of his age.

It is Dickens who never gives up his moral stand in the whole of English fiction, but here his outlook undergoes a change in his realistic account of life, the life of the age bristling with ideas and controversies of philosophers, economists and political theorists like Spencer, Bentham, Bright and Mill. In *Hard Times* Disckens, of course, does not fall in with any one of them, his line of approach is semi-ironic. He ridicules the harsh realities of life which all those people have taken into considerations. He is not a'sullen socialist' as Macaulay would call him, but a true liberal as Chesterton has acknowledged him to be.

Dickens in *Hard Times* betrays his special aptitude for a liberal view of life more than in any of his novels earlier or later. He is to be judged beside Ruskin and Carlyle of his age, although his difference with them is not too small. Dickens in this novel cares for the true purpose of life which neither improvement of science nor abtruse philosophy of life can fully uphold. Dickens's satire in the book is directed against certain evils, abuse and false evaluations of Victorian society. The target of attack in this book is utilitarianism in education, in business, industry and even in marriage greed for money. The main target of attack is Gradgrind's theory of education, which is based on 'facts' and statistics. Mr. Gradgrind is totally blind to all the liberal values. 'In this life we want nothing but facts, Sir, nothing but facts' tells the new school master. A little later Gradgrind is described as being strictly a man of realistic outlook, a man who believes in the rule of the thumb. Human judgement for Gradgrind is a mere question of figures, of simple case of Arithmetic. Dickens's scorn is for 'those who see only figures and facts of the essence of life. They are the representatives of the wickedest and most enormous vice of this time.'

The novel depicts the disastrous result of Gradgrind's long-cherished principle. He totally ignores the feelings of his daughter and marries her to a Bounderby who is another ardent follower of Gradgrind's utilitarian principle. Gradgrind's son Tom, his own Mathematical Tom, also symbolizes the irony in the context of reversal of Gradgrind's expectation as father.

Dickens is remarkable in English literature as a great exponent of humour, but in *Hard Times* Dickensian humour has changed its colour and come nearer to satire or ironic exposition. The book is as a whole great protest against the oppression of the too much of science, too much of Mathematics and too much of anything beside life. The protest may be bitter, 'but it was a protest against bitterness', it may be dark, but it is a darkness of the subject and not of the author. In this book he is dealing with hard times, 'but not with the hard eternity, and surely not with a hard philosophy of the Universe.' Dickens is for human happiness and against everything that frustrates it. All his picture in the novel, of Bounderby and Gardgrind, of O'Sleary's circus and M'Choakumchild's school, in a word the entire Coketown society, are against that happiness and so Dickens is for their overthrow.

A Tale of Two Cities: The Hero

A Tale of Two Cities is not a novel like *David Copperfield,* not as clearly a one man show as *David Copperfield* or *Oliver Twist* is. A historical novel can hardly be, even Scott's *Ivanhoe* is less so though Scott conceived it to be. In *Ivanhoe* Richard I is a greater hero than Ivanhoe, but the position of the hero seems to be reserved for Ivanhoe. The problem of ascertaining the hero in Dickens's novel is of a quite different kind.

The hero in the novel is not a historical figure, none of the leaders of the Revolution is introduced in the novel, not to speak of their attaining the hero's position. The hero here has no role in the Revolution though its impact is acute upon his destiny, this acuteness and immediacy of impact makes him worthy of the hero's position. Darnay just beside Sydney Carton is a sharply distinct figure although equally deeply in love with the heroine (Lucie Manette). Because of this triangular love effect without any apparent conflict there is either a confusion over the choice of the hero of the novel or the absurd notion that it has a double hero instead of one.

Sydney Carton is a different kind of character perhaps with no noble quality except his self-sacrifice for the sake of love. There is perhaps no noble quality in his character to deserve Lucie, even his self-sacrifice up to the last goes almost unheeded by even those for whom he made that sacrifice. All his troubles to make Darnay safe and Lucie happy are selfless and are duly strengthened by Darnay's own moral view of love, but a little more dramatic than really appealing even to the audience. Darnay's love for Lucie has essentially a different character. Darnay deserves Lucie by his noble qualities in addition to his sincerity. Darnay's sincerity is not Dickens like histrionic as in the case of Sydney, it is deeply spiritualised, all too moral to be exhibitionistic.

Darnay's claim to the hero's position is not unheroic like Sydney's claim. Sydney is all a blank with serious flaws, Chesterton calls all those 'sins of habit', a British lawyer with a French career, blank with all but a redeeming virtue, a virtue undignified in its exhibition in the course of the action. But Darnay has no sin but only a minor fault, the fault that could make him a Shakespearean hero had it not been ultimately Dickens like. His goodness to an excess could lead him into a tragic trap had he not timely been helped by Sydney Carton.

Darnay's love for Lucie is a sort of expiation, love takes its rise exactly from where hatred poisoned the soul earlier, so it is, although romantic in character, soberised by a sense of atonement. Dr. Manette was oppressed by Darnay's father, thrust into prison for 18 years, the son an Evremonde fell in love with the daughter of his father's enemy. The only thing in the holocaust of revolution instinct with true human values. Revolution has no meaning at all if it is not at least revelatory of human waste or essential human values. The position of the hero is the rallying point of these values. Sydney Carton there fails and Darnay wonderfully succeeds.

Darnay is a model of human values, his love too is a part of it. He is a young, highly refined and full blooded gentleman, his love for an equally accomplished young lady of his land is quite natural, even a bloody revolution cannot silence it. It is timely awakened as a silver lining to the dark shadows of total anarchy in the name of Revolution. Darnay and Lucie are the only hope of a future regeneration and re-establishment of human values out of the furies of oppression of a kind on the one hand and inhuman vengeance on the other that the French Revolution symbolised in Dickens's pages. Darnay inherits his blue blood from the French aristocracy but no tyranny, no habit of oppression of his stock; love and humanity make a true hero, although not of the Shakespearean type, not exactly of Scott's model, but a hero nonetheless effective for that.

A Tale of Two Cities: Plot well-made or not

Dickens has a bad name that he cannot form his plot well. Even his masterpiece *David Copperfield* is not a well-knit plot, although the story is all about the hero from first to last. *Pickwick Papers* cannot be, because Mr. Pickwick maintains the unity of all those papers only from the outside. *A Tale of Two Cities*, one of his later works, of 1859, is expected to be of better artistic coherence. Actually it is, but yet of true Dickensian stamp, its plot not well made as it should have been.

The story of the novel is based on history, so greater liberty of plot is not possible. The very fact of dependence on history must have been both a hindrance and a help to Dickens's genius. Dickens could not stray further away from the historical unity though his lively spirit may have led him that way, but history again barred his natural way of true strength. It has gained in integration of plot but lost in the true Dickensian humour. The loss of that real geniality is to be noted in the rebellious humour of Madame Defarge, which has tinged even the love episode of the story.

The plot is, however, apparently well-planned, the action is evenly distributed between the two cities, one tale partly told in London and the rest in Paris, both together make the plot. Again the cities offer a sharp contrast, a contrast between peace and revolt, disturbance and settlement, love and worries, and lastly between life and death. The two cities are linked not only by so many characters and events but also by the theme itself. The theme of the novel is not the French Revolution, it is Carlyle's theme, Dickens's is the values that lead to the revolution which again damnably dislocates all other principles. The two cities are not only like the two hands of the compass of the plot, they are the two extremes of the same truth. The truth maintains its unity.

The love episode in the story is in sharp contrast with the revolutionary history, but in Dickens's plot they are quite in place, the contrast a unity well maintained. The family that offended most makes the atonement exactly where it offended. The Lucie-Darnay marriage episode neutralizing her British lover Sydney Carton with his dissipation of life and self-sacrifice, is only one block of light in the gloomy centre of the Revolution, out-bidding all its horrors and massacre of lives. The episode is no doubt Dicken's invention although many such things could have been there in history.

Lucie's marriage with Sydney could have been not only ill-matched but also unrelated to the plot, it could never serve the purpose of the realization of the theme's objective, the emergence of human values out of the anarchy of a Revolution. Darnay's father and Dr. Manette are the two enemies, out of which the Revolution developed but developed to an extreme of waste, waste of everything, money, material and lives, ultimately to be replaced by the permanent values of love, love that knits the souls of two enemies. The unique harmony out of a chaos, a discord of souls, is the secret of the plot of *A Tale of Two Cities*.

Dickens is more or less a successful plot maker in this late creation, success partly enforced by the imposed limitation of history, and partly by his essentially human outlook on revolution. Only in some episodes Dickens still betrays his original incapacity to integrate stray bits of desperate excellences, one such is the excess of Madame Defarge's vengeance that ultimately met with a poetic justice in the last scene by means of her equally effective English opposite Miss Prossy.

Dickens perhaps felt the difficulty of controlling this desperate proclivity so that to round off the story successfully he had to invent Miss Prossy's hitherto unknown strength of body reinforced by her known strength of fidelity and love. Within the framework of this plot Dickens has thoroughly revealed his own power of thrilling externalization of human roles, as in the excess both ways of the tyranny of the upper class and the inhuman cruelty of the lower called Jacques.

A Tale of Two Cities: The Title: the role of the two Cities

Perhaps no other novel is given so significant a title in Dickensian canon as this. Practically it is a tale divided between the two leading cities of Europe. The theme is the French Revolution, but the scene of action is not confined to only the home city of the Revolution, Dickens's plan is far from that. Only enactment of the causes and the actual progress of the Revolution is not Dickens's purpose. That would have been history and not historical novel. Dickens is essentially a fiction writer, and not even a fiction writer of Scott's genius, his fidelity is more to his natural fiction than to fact.

London and Paris--these two cities assume so much importance in the plot that one can regard them as two main characters in the novel if one may. The scene of bloodshed is Paris, it has not extended to London, it cannot. But yet London has an equally significant role to play. London is also a rowdy city, Dickens has painted its rowdyism in the court scene, more particularly in the Honest Tradesman Chapter, but the Paris crowd is not rowdy, it passes beyond Dickens's usual sense of humour so totally that it gives no pleasure but unrelieved pain. A more serious excess of purpose as London characteristically does not appoint as its own ultimately object. London is the capital of Merry England, and Dickens is its true genius.

The two cities are contrasted between them, one a scene of bloodshed, tyranny and oppression, the other the sheltered scene of peace where only a fun-like the old Bailey and the mock-funeral of Roser Cly tickles light enjoyment. It does not represent any La Force or Bastille scene. These two cities are linked literally and metaphorically, Telson and Co. does it as do the major characters in the story. Dickens's plot requires it. Dickens theme is only outwardly the Revolution, his real theme is a human history revealed out of the impact of the Revolution. The first could not require inclusion of London, the second does.

London and Paris in the story are one balanced by the other, a passage up one and down another in Dickens's art. Darnay's love for Lucie could never have been a success, or at all possible had there been no echoed Soho shelter in that funny city of London where Telson offers job to a flunkey like Jerry Cruncher. Dickens is quite at home in it. Perhaps Dickens's interest in the capital city is never so intense as in this novel. Whenver Darnay and Dr. Manette cross the English channel they feel the new tingle of energy, and whenever they are in their city, then the haunted city of bloodshed, they are in a nightmare of horror, and lose, particularly Dr. Manette does, all humanity.

The story, however, is not the story of the two cities, not the history of their origin and culture, but the story of a crisis period of their history. The two cities stand out in the story with their respective roles to act, with their unique position and spirit as symbols of two different nations. The Revolution is a European problem, the popular upsurge under extreme tyranny and oppression and abominable social evil, is a good lesson to all, England learnt it already by introducing a democratic system.

Doctor Manette's role in the plot: The most tragic character retrieved

Dickens is not a great painter of psychological character, but none is so thoroughly successful as he in the portrayal of external stakes of character. *A Tale of Two Cities* is too full of external stakes, and Dr. Manette is a character, more than any other in the novel, to develop at the stakes and under their direct impact. The story is only narrowly saved from being tragic.

Dr. Manette is no doubt the greatest sufferer in the novel. He suffered at the hands of both the sides of the Revolution - the protagonist and the antagonist. Such a crucial position was Dr. Manette's and by a position like that Dickens neutralizes one by the other to make way for a different standard of values. The ruling class tyrannized over the worker class, Dr. Manette's is only the middle position, although he could easily side with the upper class. He fell easy victim to the tyranny of an Evremonde, really Darnay's father, a Marquis, when he attended another victim of his wrath, at a time he required his service. The victim was Madame Defarge's brother. The whole family staggered before the tyranny. Dr. Manette too rot in prison till after 18 years he was released by the fall of the Bastille during the Revolution. His young wife died and their only daughter was left to the care of the Bank.

Dr. Manette is a living example of the bad side of the oppression both ways, he has already lost the power of the mind, all human feelings under the tyranny of the rulers and vested interest. Defarge was once in his pay and therefore he took care of his old master till he was taken to his daughter in England. His blank mind came to be gradually revived, restored to normalcy in the warmth of human relationship which was so long withheld from him. His daughter's care and love made him a moral man, a true loving father.

Dr. Manette is not so long a psychological character as he is an subject of study under the acute stress of tyranny out of the reaction to which the Revolution was an outburst of protest, and under the infliction of the excess of the outburst itself. Dr. Manette is a study of the victim of the two opposite evils which Dickens as author seeks to cure, and there he is moral Dickens. So in the plot of the novel Dr. Manette has a very crucial position, more significant than the position of any other characters in the novel.

There is a great difference between the two main victims of tyranny of the oppressive rule in the land, Madame Defarge and Dr. Manette; Madame Defarge turned revengeful and lapsed into equally cruel evil, but Dr. Manette could not, there his human values led him to a different end. Loss of humanity made him mad, and made him sink low into a complete blankness of mind. Loss of humanity in Madame Defarge made her hellishly blood-thirsty and pushed her to the extreme of inhumanity. In Dr. Manette's case it is only a temporary suspension of normal human responses. In Dr. Manette's case the creative force is love, in Madame Defarge's case it has already passed the limit of all cure, so Dickens has met it in a different way.

Dr. Manette's revolt is exactly against evil and oppression, not against any particular class or people; he thought the Revolutionary council must honour a fellow sufferer like him, some of the members were willing, as Monsieur Defarge was, but Madame Defarge was not. His failure to secure his daughter's happiness at their hands made him demented again, he relapsed into the same blankness of mind. To get him back to normal human responses Dickens has to make a quite different arrangement, I mean artistic device to end the story on a pleasant note. It is the principle of poetic justice and the device of substitution.

Dickens is not a great painter of tragic mood, he is far from Hardy and Shakespeare in that. Dr. Manette is not really a tragic character, he is only a victim of a tragic excess of a just cause, the cause of Revolution. The death of Madame Defarge by her own bullet is Dickens's final reprimand of this excess. Dr. Manette is only the opposite extreme of victimised just cause, the cause of justice. Carton is unceremonially guillotined, and Darnay is ceremonially spared the final blow. Beside such events of the story Dr. Manette's tragic sufferings and lively escape from immediate danger and heartening recovery of normal mind serve directly no purpose of tragic loss but finally the moral recovery, which is true Dickensian.

A Tale of Two Cities : The Love theme

A Tale of Two Cities is a record of the French Revolution, not the exact history as Carlyle's is, but history as Scott's *Ivanhoe* is considered to be. It is a story of a dark revolution with a glowing centre of a love episode that ultimately moulds history into a usual Dickensian theme without distorting historical veracity.

It is the story of Lucie's love which tore off the tangled grip of a tyrannical revolution as the cause of it, rather more gory than any of its kind. Dickens's true nature as an author is fully redeemed in his treatment of this love theme. It is like him not highly romantic, but only as far romantic as can be equally forcefully, controlled by usual Dickensian moral principles. That is mainly why Lucie's love is rather equally divided between her father and husband, a husband who did not stand as a romantic suitor like any of Hardy's heroes. It is a love that shares both the classical and romantic values. In this she far surpasses Agnes.

Lucie drew too many lovers than Hardy's Tess or Thomasin did, but none of her two English friends deserved her, not even Sydney Carton who not only professed his utmost sacrifice for her happiness but actually made it, while Hardy's Diggory Venn deserved Thomasin in *The Return of the Native*. The two young British lawyers could not claim her love, Dickens would not allow it, it would have been morally repulsive to Dickens's ethics. Farmer Oak may ultimately deserve Bathsheba, but Carton cannot Lucie. It is not only not ethically sound, it is again against Dickens's plot.

Lucie's love for Darnay fulfils Dickens's basic construction of plot of this novel which seeks to outbid hate by love, revolution by permanent human solution, Darnay is a kind of lover who is ethically more exalted than David Copperfield. David passes through unavailing romantic love, one fails even after marriage, marriage with Dora, and only at long last detects his true partner of life. Darnay knows no such waste of energy, he is morally even more consistent to deserve even a more sweet lady than Agnes. Lucie's love is not French love, it has English solidity and a sweetness of a passionate ardour that timely gleams to add grace to personality.

Lucie is never like Agnes more on the side of duty, she is held in even poise between love and duty. Her duty to her father does not dry her nearly dull to her lover holding him long away from her, she is more lively than Agnes, more endowed with qualities that cannot let sleep love so long but warms it up immediately where it is. Dickens's view here seems to satisfy the claims of both love and moral principles, he knows love is no less moral with its lively freshness and grace.

None of Dicken's heroines, not Agnes at all, has been an object of love and admiration for a good number of suitors, if not for dozens of them as Lucie's maid says. She had been the object of attention in the Old Bailey, a French young lady with her physical beauty of form. Dickens has not neglected this side of beauty, rather put equal stress upon its necessity to link it up with love, rather to excite love.

He has recognised the need of the test of sincerity and seriousness of love, the one major test is sacrifice, sacrifice of money, material and personal happiness. But only sacrifice does not deserve love as it has not in the case of Carton. Dickens has provided trials and test enough, but yet has not forgotten to subordinate them all to a human good. Lucie's love for Darnay can ensure it more than her love for anyone else.

Dickens knows love as a great force, he makes it so in the novel, makes it more viable than revolution. Life is lived not because there is revolution, but because there is love as Dr. Manette can provide an example in the novel.

A Tale of Two Cities : Monsieur and Madame Defarge as minor characters

Minor characters in Dickens's novels mainly reflect his quality of humour, as Micawber in *David Copperfield* does. But Monsieur and Madame Defarge are not representations of any genial humour nor are they exactly minor characters of the novel as Jerry, Lorry are. They represent revolutionary humour eventually to a Dickensian conclusion.

The French Revolution has leaders, all figures of history, Rousseau, Robesphere and Voltair, but in this novel the leadership is taken by the Defarges, exactly the victims of the tyrannical rule, as particularly Madame Defarge. Defarge's wine shop is the rallying centre of revolutionary activities, Madame Defarge is the presiding deity there. Her knitting is a morbid type of calculation of vengeance brought to concrete evidence. Her family was awfully wronged by the Marquis of Evremonde, life and honour both were sacrificed to his will, a tyranny only waiting to be avenged by time.

Macbeth and Lady Macbeth too had their private life, but in *A Tale of Two Cities* Defarge and his wife seem to have none, except that Madame Defarge is seen often to guard the till in the wine shop and do some business. They have no issue, more inhumanly unmotherly than lady

Macbeth. They are man and wife only in the active roles in the Revolution. Defarge has his wine shop, a proletariat doing a publican business, he takes part in the Revolution to represent the working class. But we do not know any specific personal oppression to him, as we know about Madame Defarge. There he differs from his wife.

Defarge takes part in the Revolution, but he acts really no particular role of inhuman cruelty as his wife does. So far as their treatment of Dr. Manette is concerned they sharply differ. Defarge could have been a deeply psychological character in another hand, Dickens does not make him, but could if only wished. In his early life Defarge was Dr. Manette's servant, a faithful servant no doubt. Dr. Manette antagonized the Marquis by being a little more friendly to Madame Defarge's family and served long prison term for their sake. Madame Defarge practically discounted it in her treatment of Dr. Manette and his daughter. In her furies of vengeance she forgot Dr. Manette's past service. She was all too engrossed in cruelties, and definitely became inhuman and completely dead.

Defarge is on the other hand a model of gratitude. He could not forget Dr. Manette's loving care, it is he who was very careful about his master's recue in the taking of the Bastille. He was always prepared to do him good service, but he could not actually do it for fear of his wife's wrath. He was afraid to incur to the inflamed fury of his wife's vengeance and was really secretly afraid in her company, love was replaced by fear. He was always on his guard not to betray his love for the doctor and his daughter. Defarge suffered in his mind that he could not help Dr. Manette in the La Force proceedings against him and his daughter and son-in-law.

The excess of Revolution is another form of tyranny, perhaps worse than the tyranny of the ruling class. In this excess, Defarge has no main part to play, the main role was his wife's. She lost all moral scruples, lost love, even love for her husband. Dickens has no time to think of her motherhood, there is no word of motherhood in the novel as there is in Shakespeare's Macbeth. She is totally absorbed in the act of vengeance. She personally severed Faulon's head, it is she who planned secretly to meet Lucie and her little daughter for vengeance before Darnay could be guillotined.

Madame Defarge ultimately met with her death when she was after the life of so innocent a creature like Lucie and her daughter and of her benefactor Dr. Manette if possible. It was poetic justice which takes the place of Greek fate. Dickens cannot allow Madame Defarge to go unpunished and allow innocence and upright to be borne down to their tragic end.

CHAPTER XI

VICTORIAN NON-FICTIONAL PROSE

Ruskin: His Traffic and its Satiric Note

Ruskin is a true Victorian rightly to be classed with Carlyle. In his Lectures, Essays and other major writings he is not merely a theorist on painters and paintings, he takes into consideration along with art and architecture the whole moral and spiritual background of all such skill and innovations. His writings in the later half of the age, from 1857 down to the last, explore mainly the moral and spiritual values along with the aesthetic strand of human society. It is wrong to say that such works as *The Political Economy* (1857), *The Two Paths* (1859), *Unto This Last* (1862) and *Time and Tide* (1888) are essentially satiric in outlook.

Satire is not really Ruskin's method of presentation, neither in other major works nor fully in this particular Lecture 'Traffic'. Ruskin's is really justification of his ideas that conflict with the contemporary trend of British culture, at times in fairly uncompromising plain language, which seems to be a little harsh and a bit satiric. One must know the true purpose of this Lecture, it is not the model of the Exchange they would build in, buy to expose the folly of the whole nation going selfishly commercial. The Lecture is not really a 'corrective jester' which true satire is, it is all too serious to be only that, it is corrective in purpose, but the potion is provided not like a jester, it is provided as by a Prophet. Ruskin does not make his audience accept it with a smiling face as Shaw does, he recommends the remedy for his people to accept it devordly. Ruskin's conclusion is really very significant for that - 'sanctifying wealth into commonwealth'...

Ruskin starts his speech rather ironically, giving his audience notice that he must not speak on the subject, he would speak something else, he came down among the Yorkshire hills only to explain to his audience why he refused to oblige them and rejected their invitation first, and why he cannot advise them the beautification programme of the proposed Exchange. Why he cannot – the explanation is Ruskin like, only occasionally sarcastic. There Ruskin is not satiric like even Litton Strachey, neither in his ultimate object nor in his style of evocation. Strachey nibbles at private foibles as he does with Queen Victoria,

Nightingale and other Victorians, but Ruskin exposes here the national folly in its worship of the 'goddess of Getting-on' and 'Britannia of the Market'.

Ruskin is highly critical of the British commercialism which has become the religion of the whole nation and formed its literature and art and its whole culture. He does not think the Yorkshire traders can build their Exchange outside it. So it is perhaps meaningless to seek advice of an artheorist like Ruskin. Ruskin is quite satiric in his exposition how the trade people represent the whole land in their undeviated worship of one Goddess of Getting-on rather than the Greek goddess of beauty. The passages as one below are highly satiric in tone:

> 'I can only at present suggest decorating its frieze with pendant purses; and making its pillars broad at the base, for sticking of bills. And in the innermost chambers of it there might be a statue of Britannia of the Market...'

Such passages are satiric in tone and purpose because thereby the author seeks to shame them into silence and active amendment of their course from gross materialism to moral soundness.

The exact date of this Lecture is not known from the text, but *The Crown of the Wild Olive* in which 'Traffic' occurs was published in 1866. Ruskin refers to some of his earlier works as for example *The Seven Lamps* (1849) simply to suggest what his audience may expect as to his advice in this case of Exchange. As for his style of presentation Ruskin is ironical or sarcastic and at times satiric, the force of the language is derived from a conviction which is neither irony nor satire but highly moral and essentially Christian. There he differs from Strachey and Shaw and falls in line with his great contemporary Carlyle.

Ruskin's view of national religion a force behind architecture and culture

Ruskin is all through his writings and speeches either on paintings or social implications of life thoroughly spiritual even in his aesthetic outlook. He is a severe critic of his contemporary civilization, a civilization he finds all too material for essential humanity. In this Lecture 'Traffic' Ruskin tells his audience how behind all art there is an all-absorbing moral and spiritual preoccupation of not merely an individual artist but of the whole nation although it might be quite imperceptible to any surface view.

Ruskin does not take any parochial view of religion, he does not mean religion at all when he says a national religion is the secret force of the particular type of art of architecture, he means only a secret absorption or occupation, which defines with a different word 'taste' in this Lecture. He says a man is exactly what he likes. Likewise a race of nation is exactly what it worships, we should say, consciously or unconsciously.

Ruskin defines this point of national religion in the European context, and three such major religions in the past, and a fourth in his own time in England. Three in the past are the Greek worship of the god of Wisdom and Power, the Mediaeval Christian worship of the god of Judgement and Consolation and the Renascence worship of the god of Pride and Beauty. In his definition of these three European preoccupations and elaborations Ruskin is a close observer of the forces behind the trend of art and architecture there without any ironic undertone, but while defining the fourth that developed lately in his contemporary England he is full of satire and sarcasm.

Ruskin tells his Yorkshire audience that England is in the grip of a commercial culture quite against the spirit of Christianity they preach. Their faith is not in the Son of God but in the goddess of Getting-on, a God sarcastically called by him 'Britannia of the Market'. It is altogether hundred per cent prepossession of the whole nation. Nothing in the life of the nation can expect to get beyond it. So Ruskin feels he is unable to advice the art aspect of the proposed Exchange, the Exchange would ultimately take its shape as their God will dictate. The community of traders, he says, bothers less about its beauty than about the glorification of their God, no matter what he might adivse. To this God the whole nation devotes 'nine tenths of its property and six sevenths of its time'.

Ruskin is here in his true spirit of life-long crusade against gross materialism. All his works before 1866 or since then are meant for a war against the unhappy invasion of materialism which has already replaced the Christian gospel of love and faith. Ruskin does not want to advise the shape of a building the traders of Yorkshire would built but he would surely advise them the necessity for a change of outlook which would inevitably bring in a change in the shape and size of their architecture.

Ruskin's views of art as reflected in his Lecture on Traffic

Ruskin belongs to the Pre-Raphaelite movement, like the poets of this movement only influenced by the art of painting without being a painter; most of his writings are on art and painting. Whatever he writes he searches into its bearing upon art and morals, as for example his Lecture on 'War' and 'Work' collected in *The Crown of Wild Olive* volume in which Lecture on 'Traffic' appears.

Ruskin's sense of art is never an isolated issue, it is deeply involved in the question of human morals. Art is no doubt a symbol of beauty, an expression of it, not at all an activity absolutely apart from social political and economic interest of life, rather an activity enforced by the sum total of all those and unnamed many others. Ruskin tells his audience this simple truth and betrays his own feelings 'undisguisedly under the head 'Traffic'.

Ruskin does not tell the audience of the business community of Yorkshire the plain truth of the moral responsibility of the trader class, and nothing of the newest fashion of art for the design of the Exchange to build which they must spend a fabulous among of £ 30,000. Ruskin tells them that he does not care for their Exchange nor do they themselves care for it. In fact they care for 'getting on'.

The secret of Ruskin's inquiry into the basic principle of art is to be noted here. In 'Work' Lecture he does not speak of art at all, but speaks of the secret spring-head of all arts, a moral and spiritual truth. Under 'Traffic' head Ruskin speaks of it and of art also, art the total reflection of life a nation lives. He explores the three major strata of moral evolution in the world history, each laying an impact upon its artistic evolution, to which England, his contemporary England, added a fourth. England's was not the 'God of Wisdom', nor the 'God of Consolation', nor even 'the God of Pleasure' either, but simply the 'Goddess of Getting on', 'Britannia of the Market'. All art there must be shaped by this overall moral outlook, made he any recommendation of design or not.

Ruskin presents his undisguised analysis of the contemporary trend in art in England. 'All our great architectural works are of course built to her', he says. There is no escape. Rusking does not introduce any new idea of art, but none perhaps understands it better than he, not only in his age but also in other ages before him. He is by profession not a painter, he has no art lesson, but his deep sense of beauty reveals to him the secret of all that is beautiful. People say he belongs to the tradition of Keats and Spenser, but if so, his originality of outlook and deep moral sense must be an added impulse to the tradition itself.

The Nightingale-Sidney Herbert relationship episode and Lytton Strachey's biographical art thereof

Lytton Strachey is just the opposite pole of Boswell's art of biography, obviously taught by no personal experience of his subject and evolved directly from the earlier records to build a really imposing castle out of trivial bricks and mortar of life and contacts, not always to the praise of the person but to an enjoyment of petty faults of human nature.

The most interesting recorded contact in Florence Nightingale's life is with Sidney Herbert, which is Strachey's pages attains an unparalleled beauty of artistic reconstruction of a common human weakness. It is a common weakness of fascination extended to an uncommon effect. Miss Nightingale was then a young lady of thirty four only, and Sidney then the Minister of War. The contact was made mainly through correspondences during Nightingale's service in the military Hospital at Scutari. Nightingale was drafted there by the initiative of the War Minister when there was a complete mess in the Hospital administration.

Sidney deftly delineates the silent steps in their coming closer to each other in the discharge of duties, hers in the Hospitals and his in the War Office. In a later biography, *Queen Victoria* Starchey has even more satirically painted a similar relationship at a still higher level between the then Prime Minister, Disraeli, and the Queen; their meeting often painted by Strachey as a living comic scene enacted by the shrewd comedian Prime Minister in the skilled manoeuvre of his known art. But the relationship in *Eminent Victorians* between a War Minister and the so-called Lady of the Lamp is neither purely satiric nor pure fun. The relationship here deepened into a noble mission, a joint venture, which becomes a serious concern to both the parties, a subject of studies for the readers, and enjoyable as humour in the ultimate effect to all.

It is not an ordinary relationship between a young lady and a gallant aspirant, it is something altogether etherealised to an unnamed shared devotion, the male side more affected thereby, the lady presiding over the destiny of the man. The biographer tells us how she ruled his fate from a distance. The description itself becomes an excellent art, "It was through the man that the woman must work her will. She took hold of him, taught him, shaped him, absorbed him, dominated him through and through". Yet everyone knows none of them in the commonsense of the term fell in love with the other, at least not the woman.

The lady's power of bewitchment over the Minister of War was exercised in a way that recalls a similar bewitchment of Desdemona's heart by the narrative of the most wonderful exploits of war and miraculous escapes in the life of the Moor General. Strachey has duly noted how through official correspondence mainly it is done:

> "there was the composition of her long and confidential reports to Sidney Harbert. Her should pent up all day in the restraint and reserve of a vast responsibility, now at last poured itself out in these letters with all its natural vehemence, like a swollen torrent through an open sluice. Here at least, she did not mince matters. Here she painted in her darkest colours the hideous scenes which surrounded her; here she tore away remorselessly the last veils still shrouding the abominable truth...Then her pen in the virulence of its volubility, would rush on to discussion of individuals...Her nicknames were terrible. She respected no one: Lord Stratford, Lord Raglan, Lady Stratford, Dr. Andrew Smith, Dr. Hall, ...she fulminated against them all. The intolerable futility of mankind obsessed her like a nightmare, and she gnashed her teeth against it..."

Ultimately Miss Nightingale proved to be Sidney Herbert's Cleopatra, of course without her erotic passion, the only difference is Nightingale made Herbert her victim nobly without knowing it, unlike Cleopatra herself never being one. Sidney Herbert died with such words dying upon his lips in his last gasp as these:

> 'Poor Florance'... Our joint work...unfinished...tried to...'

What unfinished work one need not know, Sidney need not clearly point out, it need not be explained in Freudian terms, it was after all a venture, not to be ended in the conquest of the entire War Office for her, it was a conquest of Sidney's soul by the yet unsatisfied noble fairy, Strachey's account of the life leaves that impression. It is something more than satire, something that the thing itself can better represent.

Eminent Victorians: Strachey's art of Biography

Lytton Strachey was a Cambridge man and a regular contributor to *The Spectator*. As a biographer he ranks with the best of the class of writers like Gibbon and Boswell, but he is influenced by none of them. He plainly states his appreciation of the French biographers in his Preface to *Eminent Victorians* perhaps he was a little influenced by some French models before him, though of course he sufficiently marks his originality in the field by his three works, *Eminent Victorians* (1918), *Queen Victoria* (1921) and *Elizabeth and Essex* (1928).

Strachey outlines the particular difficulty a historian has to face in his account of the Victorian period 'Concerning the age which has just passed, our fathers and grandfathers have poured forth and accumulated so vast a quantity of information that the industry of a Ranke would be submerged by it, and the perspicacity of a Gibbon would quail before it'. To circumvent the difficulty one has now to 'fall upon the flank, of the rear'; 'he will shoot a sudden, revealing searchlight into obscure recesses, hitherto undivided.' He has also recommended a 'suitable strategy', embraced here also as his own.

Strachey's method is dispassionate inquiry, 'it is not his business to be complimentary, it is his business to lay bare the facts of the case' to quote a French master 'je n'impose rien; jen epropose rien j'expose.' *Eminent Victorians* has successfully translated this principle into practice. *Queen Victoria* is more or less satiric in approach, just the opposite approach to Dr. Johnson of Boswell, but *Eminent Victorians*, particularly the life of Florence Nightingale in it is not satiric in motive and outlook, it is an exposition in its unexpected corner.

Of the four lives in the book Florence Nightingale is perhaps the most entertaining as art. Lytton Strachey paints her, rather say finds her a woman 'possessed', which escapes the notice of the public and her other biographers. She was really just the opposite of 'the lady of the lamp' idea. The Nightingale parents thought, 'We are ducks who have hatched a wild swan.' Strachey says Mrs. Nightingale was wrong, 'it was not a swan that they had hatched, it was an eagle.' Strachey's account shows she was never in the role of an ordinary nurse discharging her duty in a military hospital so faithfully and lovingly as generally conceived. Strachey's inquiry bathes her in a different light. The account reveals her without any personal comment the female counterpart of Napoleon.

Strachey depicts her as Shaw does Napolean in *The Man of Destiny*. There one may conceive both of them guided by the same spirit, both Strachey and Shaw.

Strachey practically searches out the force that operated to make Miss Nightingale a living myth, which Shaw searches out in a different way in relation to Nepolean. The whole of the Victorian age was in a frenzy over a woman doing her difficult duty at a difficult hour of the British Army in the Crimean War. A woman in the Barrack Hospital among the wild soldiers and heroes of war, must have easily won Nightingale an extended aura of a unique role of a sisterly service to her brethren in the greatest need. Christian sisterhood, the very idea of complete dedication behind it, gave Miss Nightingale an extra glow in the essentially Christian outlook of the Victorian Age. Strachey has no satiric grin to the process of idealization, but he has definitely a sense of humour enabling him to appreciate and understand it. This very idealization gave the lady an uncommon authority in the whole of Europe and even outside, even when she was out of that hospital duty. She first became an authority in her accustomed field of activities, then in the whole area of war, then in everything else, the set process of shift and transformation is so artistically depicted by Strachey that it becomes really an enjoyable fine art that pleases even where it hits.

Strachey so astutely explores the relation between Sidney Herbert and Miss Nightingale that it attains the highest form of perfection of art, Disraelie's appearance before the Queen in *Queen Victoria* is of the same order of art only discernibly satiric, while the subtle touches in *Eminent Victorian* reach the mosts delicate form of art, highly enjoyable as humour can be. The relation is so effectively painted that the painting alone becomes a thing undefinably interesting, a thing of beauty that one can enjoy but one cannot express in words. The War Minister fell a victim to the charm of her personality and the charm secretly drew him to destruction.

Strachey's exploration shows that not all Miss Nightingale's reforms of the Hospital administration and building plan were ideal or perfect, yet like Queen Victoria she obstinately remained firm to her idea, the very tendency was extended to her analysis of the non-sanitarian subject of the Christian faith, of which she claimed the same position of authority and in the Victorian world easily passed for. Her relation to Mr. B. Jowett in later years when she was in England out of all responsible post confined to her home and bed shows how in another field she could exert her authoritarian influence upon a different personality. The whole Victorian age gave her the stepping stone to perch herself upon the topmost frame.

She is painted really a woman of destiny as Napoleon was the man of destiny by Shaw. The Victorian world made her as exceptionally powerful as destiny helped her so, although she remained as essentially ordinary as Napoleon too did. The invalid state of the living legend at her South Street apartment is another very effective means of exerting her power as Strachey depicts it. Under its sway even every newly appointed Viceroy of India easily came to play his part of discipular obedience. The last few days of her life of course became lucid, and in Strachey's delineation thoroughly of a different tone, the demon tamed, her acceptance of Knighthood unironically too resigned and noble.

The last Phase of Nightingale's Life and Strachey's art of presentation

Lytton Strachey's art of biography attains its supreme excellence in *Eminent Victorians*, and of all the four lives Florence Nightingale is the most concrete example of this excellence, and in it the last phase is still more curious in the art of presentation. It is not plain history, but history with a satiric twang. Earlier during the life time of Sidney Herbert Nightingale fought the world armed with the saddled or unsaddled Minister of War, but after his death she fought alone her pitched battle and won unaided. How?—that is satiric in Strachey's presentation and in the presentation highly enjoyable.

Herbert gone and she with no War Office to reform, practically with nothing to do Nightingale 'after much hesitation settled down in a small house in South Street'. There she remained for the rest of her life. Now she was at the peak of her glory. She became a living legend and burst upon the European scene. Here Strachey's satire is really poignant, glory made her extra-enthusiast and she sought other fields to conquer. He dropped her programme of reformation of the War Office and instead took up the programme of reformation of Christianity with her fixed idea of sanitation in a different field.

Nightingale wrote three Vols. of *Suggestions for Thought to the Searchers after Truth* (1860) and made an attack upon philosophical problems with essentially a practical mind and thought herself an authority on the subject, which predilection of the mind spared not even Mill who only narrowly escaped her virulence of temper by simply withholding his counter argument. Strachey's language is of quite satiric undertone — 'As one turns over these singular pages, one has the impression that Miss Nightingale has got the Almighty too into her clutches, and that, if he is not careful, she will kill him with overwork.'

Nightingale seems to have considered God just in the place of Herbert. This is essential Nightingale which the official historians may not correctly detect, she continued like that even when there was no war, no hospital reformation before her. But towards the close of her life she attained a different note, developed a new spirit of love and resignation. Strachey has painted it with manifest grace in which satire has no place. Both the author and his subject have reached a geniality of outlook to which such uncharitable attitude as satire or humour is quite irrelevant.

To reach that stage Miss Nightingale of course passed through an intermediate mixed stage as in her relationship with that priest scholar Mr. Jowett. Strachey says 'her feelings towards him were more mixed'. She asked him at one time to come to London and 'administer to her the Holy Sacrament' but at another 'some gall was mingled with the balm', 'Her tongue, one day, could not refrain from shooting out at him, "He came to me, and he talks to me...as if I were some one else".'

Forty-Five years she passed in her South Street apartment. Towards the close Ningtingale was altogether a changed character, there was never an occasional bout of gall in her temperament. She then reviewed her Scutari days. Strachey quoted her 'How inefficient I was in the Crimea...yet He has raised up from it trained nursing.' In such a changed mood she could accommodate an odd man like the Aga Khan, Strachey has quoted her as saying about him, 'A most interesting man', 'but you could ever teach him sanitation'.

There is yet a step further in her changed mood, Strachey has not missed it in his account: 'The thin angular woman, with her haughty eye and her acrid mouth, had vanished, and in her place was the rounded bulky form of a fat old lady, smiling all day long.' She was Offered the Order of Merit at her home, the brief ceremony of award over she recognised it with the benignity of a true Christian with the least involved irony in the words 'Too kind too kind'. The honour obviously did not make her feel proud but on the contrary feel blessed in the appreciation of the world. Strachey makes it eventually clear that his art is not purposely satiric as it was in the early 18th century writings of satirists, though sometimes in realistic exposition there might be something enjoyable like that. It is a close realistic study that leaves out nothing for any affected unreal respect for the subject.

Development of English Essays: From Elizabethan period to the Modern age

The Essay is a genre of literature that makes no less a progress than any other species in English literature. Bacon is the earliest exponent of English essays, in some of his essays European influence is quite evident, the word essay is no doubt borrowed from Montaigne, but his originality is established in his ultimate power of imbibing the Renascence spirit in a way others did not. His Essays are counsels civil and moral, the attempt other way round to realise the Renascence gospel 'Homo mensuro'. His essays of different stages, 'Of Studies', 'Of Travelle'. and 'Truth' are essentially utilitarian in outlook and aphoristic in style.

The next stage of development in the hands of the two 18th century essayists, Steele and Addison mark a curious turn in the attitude and style. Both of them, Addision most, went a bit fictional in their style and satiric in purpose tending to a happy result of humour; often their essays offer a foretaste of fiction. Addison's 'Dream', is corrective in purpose, but stylistically of the nature of a short story, and humourous in tone; so is even Steele's 'The Art of Story Telling' which could have been highly critical. Steele is rightly in the 18th century convention of the essay by acknowledging humour as a happy interpolation in the woof of truth as here: 'Those grave fellows are my aversion, who sift everything with the utmost nicety, find the malignity of a lie in a piece of humour pushed a little beyond exact truth.'

Goldsmith is already entrenched in the age of fiction, his *Vicar of Wakefield* appeared in 1766; his essays, most of them are narravative type, a good example is his *The story of the Man in Black*. The story is narrated by the Man is Black by way of gratifyng the curiosity of the author as it appears. It is a story which has all the advantages of an episode in a novel.

The next stage in evolution in the Romantic movement is Hazlitt in one way Lamb in another. Whether it is essay or anything else every production in the Romantic movement has acutely a subjective tendency of the writer's own personal reaction, moral, spiritual or any other kind. Hazlitt's 'Sun Dial' is ultimately an apparently objective survey of a time machine lost in the subjective timelessness of the author's soul. Hazlitt says in the conclusion, 'what I like best is to lie whole mornings on a sunny bank on Salisbury Plain, without any object before me, neither knowing nor caring how time passes, and thus "with light-winged toys of feathered Idleness" to melt down hours to moments'.

Lamb's subjectivity is even more curiously riddled in essays like *The Superannuated Man* and *Dream Children*, it is not the same type of soul's reaction as in their critical essays, neither stylistically as solid as in the case of Hazlitt. Lamb's personality melts down into the whole of the essay as if for a new birth there. Lamb has resurrected himself into a timeless existence for example in *The Superannuated Man*. This trend of the liberated soul is noted in all their essays, personal or reflective, in Lamb's most.

The subjectivity is almost gone in the Victorian essays, that humour of self-involvement, that kind of self-humour is almost entirely withheld from this essentially objective evaluation as in Stevenson's *El Dorado* for example. Stevenson has practically salvaged a chunk of Renascence life, but suggestively remoulded it into a different outlook, Renascence aspiration not as the spirit of a particular age but duly detected as part of the universal human nature. It is a dispassionate study of a passion, not for humour neither for correction, but for the pleasure of a discovery. There Stevenson differs from the 18th century treatment of the Dream.

In the 20th century the essay takes yet a new turn, it becomes a highly critical apparatus of inquiry, but not always in a direct approach to things, not in the usual directness of the earlier ages, particularly 18th century, not for correction of evils, not for eradication either, but evidently in a mood of revaluation of values, in the hands of Chesterton for example paradoxically to strike at the root of educated folly, learned ignorance and highly moral immoral evils. It is exactly what Chesterton attempts in *On Lying in Bed*. Chesterton and others like Lytton Strachey in this age change also the style of evocation, not earlier known to occur to that extent of excellence. They all belong to the same trend of a groping eagerness for a search in new fields of theme and style.

Stevenson El Dorado : theme and style

Stevenson belongs to the late Victorian period of English literature, in which thoughts and ideas are consolidated in one form in the fictional productions of the time and in another in different forms of critical writings, including essays. *El Dorado* although a very short essay sufficiently bears out Stevenson's style as an individual writer and the trend of the age.

One must know that Stevenson belongs to the age of Pater, Ruskin and Carlyle who are really the Victorian version of Dr. Johnson. *El Dorado* could have been a good *Rambler essay* with its thought and style, but the age in which Stevenson appears makes all the difference. It is not really a criticism of the social evil for correction, it is only a philosophic observation of human truth. His *Studies of Man and Books* (1882) clearly defines his stand and true bent of mind.

El Dorado is a close impartial study of man, it differs from Addison's one of the very characteristic essays, *The Dream*, differs mainly in style and ultimate intention. *El Dorado* can at best be considered as a symbol of human aspiration, and not at all an allegory, neither the symbolism is worked out over much, the term is only casually introduced although very suggestively - 'Our hopes are set on in accessible *El* Doraro'...'descry the spires of *El Dorado*'. In intention too not corrective. What correction does it require? It is in human nature all-pervasive.

Stevenson is deep in the late Victorian strain when Romantic fancy and personal involvement are less strong a force with an evident revival of the pre-Romantic 18th century rationalism yet with a difference. *El Dorado* is a pure dispassionate study, yet not socially altruistic as in the 18th century Johnsonian style and convention. Even Stevenson's *The Beggar* is not personal in the same effect as Hazlitt's *Sun Dial* is, The concluding paragraph in Hazlitt's essay is highly Romantically personal, Stevenson's *Beggar* is how the author's personal experience yields place to the close study of the Homo Sapiens. *El Dorado* is still more interesting a study, and closer to the trend to which Stevenson belongs.

Stevenson has less humour and more penetration, that is perhaps at the root of his moderate success in fiction. *The Beggar* has some humour that recalls Addison and the 18th century convention, but *El Dorado* lacks even that pleasant flexibility, because it completely breathes the air of Carlyle-Pater-Ruskin tradition in style.

CHAPTER XII

VICTORIAN POETS

Browning as love poet

Browning was more influenced by the Renaissance values of Shakespeare's time than any of his contemporaries was. He was greatly influenced by Shelley but in his conception of love he follows neither the Renaissance view nor the philosophy of Shelley as derived from Plato, Browning is thoroughly individualistic, he is a perfect representation of Victorian individualism, and more in respect of his concept of love.

Browning takes a philosophic view of love and it is a part of his philosophy of life, although no earlier philosophy either remotely derived from Plato, or from anybody else of recent times, can fully explain Browning's treatment of love. Only to some extent he is closer to the Renaissance view of it and in some measure he repeats some of John Donne's conceits.

We have already noted, Browning's philosophy of love is an essential part of his philosophy of life. Browning of course does not always feel that his life has fully set out the principles of philosophic love although he was a great lover and sincerely courted Elizabeth Barret Browning. *One Word More* gives us how deeply Browning valued love even in his own life. He would obviously reserve the unsullied unspoiled side of him for his lady. That is purely *One Word More*. This poem is very close to the Petrarchan tradition, although different in form.

This poem was addressed to Elizabeth Barret Browning in 1855, there is yet another poem *Prospice* where Browning is very close to his life. His outlook on love and life is always essentially objective, so even a personal poem like *Prospice* has essentially struck the philosophic view of love - If love is not fulfilled in the present life, it would be in the next. Browning has duly connected love with his overall philosophy of life as in the last two lines of the poem. 'O thou soul of soul! I shall clasp there again,/And with God be the rest!'

Browning is thoroughly Christian in outlook even in respect of his personal passion; love is always a stepping stone towards a higher attainment like the attainment of God. Here of course Browning differs from Donne. Browning is sincere about a spiritual link between this life and a possible life hereafter, and of course about the role of love in this inseverable link. Only occasionally Browning displays some of Donne's conceits of passion in some of his love poems as one here *The Last Mistress*. A passage like Tomorrow We meet the same then, dearest?/May I take your hand in mine?" recalls similar conceits in Donne's love poems.

In some of his earlier poems Browning was a little more conceitous than in the later. Mill points out *Paulina* (1833) as a poem of love where Browning's fancies are more of the order of Elizabethan period than exactly of a philosophic depth as Browning would show later.

Browning in his treatment of love and lovers is highly individualistic, and it is demonstrated in some of his great love poems like *Porphyria's Lover*, *My Last Duchess* and of course *The Last Ride Together*. In all these poems Browning is thoroughly objective in his approach to the subject of love. He is as objective here as in a highly philosophic poem like *Rabbi Ben Ezra*.

In some of his poems Browning even gets his lovers to murder their ladies even at the highest point of attainment. Critics differ in their interpretation of such accentricities. In *Porphyria's Lover*, the lover murders his lady like a mad, mad in love, as if to eternise the highly unattainable attainments in his life. In the same vein the murder in *My Last Duchess* was not perpetrated. There the murder was highly tricky, the last Duchess was murdered and the next was negotiated on terms of material gain and domestic authority. In such poems Browning achieves an extraordinary feat so far as treatment of love is concerned.

The Last Ride Together is of course a love poem of a different order. Here love and philosophy of life are so uniquely subtilized as it has rarely been done in any poem earlier. Here the last ride together is again another way of making the moment the eternity of experience even though none of the lovers is willing to consummate the courtship in a sort of marriage. The ultimate achievement lies only in making the moment an eternal experience: 'I and thee/Ride, ride together for ever ride?'

Browning delays with love as no poet in English literature has exactly done it. Love is a mysterious experience as the experience of God. Browning has taken both these experiences in a very serious vein and given them as varied shapes as he could yet not exhausting their prospects. Browning tries only to adjust love to his highly individualistic philosophy of life and he succeeds not rarely.

Browning: Words and images in his poems

A contrast between Browning and Tennyson would at once reveal the uniqueness of their artistic excellence. Tennyson is more finished as an artist than Browning. Browning's main concern was, as Eliot has stated in a different context, with his language, 'a poet's primary responsibility is exactly to his language.' Browning makes a curious use of his language to make the most of his subject matter which is also unique in itself. Browning's is always 'an incessant wrestle with words and phrases'.

Browning tries to form new combination out of the already known word stock, 'as in my serpentine beauty rounds on' in *Andreaing Del Sarto*. He realigns the grammatical and metrical syntax for specific effects. In versification he tries to break away from the established conventions in his clear effort to come closer to ordinary conversation. In doing so he very often strains the existing pattern of language, sometimes in open defiance of grammar. Browning uses words in highly original senses as does no one in his age. For example 'heaven' in Browning's poetry refers most often to 'paradise', not rarely after life, but again it suggests 'fulfilment' or 'ecstasy'.

In his own age Browning was special interest for men no less than John Ruskin and Swinburne. Ruskin in particular refers to 'Bishop orders his Tomb' as a clear evidence of his artistic uniqueness. He tells us 'I know no other piece of modern English, prose or poetry, in which there is so much told, as in these lines, of the Renaissance spirit.'

Almost in the same language Swinburne outlines the uniqueness of Browning's idiom. He refuted the obscurity charges against Browning by means of a special order of the Poet's implication which is not unoften misunderstood by ordinary readers. He is an incomparable genius who 'never thinks but at full speed'. His philosophy and his special frame of reference have given a new bone of strength to his language.

In the 20th century Browning is reassessed for adequate understanding of his theme and style. The modern symbolists and surrealists must know how language can be informal use of a poet; so it is they who made a rediscovery of Browning's artistic excellence underlining all his apparent 'raggedness' and 'woodenness'.

Browning is the Prophet of 'Victorian individualism', and his individualistic outlook is more pronounced in his choice of subjects and his method of treatment. Browning's philosophy of life is not the conventional philosophy of Christianity, his outlook on love is part of his special order of moral conception. In his whole attempt Browning extends the area of implication of his world by reference to the Mediaeval period, the Renaissance and the whole of the European movement of art; but his special order of communication follows only his own instinct and the set line of his own genius.

His use of dramatic monologue is not simply the repetition of the Shakespearean use of soliloquy, it is an evolution of a sort of interlocution which bears the stamp of his genius. The combination of villain and aesthete creates a specially strong tension in some of Browning's best dramatic monologues, particularly *My Last Duchess*. Words in such poems, as also in *One Word More* are not of the ordinary implication as in some cases Shakespeare's are not in his curious overtones.

Not only in the choice of images and words Browning is unique among his contemporaries, even his line of thought and enquiry marks a clear departure from the accepted convention. In *Porphyria's Lover*, for example, love is very close to madness, yet essentially Browingesque, and has therefore offered a taste not only of language but also of love itself.

Browning is therefore more modern in his individuality than any of his contemporaries. Words like 'bosom beats' of Rafael, 'heaven's gift', 'Earth's abatement' used by Browning in *One word More* are definitely calculated to convey a special sense not exactly attempted hitherto by any of his contemporaries and not any of the great poets before him. In *A Grammarian's Funeral* Browning's use of 'light' and 'darkness' are not designed to convey their dictionary meanings. He gives an extra dimension to their implication.

Perhaps the right calculation of Browning as a stylist is attempted in the context of modern stylistic innovations in poetry. Browning is better placed beside the modern poets who try to invent their own pattern of expression for the adequate justice to their own special ideas and thoughts.

The Second person in Browning's dramatic monologue

It is Browning who popularised the literary form called Dramatic Monologue. Consciously or unconsciously this form was adopted earlier and even later by different poets more or less under his influence. The main contribution to this form was of course made by Browning.

Robert Langbaun has made a thorough study of dramatic monologue all through and has pointed out specifically Browning's place in it in 1957. The question of the role of the second person in Browning's dramatic monologue is a vital issue which Langbaun has taken up.

Browning's dramatic monologue is essentially very distinct with a shift from the personality of the poet to the personality of another narrator or speaker. This speaker objectively viewed is however the second person, often very close to the personality of the poet yet not the poet himself.

Browning makes this second person highly dramatic, and the drama lends itself to the dramatic pattern of the narrative which often includes yet another person. Some of Browning's critics regard him as the interlocutor. So Browning's personality as a man is two removes from the objective narrative of his poems.

There are of course varieties of use of dramatic monologue in Browning's remarkable poems of this order. There Browning is far different from his great contemporary Tennyson, although the latter has also adopted this form in some of his poems, at least in poems like *Maud* and *The Lady of Shallot*. Browning has his special quality as a poet of the dramatic monologue, he is less lyrical than his contemporary and more dramatic in execution.

Among the modern poets Eliot has made use of it in at least some of his great poems, for example *Prufrock*, *Gerontion* and *Marina*. Eliot of course, attains modern complexity by means of his very effective use of dramatic monologue. Yet Browning remains the stalwart in the field. In some of the poems the rule of the interlocutor is almost faded, for example, *Porphyria's Lover*. The other great poem *Rabbi Ben Ezra* has the same blurring of the role of the interlocutor. It is a poem really to be termed dramatic monologue by virtue of its title only; otherwise it is a direct statement of philosophy.

In most of the best poems of dramatic monologue the role of the interlocutor, is more or less that of a passive listener, always giving rise to the curious exposition of the mind of the actual narrator. His poems of Italian artists, *Andrea Del Sarto* and *Fra Lippo Lippi* are dramatic monologues in the very special reactions in which the artists are caught as Browning's model.

The best poems of this class are of course *My Last Duchess, The Last Ride Together*, and *Bishop St. Praxed.* In *My last Duchess* the interlocutor is clearly defined whom we may term as the second person, the recipient of the Duke's confidences. Here the monologue is so very complex that it reveals not only the person at the centre but also his artistic sense and depraved psychology at the same stroke. The Bishop in the *St. Praxed* poem is so much representative a narrator, one remove from the poet himself, that Ruskin has found no parallel to him, neither in the whole of the Victorian period nor outside. The complexity of the personality is almost bewildering.

The Last Ride Together is again a Dramatic monologue in which the poet himself is shaded away, and the whole stage is left to the disappointed lover to enact the drama of his disappointment which is very close to reconciliation in a philosophic outlook. In the execution of such a complex method the role of the interlocutor is practically dwindled into nothing.

Now Browning as a poet of dramatic monologue makes a wonderful use of the second person either as an objective type of narrator subjectively involved in his own curiosities or as an interlocutor who appears at times in the role of a passive listener. Browning's dramatic monologue is wonderfully explained by Mac Callum in his 1925 Warton lecture as instinct with certain amount of 'a dramatic understanding of the person speaking which implies a certain dramatic sympathy with him'. Browning is essentially a poet with such a dramatic sympathy as made him a great poet.

Browning's philosophy: the theme of failure or success

Browning is most remarkable in Victorian literature for his philosophy of life. The two other great poets of this period, Arnold and Tennyson, took their own line completely diverging away from

Browning's individualistic outlook. He is the true representation of Victorian individualism. And it is right to say that Browning's philosophy of life and his conception of love sprang from this curious individualistic outlook.

In this stage of Browning's achievement his philosophy of life passes through a sort of uncertainty. In his three early poems *Pauline, Paracelsus* and *Sordello* – Browning explores avenues of individual fulfilment of life. In *Pauline* self sinks into selfishness cleaving only to desperate hope of salvation through a woman's love. In *Paracelsus* Browning seeks the means to rear up individuality into a spiritual achievement. In *Sordello* the quest is followed further – selfhood is attained through service, man gains his own soul by sacrifice.

Browning is still not clear how he should deal with the question of self to attain the supreme success. His philosophy takes a queer turn in which most failure is considered as most success. Perhaps no other poet in English literature evolved so complete a philosophy of failure as Browning does. In the light of his philosophy Browning estimates the whole picture of love, even his own love for Elizabeth Barret Browning. Love is an indispensable factor in the philosophy of Browning. Whether it is love or faith Browning's philosophy is a philosophy of failure or unsuccess.

In *The Last Ride Together* the disappointed lover is a picture of failure, but the failure is not a matter of great sorrow. It is simple a stepping stone towards a great success, and the lover is for that. The proposal for a last ride together with his unwilling lady is what Browning wants to make it, a great test for the self.

The philosophy of unsuccess in our present existence on earth is a part of Browning's total view, of which the present life is only an incomplete half. Under this impression Browning's only elegy *Prospice* has developed an idea of bright future on the other side of the grave. "No! Let me taste the whole of it." "I shall clasp thee again,/And with God be the rest".

Love although individualistic in all Browning's poems where it is treated is not an end in itself, it is again a road to a higher spiritual perfection, to attain which not only love is necessary but faith is indispensable. In Browning's philosophy of life faith is not simply in the existence of God, it is also in the whole mechanism of the universe, in which success and failure, light and darkness, are inevitably included.

In all those clearly marked philosophic poems, as one *Rabbi Ben Ezra*, Browning develops his idea of faith, his philosophy of a total picture of moral order in which old age is better than youth, and death itself is no less covetable than old age. Browning holds this view because his conception of life is an unending journey towards a higher perfection. Even that journey takes death only as a passing phase. This is what is called robust optimism of Browning. *Rabbi Ben* is a philosophy of optimism, a philosophy of such an unshaken faith.

The Jewish Rabbi does not grumble with all those throes of life, nor even old age and death. For him life is a 'potter's wheel', time spins it "Time's wheel runs back or stops: Potter and clay endure."

Poems like *Rabbi Ben* and *Garammarian's Funeral* reveal the highest achievement of Browning's philosophy. Browning considers life only as an incomplete half. The other half is to be rounded off in the existence beyond. How we shall fare in this life, that is not the ultimate test of our success or failure in knowledge, love or spiritual attainment. Browning's philosophy is 'try and test' and thereby scale upon the road to perfection. So life, in whatever shape it is, not at all an object of either sorrow or easeful complacence.

CHAPTER XIII

MODERN POETRY

Hopkins the poet priest

Hopkins historically belongs to the late Victorian period, a handful of poems placed in anthologies by his friend Robert Bridges were brought out not earlier than 1893; but a full collection of his poems was out only in the year 1918.

Hopkins was first appreciated by Robert Bridges; he saw in him all symptoms of a successful modern poet, although he died in 1889. Hopkins was a painter originally and a musician and later became a Jesuit priest. He was converted to Roman Catholic faith in 1868 when he was only a young man of 24, sensuous to a great extent and responsive to outside influence even then.

The fact of early conversion marked a turning point in Hopkin's career as a poet. He is indeed a poet turned priest, but a priest of an exceptional kind. No doubt he abjured the earlier enthusiasm, the enthusiasm of almost Keatsian sensuousness, as a result of his conversion. He joined the society of Jesus and adopted the rule of its founder St. Ignatius. This of course coloured his verse although something of youthful sensuousness still lingered.

Hopkins as a young man imbibed the spirit of Matthew Arnold and Walter Pater at Oxford. He came also to appreciate Ruskin. All these have already coloured his vision. A painter, musician and a great admirer of the people who appreciated best the beauty of form and the beauty of art, Hopkins already built up a beauty cult for his pursuit. But his conversion to Roman Catholic faith turned the tide.

Hopkins came later under the influence of the Mediavel philosopher Duns Scotus, particularly in 'the metaphysical significance of the individuality of the created things'. Every particular manifestation of the creation came to represent to his view a piece of beauty as also a metaphysical essence of creation. This led him to an idea of 'inscape', a word which was defined by him as the essential individuality of every created thing formed from within as a result of propulsion of something of the Creator from within.

Hopkins's priestly outlook is at the same time highly poetic. His religious feeling as a result of his conversion is not exactly that of any conventional religious poet, say Crashaw and Herbert. The poem that establishes him as a priest under the mask of a poet is the *Wreck of the Deuschland* commemorating the shipwreck of five German nuns on Dec. 7, 1875. In this long poem Hopkins does not paint this great tragedy absolutely tragically. So it has not become a conventional elegy. It is manifested in extracts like this "Thou hardest me truer than tongue confess/Thy terror, O Christ, O God."

Hopkins's concept of beauty underwent a great change, and the change was no doubt the result of his change of outlook. He viewed every specimen of beauty as essentially with an element of God in it, which made everything more beautiful than without it. This is a thing which we do not trace in Keatsian sensuousness. Felix Randal is a common farrier whose death is at once mourned by the poet but the mourning note is at the same time coloured by the appreciation of God's mercy: "Ah well, God rest him all road ever he offended."

The Keatsian sensuousness as regards the enjoyment of beauty made a priestly invocation of God in every manifestation of beauty in the outside world in Hopkins's poems. We find it no better in any other poem of our time than *Pied Beauty*, "Glory be to God for dappled things."

Often Hopkins is compared with Donne. All Donne's devotional sonnets are of a special kind to which any of Hopkins religious sonnets are rightly comparable. *The Windover* is a poem dealing with Christ, but it is not plainly all about the Saviour of mankind. Here Hopkins does his priest's duty in such a way that he makes his position as a poet-priest sufficiently clear. All his imageries duly coloured with the spirit of modern symbolism, in which he essentially represented as a poet, his ecstatic exclamations are all devotions, perfectly in tune with his poetic fervour. "My heart in hiding stirred for a bird, — the achieve of the mastery of the thing."

Hopkins manifested his individuality all through even in his priestly outlook in all appreciation of beauty and in his sympathy for everything in distress. Ultimately it remains a great inseparable link between his poetic self and his priestly sympathy. His justification of the Lord in discrete thing is to be noted in sonnet "Thou art indeed,/'just Lord' if I contend with thee." Hopkins is a religious poet no doubt, but his religious outlook is not at all comparable to that of the earlier 17th century Christian poets like Marvell, Carew, Crashaw and Herbert.

Hopkins: His poetic journey

Hopkins actually belongs to the late 19th century of English literature, born 1844, died 1889. But his poems are not published until 1918. So in him is clearly to be noted the late Victorian evolution in the field of poetry and a reflection of the early 20th. Hopkins is to be estimated just in the curious blend of these two tendencies. It was Robert Bridges who took note of the genius of Hopkins and just in time aroused interest in his work.

Hopkins is regarded more as a part of the 20th century, just the beginning of it, than his contemporary trend of English poetry. The uniqueness of his position ultimately remains in his individuality that transcends all such classifications as Victorian or modern.

Hopkins was in the earlier stage of his life, a painter and musician. Then he became a scholar and Jesuit priest. At Oxford he was under the influence of Arnold and Pater and his conversion to Roman Catholicism in 1868 gave him a total change of outlook and attitude. He sought an identification in every respect with the ideals of Jesus thereafter.

Now Hopkins started to make a synthesis of his concept of art and the ideals of his faith. There he came under the sweep of Ruskin, his affinity with the author of *Modern Painters* is to be seen in his idea of an 'indwelling presence' of God in everything, in every particular object of the phenomenal world. All his poems are in a way written in an attempt to objectify this subjective feeling of the poet.

In his earlier stage of writing Hopkins was more interested in the Mediaeval philosopher Duns Scotus in his obvious emphasis upon 'the metaphysical significance' of the individuality of the created things. To some extent Hopkins imbided in his blood the sensuous beauty of Keats's concept. This element never left Hopkins, even not in the later stage when he was already a devoted Christian with a God-sense in everything he viewed.

Hopkins is a great innovator, but his evolution as a poet from the earlier stage to the later is really a curious evolution in which his excellence is to be realistically judged.

The earlier stage of Hopkins is clearly to be seen in poems like '*Two Boyhoods*' in which the poet is more or less in the tradition of Keatsian sensuousness, the supremacy of passion in two defined forms is readily recognised—'Fair love' and 'love of Nature'.

Hopkins took note of both Wordsworth and Keats in his earlier studies of life and nature; but in his already changing mood he took into serious consideration a spirit of God in all such phenomenal manifestations, either in human mind or in outside nature. The change is to be noted in poems like *Pied Beauty*. In this poem the poet felt - "Glory be to God for dappled things."

In his passage from one stage to another Hopkins could not escape inevitable struggle in his mind. The stage is represented by poems like *Carrion Comfort*. It is the struggle of a new convert, reorganising his ideas about something of a new discovery. The struggle is rather terrible, his mortifications and frustrations are realigned with a new stake. "Nay in all that toil, that coil since I kissed the rod,..."

Now Hopkins is on his way to his Jesuit destination, the ideal of Jesus; but his passage is through the ordinary world of beauty, beauty in every created being and all created things. *Felix Randal* is a good record of this reaction in Hopkins. The poet is endowed with a godly feeling that could have been in the Son of God. "Thy tears that touched my heart, child, Felix, poor Felix Randal".

Hopkins is entirely of the 20th century, although not historically, with his stylistic innovation like 'sprung rhythm' and his conception of 'Inscape'. Almost in every important poem Hopkins has shown the excellence of his ideas and stylistic devices of this order. But even more interesting is his evolution at the later stage of his life when he leaves behind his secular outlook for a deeply religious sentiment. We have noted it in some of his semi-devotional sonnets like - Thou art indeed just - the sonnet that recalls some of the best devotional poems of Donne; it is more clearly noted in Hopkins's masterpiece *The Deuchland*. It is a poem that celebrates and 'vindicates the way of God to Man'. It was written to commemorate the disaster in which five German nuns were drowned off the English coast. The story rather awakened the poet to a new idea of reconciliation with the Decrees of God.

Hopkins is rather a controversial poet who belongs actually to the late Victorian period, yet who foreshadows some of the best qualities of the modern period. In his early poetry he followed Keats and the pre-Raphaelites. In his later stage of writing he tended towards Dryden and Donne, particularly Donne of his Holy Sonnets. He is a little Miltonic in his reconciled state of faith in this period.

Yeats: Adam's Curse: a critical analysis

Yeats is one of the modern leading innovators of his time, but in 'Adam's Curse' he employs no such innovations. He sails free of any modern device of style. He maintains utmost simplicity of language and allows no complex imagery to burden his mind and obstruct his feelings. The poet's theme is directly introduced, the theme of poetry and love, both blended together, wearing a withered look in our civilization.

Poetry is just the poet's care, love the care of the woman who is called upon to trim her beauty up for love; but the poet knows a different story. The poem opens like a modern short story, exactly as Conrad's *Heart of Darkness* started. 'You and I and mild woman' — these three appear together, very familiar in their talk and very close in their acquaintance. The poet talks about his familiar subject, how a true poetic line can be composed; he knows it is no easy matter, only care calculation and industry cannot ensure it; a spark of genius is necessary to produce a true poetic line. Creation is the stroke of a moment although the preparation may take ages, so is poetic creation, the work of hours but the creation when it is really so is fortuitous, giving the idea of a lucky effect of a moment.

If poetry can strike no such impression of a moment's lucky gift it is the work of drudge, and the poet should better work as one without much bothering about versification, it is not his true sphere. The sweet sound of verse, and the sound that strikes the sense it is a job far more stupendous than anything great achieved on earth.

The woman speaks of the old tradition of love and beauty, to which the modern stage of evolution is a sharp contrast. Today one need not undertake much pruning for beauty, the old curse is no longer applicable to women. The poet was ready to make love to this lady with the old sincerity and in the earlier majesty of style, but it does not suit his time. The Mediaeval and Elizabethan pompous style of love is no longer valid in the modern period. Love in the Elizabethan period turned the lover to the studied method of effusion as in their sonnets. Sidney, Spenser and Shakespeare—all of them took the bookish way of making love to their ladies. Yeats is not literary in his courtship to his lady.

Modern life has its own quality and character; in most of his leading poems Yeats has studied it to his utter disillusionment; he has, however studied it right. In 'Adam's Curse' he has done it no less effectively. Now lovers are tired, in spite of the sincerity of love they are tired like the wan moon. Time's repeated wash has left the moon a sea-washed shell upon its beach, with a subdued beauty to excite a love that is daily like all other common thing of everyday experience.

Like all other truths of life love is also a dun grey thing in modern complexity of life. It has its validity only as a basic truth but not as a new surprise exclusive in character and explosive in force. The pattern of expression is devoid of any extra padding or any kind of concealment, it has the force of direct communication, no symbolism or surrealism, any indirect evocation has not stood in the way of Yeats's direct hit.

Byzantium: Representation of Yeats's last stage of maturity

The Romantic predilection of Yeats's mind is readily a propelling force in all his crisis of feeling, some owing to the condition of the whole of Europe, especially Ireland, and some of his private and personal sense of devitalized drooping state of old age. The phase is started by 'Sailing to Byzantium' and ended in a disenchantment of the city itself when reached.

'Byzantium' belongs to *The Winding Stair* volume of 1933. The poem is comparable to Eliot's *The Waste Land* in complexity of thought and style and also in subtlety of symbolism. The five stanzas of the poem are varied in images and sweeping in shiftiness, the unity of effect is in one way maintained by a 'Kubla Khan'—like rareficaction into apparent insignificance in terms of ordinary language, in another by a 'Waste Landish' phantom quality, infusing into the mind the idea of an unreal city.

The poem is an evidence of Yeats's excellence of art and symbolic interpretation of modern life. It is not the plain analysis of '*The Second Coming*', the mastery of the intricate structure is only an evidence of genius. It is true the poem betrays the poet's disillusionment, the city when reached is found not exactly what he was sailing to. The first stanza of the poem depicts the city in ironic touches, neither the day scene nor the night scene is encouraging:

A starlit or a moonlit dome disdains
All that man is, ...

It seems to him:

All mere complexities
The fury and the mire of human veins.

Hell is introduced in the second stanza, because man now appears to him not merely false complexities, but simply a shadow of the underworld 'Shade more than man'; then the poet feels it is yet not the correct definition, better call 'more image than shade'. It may even represent the reverse process of evolution 'Hades bobbin bound in mummy-cloth/May unwind the winding path'. The image with a mouth but with no moisture no breath, a gruesome image, invokes 'the superhuman', just the grotesque Second Coming of half-man half beast type of an earlier poem. '*The Second Coming*', even more horribly undefined – 'death in life, life in death'. Yeats's symbols here suggest a grimmer picture than Eliot's '*Preludes*'.

In the 3rd stanza the miracle of art, which was an object of adoration in the earlier *Byzantium* poem, represents only a premonition of grave consequence. The Byzantine art, 'bird or golden handiwork...although planted on the star-lit golden bough', signs only of owlish omen, 'can like the cocks of Hades crow, ...in glory of changeless mental...all complexities of mire or blood.' All the romance of the poet of the earlier 'sailing' to the city of art is gone. It yields place to an ominous destiny. Man is now a useless complexity, there is doubt whether of blood or simple mire.

In the 4th stanza the creative mind takes altogether a different turn. There is no question of art or its detraction, the question does not arise at all, the mood of the poet changes to a depiction of devil's dance of death's fire, a fire fed by no faggot. It is 'flames begotten of flame' only, 'blood begotten spirits come' and 'all complexities of fury leave'. It is no ordinary fire, it does not burn anything, it 'cannot singe a sleeve'. It causes only the 'agony of flame'. The poet thus symbolically suggests the holy city's agony of physically unburning flame that does not spare even the palace.

The dolphin symbol of the last stanza suggests its placement and displacement, the spirits take its place, the gold smithies of the Emperor make all the difference, the dolphin is dead, yet it has 'mire and blood', the blood is water the smithies release. The dolphin is not in the sea, the sea is gong-tormented everything is out of place, yet smithies of gold in the old city put each in its place, artificially arranged - just the idea of is and is not, is not yet is. The world is viewed like an unsure surety, an inconceivable thing like that.

Yeats's *Byzantium* is a rare symbolistic poem in which the set colour of the mind is withheld giving way to an open jigsaw puzzle. The idea is not what it is, but of what it is not. There the poet's mind transcends all limitations.

Sailing to Byzantium—a representation of the movements of the poet's mind: the stages in evolution

Yeats belongs to the late Romantic and the pre-Raphaelite tradition of English poetry, only readjusted to the truth of Irish acquisition of his life. He is a symbolist as most of the leading poets of his time are, but his symbolism is steeped in Irish obscurantism. A new simplistic strand out of his Irishism can clearly be noted in his major poems.

Maud Gonne's appearance in his life and a sort of betrayal about 1903 at her marriage and later her reserved widowhood in 1916 left Yeats at his already advanced age (52 years then) scurrying about for a steady foothold. This must have secretly moulded his outlook which is reflected in his poems of this period and of even later stage of composition.

Yeats's '*Sailing to Byzantium*' belongs to *The Tower volume* of verse, published in 1928. The poem opens the volume and is followed by a sequence of three poems collectively called 'The Tower'. '*Sailing to Byzantium*' reflects the mood of the poet, which is the result of the European situation, the Irish problem as also his private problems. Yeats detects now his old age disenchantment which he wants to overcome not exactly like Keats with a timely conceived world of beauty, but by sailing to a city of Romantic values, a city of youth and exuberance.

'That is no country for old men'.

The poet at the old age of 63 revives all the values of youth and eternal summer, he knows 'An aged man is but a paltry things'. With a magnificent symbol Yeats represents old age - 'a tattered coat upon a stick'. The only difference made is by means of only the existence of soul, clapping its hands and singing song of life. The singing now yields place to studying, which makes the 'monuments of magnificence' of his old age. The poet sails off 'to the holy city of Byzantium' 'to escape calculating dreariness of old age. The poem is not really Coleridgian 'Youth and Age'. It is the reflected glory of youth and all those Romantic values, the lack of which makes the present age dead, just the symbol of 'tattered coat upon a stick'.

The 3rd stanza of the poem bears evidence of Yeats's pre-Raphaelitism which marks his difference from Keats. Keats wants an illusion as in '*Lamia*', but ageing Yeats wants permanence of art, not exactly beauty of it as in Keats's '*Ode on a Grecian Urn*', but a world far apart from the real world of youth and age. Yeats invokes the 'sages standing in God's holy fire' to 'be the singing masters of my soul'. 'He wants them to 'gather me into the artifice of eternity'. It is not Keats's 'beauty is truth truth beauty', it is the eternity of art that knows no age.

Yeats's conclusion in the poem is not a Keatsian conclusion although Yeats is like Keats in a mood to escape this world of sorrow and sufferings into a world far beyond it, for Keats of beauty and for Yeats of art. Once released from this human body Yeats would never like to assume a 'bodily form from any natural thing. But would really assume 'such a form as Grecian goldsmiths make of hammered gold and gold enamelling/To keep a drowsy emperor awake'. Perched 'upon a golden bough' he would sing to lords and ladies of *Byzantium* of what is past, or present, or to come'.

'*Sailing to Byzantium* 'ultimately proves to be the poet's long entertained concept of art by which he seeks to cure the malady of the 20th century life, the malady that prompted him to write '*The Second Coming*' in 1919, and cure also the desolating worries of his personal life almost like Keat's if he could live longer. Keat's only temporary illusion of the world of the Nightingale gets permanence in the world of art, to Yeats Byzantium only offers a perfect symbol of it.

The second Byzantium poem of even a later volume (1933) is only the next stage evolution of this mood, a little more intricate in technique and a bit more difficult in its psychological bearing. '*Sailing to Byzantium*' is only a journey, '*Byzantium*' the journey's end.

Symbolism in The Waste Land

The 20th century is an age of unknown complexity in life and evolution which claims a similar complex method of communication in art. Symbolism is a stylistic innovation of the modern period, a clear departure from the conventional meaning of word. Word has its original meaning of sound or objective symbol. Eliot has made the most of this method and truth in *The Waste Land*. It is perhaps the more adequate expression of modern life than the ordinary style of rendering could make it.

The Waste Land is in itself a symbol of barrenness in modern life, against which Eliot's 'fertility rituals' are deeply ironical, particularly when the ritual is not straightforward; the ritual too is suggestive, and symbolic. That is perhaps the reasons why the poem requires a different style of comprehension.

The poem is full of symbols, the general trend of which is an evocation of sense by means of an object emblem or sound emblem. Dead 'Lilacs born out of the dead land', 'branches grow out of the dead rubbish', 'dry stone', 'dead tree'— all these are symbolically odd company yet true. The idea of 'neither living nor dead' leads through 'the pack of cards' symbol to 'the unreal city'. by close-set symbols of unrelated disjointed things of the city its unreality is brought home to us.

The chaired lady with lascivious elaboration of carousal is sick in body and mind - 'My nerves are bad tonight', she says. She seeks company, seeks words of sympathy. A symbol like this is the true expression of modern poverty in plenty, hollowness in gaudy elaboration. All our high roads are 'rats' alley' all our noise is 'the wind under the door'.

Eliot's use of proper names is unspecified generalization as unnamed objects can be. Lil's husband, poor Albert are not names, they stand for generic truth. Something is impatiently awaited —'Hung up please its time', so they all bid good bye, good bye is all their end —

'good night Bill, Good night Lon...Good Night.'

The poet need not say clearly what is awaited, and why so impatiently? Perhaps it cannot be made clear, as today the horror of the Third World War. In this awful suspense no evening party can run its full course, it breaks in the middle.

The unreal city and the real river as in the Fire sermon part of the poem together make the symbol of the truth of modern civilization. The glossy city with the grimy river with filth and wastes is the fit home for the 'human engine' 'throbbing like a taxi' in exhaustion. The poet points to so much filth that it makes so apparently blazing a city quite unreal. The river is the real history of the unreal city: 'The river bears no empty bottles...summer nights'. The city of London with all the daily truths remains untrue in its hidden history.

The thunder part of the poem is symbolically even more subtle, the whole piece seems to be a symbol *en bloc*, the sense stirs in the symbol itself, no word in ordinary terms of language seems able to communicate it. Let us take one small patch out of the whole–the first passage without any intervention of punctuation, because you don't know where you begin and where end - note only the rumble and 'reverberation of thunder of spring over distant mountains's, 'He who was living is now dead we who were living are now dying...'

Eliot himself explains some of his symbols, refers even to Jessie Weston's book on Grail legend, *From Ritual to Romance* for his main source and many other European originals and Asian too; but symbols as they are in this poem, with their disjointed awkwardness and coherence by turn suggest something deeper than those originals. Even Eliot's explanation of 'the third who walks always beside you' as Jesus is not what exactly the imperceptible shadow means to every individual with a feeling of another he needs and always finds. India can easily explain it as the shadow of the eternal presence that makes even the so sincerely coveted union of the two possible, a presence just in-between the two, just beside both and even beyond. This is better explained by Indian spiritual tradition when in the rest of the piece Eliot falls upon some clear Indian myths for symbols.

Eliot in his choice of symbols explores a wide field of European and Indian literature, for an idea exceptionally his own although it represents a truth of the whole age and even something beyond.

Easter 1916: A Representative Yeats

The poem is a true representation of Yeats's genius. Yeats is an Irishman, but he is not really an Irish poet although he makes the best use of Irish materials. Yeats dilutes his Irishness in the real excellence of poetry, his Irishness contributes to the greatness of his poetry, and lifts him far above low nationalistic outlook.

The poem *Easter 1916* is an occasional poem, the title suggests it is so, it seems to commemorate the Easter rising of 1916, the poem was composed on Sep. 25, 1916 obviously in the heat of that national rising. The poet mentions some of the leaders of the rising in the poem, but except those few names the poem hardly bears any evidence of any political predilection. His patriotism is without any parochialism.

Save only the occasion of its composition and title the poem has nothing to do with the Easter rising. This gave Maud Gonne, the lady he loved, great offence. Yeats politically contributed to Gonne's line of thought because of the person but not for the principle. *Easter 1916* is therefore his liberation, he is not against the British, but with the men of the world as with his people. This parallels Rabindranath's line.

Easter 1916 is better not treated as an occasional poem, not revolutionary at all, neither narrow-minded, it is what excellent poetry can make it. The poet can be considered politically non-committed, he is taken to be so here by even his love, an extremist partisan; but he is committed to his cult, his craft as a poet. *Easter* is a poem in which Yeats has attained international status by a serious study of the trend of our life and civilization in which just like his study of this in a later poem '*The Second Coming*' (1919) he detects 'a terrible beauty, beauty is born', 'all changed, changed utterly'. In the study he recalls even the role of a woman, not even woman, but a particular woman –'that woman's days were spent/In ignorant good-will.' Evidently the poet has single-minded love for her 'what voice more sweet than hers'. One may identify her as Maud Gonne, if one likes.

The inquiry based upon the poet's personal acquaintance and experience reveals one great truth that he is in a mind to evaluate the crisis of the present civilization not necessarily confined to a particular area, as for example Ireland, but of the whole of humanity although with the help of specific symbols. The poem belongs to the *Second Coming* trend of thought and outlook. War, in the atmosphere of which he writes, and uprising in his land are considered only symptoms of the distemper of our civilization. *Easter* does neither belong to the obvious category of Owen's war poems nor Pound's *Pour I' election* type viewing war as a depleting force affecting values of art, Yeats's study is yet more deeply searching, study of a deep-rooted malady in which war is only a symtom.

A study of Pound and Owen as war poets

Pound never took part in war although he broadcast was commentary over the Italian Radio during the Second World War and was charged with treason. His link with war is really very slight, not at all so deep as with Owen who fought in the front and was killed in 1918. Owen's collection of poems was published by his friend Seigfried just in 1920 when Pound too completed his Mauberley Collection.

The first poem of Pound's Mauberley collection has clear reference to the war, particularly in the 4th and 5th piece; the poem itself bears evidence of the ennui of war. *De Son Sepulchre*—the title apparently does not immediately given any idea of its link with war, it deals with the sepulchre of rhyme which is caused by lack of vitality and verve. As a depleting agent in this effect war acts its role. *Owen's Strange Meeting* is thoroughly a war poem, and all his poems are out of a reaction to his experience in war, his *Strange Meeting* voices the pity of war.

Pound's theme in *De Sepulchre* is his art, poetry which he means to have been already a 'dead art'. Some one, he need not name him specifically is engaged seriously to 'resuscitate' it, 'to maintain the sublime'. The atmosphere in which one is to attempt it is highly uncongenial. War is one very devitalizing factor to make the standard of art fall. In Owen' case war made the poet sing the pity of war. All Owen's Poems are trench-effusions of a soldier, *Strange Meeting* most.

Strange Meeting evokes a meeting in hell between a killer soldier and the killed and thereby the pathos of the war machinery; war is only a mess of things and massacre of lives, victory or defeat is meaningless in such an irreparable waste. The poet shows in this poem, the soldiers whether they kill or be killed, are not normally enemies, in hell they are not, but they are made so by the devilish tricks of the war lords. Although Pound's subject is not war as it is Owen's, it is an affecting force in the degeneration of culture and civilization and in it art. War invites only a similar mess on earth and sends and all those to hell 'walked eye-deep in hell, believing in old men's lies.'

Pound writes this poem with the first world war's bitter experience of massacre of life and property fresh in his mind, so comes to the same conclusion as Owen does. War is an irony of human civilization and a total waste of life and values, in which the war lords are only satanic leaders of death – in Pound's words:

For an old bitch gone in the teeth
For a botched civilization.

CHAPTER XIV

THE TWENTIETH CENTURY NOVEL

The Rainbow: the problem of education

In English fiction the problem of child education has been a popular theme, particularly during the Victorian period, when Education Bills were passed one after another in British Parliament. Even contemporaneously Dickens took it up in *David Copperfield* and *Hard Times*. In the 20th century it is taken up still more psychologically as in *The Rainbow*.

Lawrence has before him Dickens and Hardy mainly, but he makes it a different issue, it does not even compare with Hardy's treatment of it in *Jude the Obscure*. Jude, Sue and Phillotson are three different pictures, Phillotson was normally in the profession of education, Sue was only brought to it, and Jude could not be though he desired it. Their problem too had a different root.

Lawrence widely differs from Hardy, differs from Dickens too, though Mr. Harvy's school comes closer to Mr. Creackle's Salem House and Miss Brangwen's position under Harvy in a way recalls Mr. Mell's position under Creackle. Of course Mr. Creackle and Mr. Harvy are widely different as Ursula is from Mell. The children in St. Phillip's School in *The Rainbow* are a little more officious though Steerforth is still lacking there. The children of St. Phillip's School are a wicked band.

Mr. Harvy's and Mr. Creackle's position are the same but as persons they differ. Lawrence does not paint a noble figure of humour like Dr. Strong of *David Copperfield*. Lawrence is too serious to introduce Dickensian humour in *The Rainbow*.

Ursula is the crucial figure for a close study of the issue of education in hand — Ursula as scholar and Ursula as teacher, twice over. The Ursula-Inger relationship must have laid the basis of Ursula's outlook on education when she went to serve as a teacher of Harvy's school. Ursula's study of her own nature and Inger's very personal touch in her life, of whatever nature the touch may be, gave her an idea of human instinct and prospect of its free and unobstructed evolution. But Ursula's plan completely failed in the artificial atmosphere of imposed discipline.

Mr. Harvy is the modern version of Mr. Creackle, so Mr. Harvy need not change his profession to a prison Governor, he must continue to govern the school with prison like austerity of discipline. Ursula cannot fit in well there so she antagonised both the authority and the scholars. Ursula's experience is, "in school it was power, and power alone that mattered" (p.377). In-between these two forces she was about to be sandwitched, because she could not exert power.

Her theory of education although in principle right is inoperative in an atmosphere of almost total distortion of human instinct. The cloak of education is shiny and attractive with all its paddings but the body inside is rotten. Mr. Harvy and other masters and mistresses and with all those accessories living and non-living are only the cloak of the system, the mind and heart and other human values form the body within and get rotten in the process. Miss Brangwen is the unlucky observer, the representation of the author's entity.

The Rainbow: Social Evolution

Lawrence is not a writer like Galsworthy. Lawrence is rather a severe critic of Galsworthy and his theme of society. Lawrence has never attempted anything in the manner or a *Forsyte Saga.* Galsworthy has studied the changes of social forces in several generations of a late Victorian family. Lawrence has, of course, studied in *The Rainbow* and its sequel *Women in Love* at least three generations of a family, but not with the same objective as Galsworthy has.

The Rainbow is a novel that deals with the man and woman relation within a limited area. Some of the episodes in the novel are more or less blurred by the writer's search deep inside the individual instinct. This is mainly so because Lawrence does not present us with the exterior view of a society, he depicts the inner mechanism.

The novel in not exactly autobiographical as *Sons and Lovers* is. Of course the background of life is nearer Lawrence's own background, is the same Nottinghamshire, the same colliery area, and almost the same countryside life with a family problem that was essentially Lawrence's own.

It was a story of life about the year 1840, a life mainly confined to Marsh Farm, connected with the newly opened collieries of the Erewash Valley. Lawrence has not thoroughly depicted the background of life that could have been done by either Hardy or Galsworthy.

Lawrence's emphasis is upon the individual life as developing in the common social background with no help coming from there but with some obvious obstacles in the way of normal emotional growth and the free expression of instinct. The marriage between Lydia and a Polish doctor is ultimately not at all a happy marriage, it comes to the mixture of blood of two different races, German and Pole. When Lydia crossed into England with her husband it was surely due to the political troubles in the Russian and Polish mainland. But Lawrence has not elaborated the political scene or its impact upon the life of his characters.

The next generation of the family came to be acclimatized with the English society. There was yet another mixture of blood of two different races in England, the Lenskey became Brangwen in England, the language became English, although the elderly lady Lydia still retained in her blood a Polish strain. So her friendship with Baron Skrebensky, a Polish refugee in England, was very easy.

Lawrence had neither one land in view nor the other, when he wrote *The Rainbow*; his attempt was confined to the delineation of a secret conflict between the ordinary culture of the society and the eternal human instinct.

Lawrence took of course the common cultural unit of society, the family and the essentially accepted form of human intercourse in the institution of marriage. But Lawrence did not like Galsworthy or Hardy or any of the modern novelists take them as the unrocked foundation of the society. He simply took them to paint the unavailing incompatibility of their agencies in the work.

In the context of common conventional society Lawrence has placed his family and young men and women to show only their ultimate conflict with the forces of traditional values. Mrs. Brangwen's position in the family is in direct contrast with the young boys and girls seeking fulfilment of their life, as mainly the life of Ursula Brangwen.

Ursula Brangwen definitely passed through all those commonly accepted forms of cultural and educational attainments; but in spite of so thorough a training she ultimately remained a unfulfilled young woman to whom Anton Skrebensky offered only a timely encouragement ultimately to leave her quite in the cold.

Lawrence is all along a writer of life not so much social as individual. Although in his view society forms a part not as a helpful force to exert itself but as a hindrance to the life of pure instinct and in coloured emotion.

A Passage to India: Symbols and images

E.M. Forster is not regarded as one of the leading symbolists of modern literature. He belongs to the Bloomsbury group of writers. In none of his earlier novels he adopted any striking symbols, not up to 1911; but in his last novel he has developed a method nowhere to be noted so significantly effective as here.

A Passage to India is in a way a deviation from Forster's usual method as also his usual theme. In this novel Forster has exhausted all that he has to give to the world in his creative writings. *A Passage to India* has attempted more or less a symbolic method of representation. We know the Bloomsbury group inculcated liberal humanism, Forster obviously did. But his symbols used in the novel are not of a kind used by another of the same group of writers, Virginia Woolf.

Forster's symbols and images betray a quality of his own mind and culture, he particularly continued Arnold's idea of culture, which gets a clear shape in *A Passage to India* when effectively the three major symbols are estimated in the proper perspective of values.

A Passage to India brings out Forster's theme of apparent racial conflicts and his underlying essential humanity. Apparently the novel deals with three communities steeped in three different kinds of narrow outlook and convention; Christianity parochial, Islam ethnocentric, Hinduism incomprehensible. Of course the three symbols only outwardly stress a description like this.

The novel starts with the symbol of Mosque, then followed by two other symbols, Cave and Temple, all representing the Indian tradition. The symbol of Mosque is of course a modest and subdued symbol. The Muslim community in India under the British rule is thoroughly and very faithfully studied by means of this symbol. The English lady Mrs. Moore only accidently met Dr. Aziz in one corner of a Mosque. Dr. Aziz was to maintain the sanctity of the Mosque, and so he asked Mrs. Moore to enter it without shoes.

The Mosque is practically without any major racial conflict, if there is any it is only between the two main religious communities of India, Hindu and Muslim. The controversy deepened under the Cave symbol. Here is a rare racial disbelief and dissension between the ruler and the ruled, practically between the British India and the European ruling community in India. The symbol attains its deeper significance by means of its total incomprehension of the truth of hard realities of the caves and hills which forms an essential part of India.

The funny thing is the British people wanted to understand India, yet they were not ready to understand some very essential things of India which appeared to them quite awkward. The last symbol the Temple, is again an object the European people would hardly understand because it was beyond their experience.

Professor Godbole in this novel is not a character only but also a symbol of Hindu eccentricity or, you may say, an eastern oddity which the European people could only make an object of fun without any sufficient patience to understand it sympathetically. Aziz is likewise a modest symbol of the educated Indian of his own community, not Islamic so much as he is poetic, neither sticking to the strict Islamic principles as Professor Godbole did in respect of his own religion, nor getting ultimately to be highly liberal as Forster may have expected. All the European characters are more or less typical of their colonial sentiment, the only rare exception was Mr. Fielding.

Forster did the same thing by means of his characters as by those chosen symbols in the novel. His study of India is essentially the study of racial oddities, sometimes in the form of conflicts between them, indirectly only leading to the basic unity of humanity.

Professor Godbole under the symbol of the Temple is the side of mystery that often India is to the uncomprehending British community in India. Forster of course is quite comprehending when he has got to accept this mystic side of India's culture and tradition.

A Passage to India: The Cave Episode

E.M. Forster wrote at the end of his career as a novelist his masterpiece, *A Passage to India*, a real departure from his usual theme. In this novel he elaborates his subject matter by means of mainly three symbols, the most important of which is the Cave. The Cave episode of the novel takes more space than the other two.

It has not been sufficiently clear to the Western readers what is the meaning of this elaborate description of the cave experience of the two European ladies. Did Forster want to make them simply a laughing stock to the non-European world or readers? Forster does not really have any such motive. Did he then make the episode a grotesque savagery of Indian culture? That also seems not to be Forster's ultimate end.

A Passage to India is Forster's masterpiece; it is all too serious a novel for simple fun. The cave episode of the novel is not at all a fun although it comes closer to it. The episode itself is Forster's favourite device to bring out serious meaning of underlying essential humanity in all apparent difference and disunity.

The episode is apparently full of fun. Two European ladies are taken into the Marabar Cave, one elderly, the other quite young, and taken by an Indian, Dr. Aziz, as his guests. The Cave is the meeting place for the three different races, at least it is proposed so, two of the Indian communities, and the third the ruling European race. Dr. Aziz meant only an adventure and he selected the Marabar hills as it was already on the tourist map of India, quite a sight-seeing spot. Dr. Aziz was quite an innocent person and he wanted to entertain his English friends.

Things so happened in the Marabar Caves that it passed beyond his control and of course beyond his expectation. The simple story is, Miss Quested, as also Mrs. Moore, had only a traumatic experience inside the cave. Mrs. Moore at last kept outside the cave enjoying the free air above ground, Miss Quested was taken down into the cave by Dr. Aziz as she was more adventurous than the elderly lady.

Adela Quested had this time so maddening an experience in the interior of the cave that it was simply stunning upon her nerves. She could not clearly form her idea as to what exactly happened there. In Chap. XIV towards the close an excellent description of Miss Quested's experience in the cave has been given. The young lady practically jostled with an unspecified number of people rushing in and throwing her deep into the cave, where she did not know. She heard a terrible sound, what it meant she could not tell. She was absolutely helpless and dashed against a good many naked bodies, one in particular striking upon her face. She struck perhaps against Dr. Aziz, but she did not know, although she struck Dr. Aziz with her camera. The terrible sound with its endless echo simply made her mad. She came out only to escape as quickly as she was taken into the car of her betrothed.

Forster has given all the romantic fervour possible to this adventure, made it a little funny, but ultimately made an emanating centre of his own ideas about the apparent racial conflicts which took an awful shape in British India.

Forster depicts in *A Passage to India* not only the communal conflicts that wrecked the peace and tranquility of the Indian sub-continent, he depicts as well the conflicts between the Indian community and the ruling community of England as they behaved in India.

The Cave episode did not all end with the traumatic experience of the two European ladies, particularly one; it involved a sorry and sad conflict between the Indian and the English, a different kind of racial conflict, over as filmsy a matter as it is absolutely false. Adela was under a delusion that she was assaulted by Dr. Aziz, she was perhaps made to feel so by the excessive exaggeration of the prestige issue of her own community then stranded in India.

Forster has attempted so unique a picture of the colonial rule that he has in some way surpassed in his thoroughness and enquiry the most outstanding writer of colonial rule, Rudyard Kipling. If there be any fun that Forster may have attempted in a serious novel like this he must have attempted here in the false prestige issue of the ruling race centering so insignificant an experience in one curious part of India which the European people could hardly understand. "Yet the Marabar Cave had been a terrible strain on the local administration."

The temperamental affinity between Mrs. Moore and Prof. Godbole in A Passage to India

The reader of Forster's novel, *A Passage to India*, must be struck by the note of mysticism in it. Mrs. Moore and Professor Godbole as characters have essentially a mystic outlook. Both go beyond the scope of facts and converse with the transcendental realities. A temperamental affinity between the two characters is a part of Forster's craft. Forster's treatment is attuned to the spirit of mysticism, their temperamental affinity is not brought out in clean terms but only suggested by evocative touches. In the novel they have one important point of contact - a depth of spiritual realization. As mystic they, however, differ, Professor Godbole represents the oriental tradition and Mrs. Moore only the Western. Professor Godbole has a religious mysticism, a mysterious God at the end of the journey of life. Although an educated person like Kipling's Purun Bhagat, educated in the English system, remains basically Indian with a vision of God as a final dispenser of our destiny. Mrs. Moore's mysticism is deepened by her Indian contact, perhaps she fails to adjust her European ideas with Indian values. Mrs. Moore fresh from England felt awkward in a land which revealed something to her she could not at all understand. It begins right from her contact with Aziz in the mosque. This mystic approach to a land not earlier known to her deepens in the cave episode of the novel. Mrs. Moore appears to be the modern version of Dickens's Betsey Trotwood. But Mrs. Moore's eccentricity, rather apparent eccentricity, is a kind of mystic anticipation of values not clearly known to her. With regard to Aziz Mrs. Moore was not sure, whether she should hold him responsible for the supposed guilt, she was not at all sure. When later she was approached by her own son for an effective witness for prosecution she flatly told him she was not at all interested in any court procedure. She thought Aziz was not guilty, the whole lot of the European protagonists could not make her one of their party. She had different source of knowledge rather an unidentified source. She was completely isolated from the whole lot as she would be in her study of India too. She was not sure what India actually was, but she was no doubt very close to India, more close than any body else among the British people. Her abrupt decision to leave India for England at a crisis moment for the whole set of European rulers in India is a symptom of her unknown source of inspiration.

Mrs. Moore's ideas of love and marriage have also a mystic note:

'Why all the marriage, marriage?. . . the human race would have become a single person centuries ago if marriage was any use. And all the rubbish about love, love in a church, love in a cabe, as if there is the least difference, and I held up from business over such trifles."

Professor Godbole has a thorough mystic outlook, wholly in the Indian tradition of it. For all his education and knowledge of Western culture he remains a pure Indian in his outlook and understanding. Although Mrs. Moore comes closer to a temperamental affinity with

Professor Godbole she lags far behind the Professor. Mrs. Moore does not survive her cave experience. The last part of the novel is entirely given to Professor Godbole's mystic approach to life and knowledge.

Professor Godbole is a Minister of Education just like Purun Bhagat, but he has a mystic apprehension of values of life in which the ultimate goal is God. Professor Godbole's highest discovery of truth is 'God is love'. It is love that links up man with his God, and it is God that has given India a mystic glory of her own.

Professor Godbole forgets everything, has everything blurred, in his highest thought upon that ultimate Creator embodied as Lord Krishna at the Gokul Astami Festival. Significantly enough he has a faint memory of 'an old woman he had met in Chandrapore days', this lady with her whole association comes back to Professor Godbole with a different identity mystified in a whole order of things in his exalted mood. Professor's Thukaram and Lord Krishna are a mystic representation of essential India in its very Hindu conception, it is an India which knows no exception but upholds an embracing unity, although very mystically: 'God is love' 'looking back upon the great blur of the last twenty four hours, no man could say where was the emotional centre of it, any more than he could locate the heart of cloud.'

European approach to India in the modern age is more or less of the same mystic character as in the quoted line above. They have seen India a vast entity yet not knowing its very fixed centre. Mrs. Moore seems to be in this respect Forster's own anticipation of India, and Professor Godbole is its perfect symbol. This is perhaps the reason why Forster has brought Mrs. Moore and Godbole closer to each other in temperamental affinity in the novel.

Heart of Darkness: The Narrator Problem

The narrator in Conrad's novels has assumed an exceptional point of special nicety in the artistic evaluation of his themes. Very often in Conrad's novels we come across more than one narrator, Conrad's use of Marlow as narrator in a good number of his novels has assumed a special character. Conrad does it as the recent critics think to meet a curious artistic problem in his writing and at a time when he felt the need of a special attention to this problem.

Heart of Darkness is of course the second story in which Marlow appears as the narrator. He picks up the thread of the narrative from the original narrator of the story. Conrad significantly abandons the method, of omniscient narrator as he has already felt the special need of a change. In the earlier two novels Conrad employed the omniscient narrator, but in *The Nigger of the Narcissus* Conrad shows signs of ineffectiveness of the omniscient narrator method. In *Youth* for the first time Marlow appears. In *Heart of Darkness* Marlow's role as a narrator is a little more complex and artistically a little more significant.

Why Conrad invents Marlow has been a subject of endless debate among his critics, but they more or less come to an agreement on the point of Conrad's special necessity for such a device. So far as *Heart of Darkness* is concerned it is clear that Conrad wants to conceal his personality behind his character, and if possible in a surrogate figure among the characters of his novels. Marlow appears as such a figure in *Heart of Darkness*. At least Schwarz and Sherry explain it like this.

In *Heart of Darkness* Marlow makes a journey into the interior of the dark continent and by means of such a journey Marlow gathers experience as a civilized man of the still savage stage of things in a continent far away from the civilized world. It is essentially the experience of Conrad in this Congo expedition.

Heart of Darkness is the first novel where Conrad has perhaps managed to think out a subject for his writing, his idea of art has already gained clarity in the *Nigger* Preface, but his theme has not yet been clearly thought out at that stage. Some critics think, Conrad has at least made out his subject matter in *Heart of Darkness* - a contact between two civilizations, two different races.

Conrad's narrator in *Heart of Darkness* has a special role to play in the context of such a changed view of his theme. It is clearly different from the role of the narrator in the earlier story. There Marlow is only a keen observer although as a character; but in the present story Marlow's impartial disinterested observation is not only highly dramatized but also deepened into a spiritual significance, as we might term it as journey from the Id to Ego.

Marlow's meeting with Kurtz in the interior of the Congo is the meeting of the two sister cultures of the same civilized world with a keen sense of contrast with the purely uncivilized savage background of life, where darkness was not only physical but also moral and spiritual.

Conrad as writer wants perhaps to shift his responsibility of final judgement to one who might serve as his own representation yet not directly involving him as a decisive factor.

The narrator in *Heart of Darkness* has such a special role to play and at a time when Conrad as a writer was surely in a flexible state of mind as to the final judgement of the validity of his account.

Heart of Darkness: a study of evil, decay of modern civilization: Kurtz its symbol

Conrad completed writing *Heart of Darkness* in 1899, it came out of his pen subjectively with his experience in the Congo and objectively with the gathering gloom of 1890's. In an objective analysis the story seems to be an allegory of evil, a symbol of decay of modern civilization, and Kurtz its springhead.

Conrad's study of evil in the story is not exactly in the form of moral allegory, though there is something allegorical in it. It is rather of a story of one culture in conflict with another, civilization of the modern world contaminated by the savage principle of the Dark Continent, the decay of moral values rightly the work of evil, better the expression of it.

Kurtz is the central figure who combines both culture and crime, solemnity and sin. Conrad's study of this character is objectively an inquiry into this complexity of human truth that transcends easily the barrier of his own experience and the decadence of his age. Kurtz is a symbol of human evil steeped in the imposing superstructure of civilization. He is power of the European civilization with a soul of human weakness. With that power he conquers all he meets, at least three in the book, the Rusian youth, Marlow and his Intended, but he is conquered for that Weakness, his animal passion.

The Savage sweetheart and the civilized Intended are the two poles of his career, conquest and defeat. Kurtz's whole mission of civilizing the savage is a sad failure, a clear flop. His civilization proves servility to him. Conrad seems not be believe that the Dark Continent is all dead, and so-called civilization would do it more good than harm. Civilization of Europe and savagery of Africa have ultimately a common basis of human nature and its essential animality. *Heart of Darkness* explores that secret corner. The Savage sweetheart and the civilized beloved could meet at that point.

In Conrad's conception evil is better not considered as an ethical principle, it is rather regarded as a part of life and human nature; and it is allowed its freeplay in the unregimented rule of the forest in *Heart of Darkness*. Kurtz could pass well in regimented Europe, but in the forest of Africa where there is no fixed rule of law he could take law in his own hand. Europe is a continent of regimented civilization and therefore shows cracks when tight rule is relaxed. Civilization is only a forced imposition upon underlying animality.

Kurtz dies in that dark forest, dies with his dark soul revealed to the world, revealed in the last hour under yet a veil of mystery, the mystery of his enigmatic utterance. In *Heart of Darkness* Kurtz's last word, a single word repeated twice, attains the highest point of soul-searching and conveys a meaning which Shakespeare's dying heroes convey being themselves convinced of it. Kurtz is likewise convinced of his folly in the last hour, the poignant hour of clear vision of truth.

In that word repeated twice The Horror! The horror!—twice because his breath did not allow more—is an introspective and retrogressive review of his life. All his impassioned scrutiny breaks into an outburst in this word. Perhaps no better interpretation of evil in him and in humanity as a whole is possible by any amount of close scrutiny. Marlow has attempted an interpretation very near Kurtz's own meaning, but only very near, and not exactly what Kurtz meant in his life's experience. Marlow believes, Kurtz had pronounced a judgement upon the adventures of his soul on this earth (p.150). His meaningful stare'...was wide enough to penetrate all the hearts that beat in the darkness. He had summed up—he had judged the Horror! Marlow thinks.

Heart of Darkness is better considered an objective study of evil in man under the varnish of civilization, evil that breaks into all signs of decay and loss of values.

Heart of Darkness: Its narrative art: The role of Marlow

Conrad's narrative art is brought under the impact of his personality, which necessitated introduction of a narrator, first an unnamed one as in the *Nigger*, then from *Youth* one named Marlow. The omniscient narrator in *Heart of Darkness* yields place to Marlow for him to relate his Congo experience and introduce a theme he does not take the responsibility of.

The omniscient narrator starts a story in which Marlow narrates another. The plot comprises a story within a story; four chums in the yawl came down to the Thames reach for a dinner hosted by the Company Director and talked; the first narrator is one of them without any name, the second narrator Marlow, one of the group.

The story which is narrated by Marlow is of the nature of the Ancient Mariner, only the listeners are unlike the unwilling wedding guest and four instead of one. The unity of the plot is the singleness of the narrator's account of his experience, which otherwise breaks off almost in the middle of telling. Marlow starts sitting like the mediative Buddha and ended by assuming the same pose; 'Marlow ceased, and set apart, indistinct and silent, in the pose of meditating Buddha.'

Marlow's story was narrated and the first narrator resumed and rounded off the story as he started it leaving the blank in the middle to be filled in by Marlow's narrative. Meanwhile in the narrative, the Director said, "We have lost the first of the ebb", and the original narrator chum ended by saying:

> 'The offing was barred by a black bank of clouds, and the tranquil waterway leading to the uttermost ends of the earth flowed sombre under an overcast sky - seemed to lead into the heart of an immense darkness.'

The story is a well-knit plot only because of the outer framework of the narrative pattern, otherwise 'It is an interminable analysis' of Marlow's experience which breaks off eventually to yield place to the original narrator. Marlow passes through the whole course of the story following closely the secret of Kurtz's personality and comes to an almost clear understanding as he will not perhaps in relation to Jim later. In *Lord Jim Marlow* has Stein to help as also Jewel but in *Heart of Darkness* he has none; but yet he understands Kurtz and attains illumination. That final lie he told the Intended is a sure proof that he did. The passage is true wisdom:

> 'I heart her weeping; she had hidden her face in her hands; it seemed to me that the house would collapse before I could escape, that the heavens would fall upon my head. But nothing happened. The heavens do not fall for such a trifle. Would they have fallen, I wonder if I had rendered Kurtz that justice which was his due? Hadn't he said he wanted only justice? But I couldn't I could not tell her. It would have been too dark — too dark altogether ...'

Marlow's lie is more than truth, the meaning of his tale, he proposed at the start, does not lie within but hangs loose outside as a curtain of mist. Marlow attains complete hold of his meaning though it surrounds his story more than conceals itself inside its mysterious folds. Conrad gives him the Buddha pose not without reason. He wanted to go free under the mask of Marlow's wisdom. Marlow adopts the flash back method of narration, in disquise the author's experience, which Sherry has thoroughly explored in his *Conrad's Western World*; even the symbols are mainly from his life experience, as significantly the knitting woman and one he calls Marlow's Aunt. This Aunt is also the shrewd trick for introducing Poradowska as the two Yale University editors of Conrad's letters believe.

To the Lighthouse: Mrs. Ramsay: Her role and character

Virginia Woolf stands for a different artistic value of the novel, just a significant starting point in the 20th century English fiction, in which characterization undergoes a total change. Character is not at all painted in the conventional time sequence, nor in the traditional psychological framework, character is also a gliding meandering course upon the uncharted vast sea of the unconscious.

> And shines out...in the face of the flowing,
> the fleeting, the spectral, like ruby...

This is how Mrs. Ramsay perceives a pattern in a flux. Her intuitive perception of truth is more dependable than the factual evidence of Mr. Ramsay. While the other characters of the novel are encased in their own selves, Mrs. Ramsay comes out of her own self and builds up a bridge of sympathetic understanding between herself and others in the story. She brings people together and affects one 'almost like a work of art'. She serves as the structural and psychological centre of the plot. It is she who gathers the various characters of the novel into a homogeneous community. At the dinner party she acts as a perfect hostess and creates an atmosphere of peace and solidarity.

In a stream of consciousness novel there is not very much scope for offering full length portrait of character. Very often characters become sketchy and only a bundle of reflections. But within the limitation of this kind of novel, Mrs. Woolf has been able to provide her characters with distinct individuality. Mrs. Ramsay is presented essentially as a feminine figure, full of pity and sympathy for the poor, the needy and the suffering. She knits a brown stocking for the Lighthouse keepr's son, because he is sick. She often goes out of the town and provides the poor people with food and clothings. She has motherly affection for Ramsay and Lily and Bankes. She has perfect understanding of human nature and, therefore, she knows how to treat people properly. She understands her husband very well and makes every effort to make him happy. Mrs. Ramsay maintains a healthy relationship with her husband and children, and with all others with whom she came into contact. She is loved and respected by her children because she is well aware of their psychological needs. While Mr. Ramsay alienates his children by hid cold shouldering indifference, Mrs. Ramsay however wins their hearts by her sincere concern for them.

Mrs. Ramsay stands for fancy while Mrs. Ramsay represents fact. Mrs. Ramsay tells James that it won't be fine tomorrow so he won't be able to go to the lighthouse. This is fact, that shatters the hopes of the poor. Mrs. Ramsay at once assures him that the wind might change and they might still be able to go on the expedition. This is a lie, but a white lie to use for a boy's happiness.

It is sometimes believed that Mrs. Ramsay has not been individualized, and that she serves only as a symbol. But Mrs. Ramsay is more than a symbol, she is a living presence in the story. She is not physically present after the first part, but her spiritual existence still continues. She is seen through the eyes, of her husband, her guests, her children, and above all through the eyes of Lily, and the result is an extremely complex, rich, fascinating and life-like personality. After Mrs. Ramsay is dead, Lily feels her absence deeply: "how aimless, how chaotic, how unreal it was...a house full of unrelated passions". She remembers Mrs. Ramsay as a woman who resolved everything into simplicity. She thinks of the multiplicity of the personality of Mrs. Ramsay: her beauty, her aloofness, her friendliness and so on.

Mrs. Ramsay comes back into Lily's picture, it is she who provides her with the inspiration to complete the picture. This picture is symbolically the spirit of Mrs. Ramsay only reshaped into a work of art. At last Lily finds the meaning of life, she puts her finger on the fixed point in time. She perceives: "In the midst of chaos there was shape: this external passing and flowing...was struck into stability."

Thus Mrs. Ramsay remains a potent force in the novel. She stands for the values that the Lighthouse symbolizes, the chief of which is guiding from a safe position the erring humanity at large as the vessels upon the high seas. In a sense, Mrs. Woolf seems to place Mrs. Ramsay in the same position in the story as the Lighthouse occupies in navigation.

To the Lighthouse: A stream of consciousness novel

William James used the very term 'Stream of Consciousness' in his *Principles of Psychology* (1890). The term itself laid an impact upon the art of Henry James, his brother. According to Leon Edel James's first outstanding psychological novel is *The Ambassadors* (1903). Virginia Woolf of course marks the next stage in the evolution of the stream of consciousness novel.

Virginia Woolf in her article 'Modern Fiction' has defined the difference between the conventional novel and the modern novel called rightly the Psychological novel. The difference is as sharp as between materialism and spiritualism. Mrs. Woolf calls the earlier three novelists (Wells, Bennett and Galsworthy) 'materialist', and modern fiction as 'concerned with spirit'.

Virginia Woolf's masterpiece, *To the Lighthouse*, must be estimated in the light of this evolution. As Virginia Woolf tells us, 'the point of interest lies very likely in the dark places of Psychology' among the moderns, herself obviously included. The clear distinction between the conventional technique of the novel and the technique adopted by Virginia Woolf, particularly in her *To the Lighthouse*, is clearly indicated by Erich Auerbach under the title 'The Brown Stocking'. Auerbach, just quoting a substantial portion of the part I of Virginia Woolf's novel *To the Lighthouse*, gives her own summary and thereby marks out the clear distinction between the conventional trend of writing and the new method adopted by Woolf.

Virginia Woolf deals with a subject very meagre in substance and very tenuous as a thrend that may link up materials into a good plot, yet her novel makes for a unique success. This success is mainly due to the shift of accent from the ordinary time sequence to the living flux of the semiconscious mind of man. Virginia Woolf wants to follow the actual movements of the mind which of course differ from the ordinary concept of psychology. It is the stream that flows in the very conscious and subconscious levels of the mind that represents real life. A systematic reconstruction in the outside would only belie actuality. With this view Virginia Woolf rears up a new model of Psychology which William James has already suggested and which Prounch only a few years earlier adopted in his novel, *A L'Ombre des Jeunes*. Prouch only indicates in a stray form the *raison d'etra* of the method.

To *The Lighthouse* is far from an ordinary novel. It deals with a flux of the mind, not all 'symmetrically arranged', it cannot be in view of the realities of life. Virginia Woolf takes stock of a new reality of life as she has pre-eminently done in the present novel. The plot of the novel is really to be described in terms of psychological 'inconvenience' - the three parts of the novel are described as the Windows, the Time passes, the Lighthouse. All these three parts are only psychologically connected, connected in the stream of consciousness particularly of a character Mrs. Ramsay. It has definitely disturbed ordinary arrangement of matters around a clearly defined centre. Here is a method of arrangement that attains a central significance out of a lack of actual centre.

In the novel there is Mr. Ramsay with his family, rather a modern family of London culture, shifted to a residence as far situated as the Hebrides, with visitors like William Bankes, a Botanist, Lily Brisco, an artist, with all these a link is established between life and art. The problem of life and art is practically the same. 'To make the moment perfect, to harmonise discord, to attain a central significance.' Life Flows through the book like light through a web.

Virginia Woolf maintains all through the books a central significance of life, of consciousness where no systematic arrangement is possible and where everything is of lasting inconsequence to which life leads. Virginia Woolf achieves perhaps the greatest success in this art in English fiction.

Heart of Darkness: The Title

Conrad's *Heart of Darkness*, one acutely controversial novel of the late 19th and early 20th century, has equally a title of much debate. It is Conrad's second story in which Marlow appears as the narrator. Both Marlow and Kurtz are European, one an English man, the other Belgian. They come to the dark continent of Africa. Conrad's treatment of the theme is a little more significant than his theme in the earlier novels of the Far East.

Dr. Sherry in his *Conrad's Western World* has made an elaborate analysis of the genesis of the story. He takes simply a realistic view of Conrad's adjustment of material. He tells us, Conrad had his Congo experience in the year 1890 and maintained a Congo Diary the only diary maintained by him, and wrote this novel 9 years after on the basis of his actual experience. Dr. Sherry brings out a new character to replace Klein as the origin of Kurtz. In his view Heart of Darkness is a geographical region of the continent usually called the Dark Continent.

Just side by side with Dr. Sherry's realistic interpretation of the title as late as 1971 there is again a spiritual interpretation of the physical journey of Marlow into the interior of Africa, actually undertaken by Conrad himself, psychologically interpreted the journey can be described as a journey from Id to Ego. Of course this must have been the journey of Kurtz. Kurtz fell a ready victim to his animality. It was no doubt the picture of a lost soul, lost in the darkness of his passion. Conrad may have suggested this idea of an inevitable transformation from solid humanity to gross animality, that was a change which Kurtz underwent.

Marlow and Kurtz seem to have been psychologically related, at least Marlow felt like that. Marlow knew, it was all a moral squalor to which Kurtz completely surrendered himself, yet he felt a sort of inseparable link with that lost soul. Kurtz's words had so strong a fascination that they not only conquered the savage people of Africa but conquered even a cultured Englishman like Marlow. The close relationship between Marlow and Kurtz, actually psychological relationship, seems to betray a side of human enigma, which an impartial observer like the present narrator (Marlow) could not absolutely explain away as simply irrelevant. Is it then the darkness of human soul remaining still impenetrable?

The darkness episode, which has lent deep significance to the little, may then be related first to the character of Marlow, then to the character of Kurtz. The uniqueness of Conrad's treatment of the subject is to be seen in the equal validity of both these relations. Marlow's is the journey of an impartial observer; coming from the best of civilizations, he could rightly probe the depth of darkness that gathered first in the geographical conditions of the continent he visited. Again it is the journey of Kurtz who is considered in the novel as the best fruit of European culture, but this time the journey is spiritual; in spite of Kurtz's great genius, best of attainments, perfection of manners and academic achievements he completely surrenders himself to all animal propensities rising their ugly heads in close contact with the savage people. It is a journey from the light of culture into the centre of the darkness of pure animality. Just in the moment of inevitable crisis only a few seconds before his death Kurtz pronounced his confused reading of the whole drama of degradation in words—'the horror ! the horror!'

In whichever way we explain the theme of the novel, *Heart of Darkness*, and whichever way we try to assess the validity of the title the fact remains that it is a novel that deals with the contrast of two cultures, the contrast between the two extremes of human attainment, best symbolized in the two races, in colour and complexion diametrically opposite, one a white race the other black, one full of the fruits of modern culture, the other absolutely with no culture at all. It is a picture of the impenetrability of darkness where the conquest of civilization against the savage turns absolutely a picture of civilization conquered by the savage to a finish. Kurtz is rightly a symbol of such a possibility in the dark continent.

Conrad has delineated in the story the realistic background of the Belgian Congo, the proverbial river of darkness flowing through almost a sunless forest with the people of primitive habits and manners. This elaborate detail of the background of life agrees well with the symbolic interpretation of darkness that may be stressed in the deeper level of human consciousness where man is simply a naked animal. Considered all these aspects the title of the novel seems to be highly suggestive.

CHAPTER XV

TWENTIETH CENTURY CRITICAL ESSAYS

Aldous Huxley: Tragedy and the Whole Truth: The prospect of Tragedy

Aldous Huxley writes this essay to examine a modern trend in art and literature. He seems to take note of life and bring art closer to the true nature of life. The gap between life and art is narrowed down in his attempt. In his treatment Tragedy and the Whole Truth are two contrasted ideas, mutually incompatible. In spite of this incompatibility both are sure to exist, they may co-exist even in the same design of art. The essay weaves these two strands into a consistent account. Here lies the excellence of Huxley's view.

Huxley has a clear view of both the types of truth, whole and part, the literature of the Whole Truth and of the partial truth of tragedy. Both have their own sphere of significance, completely different, Huxley tells us. In modern period the trend is towards the Whole Truth in drama and other species of literature, so there has been naturally an eclipse of the tragic art. This may tempt one to believe that tragedy would have no place in literature in future, but Huxley foresees no such prospect. Tragedy has a different taste, a different flavour which the Whole Truth literature cannot offer.

Shakespeare is the highest attainment of tragic art, particularly in his high tragedies, *Othello, King Lear, Hamlet* and *Macbeth*. It is not Whole Truth, but yet it is truth, truth of a different order, Huxley calls it 'chemically pure' and therefore sharply contrasted with the impurity of the Whole Truth literature. I.A. Richards's claim of tragedy as being 'proof against irony and irrelevance' and capable of absorbing 'the untragical and anti-tragical' is not wholly accepted by Huxley. All Greek and French and most Elizabethan tragedies, he says, 'cannot stand the test'. Only high tragedies of Shakespeare can.

Huxley does not clearly say but surely he suggests that Shakespeare is the future of tragedy, although in our time, he notes, none of the great writers, either in England or across the Channel, is a true example of pure tragedy. Huxley in this connection subjects to close examination some of Shakespeare's scenes. The future of tragedy is Shakespeare and

Shakespeare with his unique quality of intensity and depth of tragic passion which has absorbed a good deal of 'irony' and 'cynicism', Huxley tells us, and heightened the effect of the passion to a grand universality, universality not by widening its area but by deepening it to the heart of humanity. This is what Huxley means here: 'Shakespeare's ironies and cynicisms serve to deepen his tragic world, but not to widen it.'

Tragedy is a world apart from the wholly truthful art. It has a different art and a different taste and different discipline. An Othello, a King Lear, a Macbeth, an Ophelia and an Iago have their own reality to live with, their own law to be guided by, Odyssean or Fieldingesque design will not suit them. Desdemona cannot tumble down like Sophia upon the bumpkin inn-keeper's pouchy belly, far less can have her posterior exposed to view, Huxley is sure.

Tragedy is a part of life experience, even when Odysseus with his followers wept for the lost friends after a good meal they had a tragic experience which of course dwindled in the total values of life. Tragic art knows how to isolate it from the whole and make the part a whole within itself. Artistically then it is more ingenuous than the wholly truthful art. Huxley observes that today art passes through a period of eclipse, but he is sure it cannot die, and it must not be allowed to die. When it would be so allowed it would be a great loss to the literary world.

Owing to its very distinct flavour and taste tragic art will not only survive this literary slump but retrieve its old glory and even open up new avenues in future when the suitable genius will arrive. Huxley rightly ends his essay with:

> Tragedy is too valuable to be allowed to die. There is no reason, after all, why the two kinds of literature - chemically impure and the chemically pure, the literature of the Whole Truth and the literature of the partial truth - should not exist simultaneously, each in its separate sphere...

Tragedy and the Whole Truth: compatible or not: With reference to the Odyssean novel *Tom Jones*

In this Huxley elaborates his view of Tragedy and the Whole Truth with special reference to the *Odyssey* and *Tom Jones* on the one hand and Shakespeare plays on the other. In this analysis of the subject Huxley finds tragedy and what he calls the Whole Truth are not compatible, but surely with distinct tastes of their own. So one need not cause the destruction of the other, they may exist in literature as two different forms, and Huxley ultimately tells us they should.

The Odyssey tells a truth which Shakespeare does not tell at all, but he tells a truth no doubt. These are two different kinds of truth, one is the truth of life which includes everything, joy and misery almost in an odd company. In life there are irrelevancies, the art of the Whole Truth deals with apparent irrelevancies for a conformable design, more or less flexible. The tragic art cannot be that flexible, it must be compact and concentrated. That is why Huxley calls it chemically pure.

In this connection Huxley defines truth. By Whole Truth he does not mean the overall truth of entire life. It is the truth of life, but not exactly all that occurs in life, it is the impression of life, in its entirety, attempted to convey by means of 'an acceptable verisimilitude'. This is the art of the Whole Truth. Huxley offers an example from a relatively recent time, *Tom Jones*. He refers to the heroine's falling upon the flabby belly of an inn-keeper head first with the posterior exposed to gathering urchins' view, a thing which only the Whole Truth concept of art can accommodate. To think of a thing like this about Shakespeare's Ophelia or Desdemona is a travesty. Tragedy is more refined an art as a tended garden is more adapted to taste than the rank growth of the forest.

Huxley knows good art is not a copy of life, even the wholly truthful art is not, it only gives an impression of the embracing completeness of life, how it will be ensured the artist knows better, he knows his method, and only he. Whether it is the Whole Truth view or the tragic view of art, it is an art after all, and every good art, whatever it is, 'possesses a kind of super truth - is more probable, more acceptable, more convincing than fact itself' Huxley tells us. This is so because the artist has, Huxley says, a greater power of transmission than ordinary people. 'They receive from events much more than most man receive, and they can transmit what they have received with a peculiar penetrative force, which drives their communication deep into the reader's mind.'

This general truth underlines both the arts, the art of Whole Truth and the art of the limited truth of Tragedy. Homer and Fielding are the two authors of the Whole Truth, because they uphold the overall impression of life in which thousands of irrelevancies are adjusted and together form into a unit of expression. Sophia is the perfect example of the Whole

Truth attitude; she is the most loved heroine modelled after the author's first wife, but she is not made another Pamela morally pure; she is not at all a dull Ophelia, she shares unvirtuous impulses with a sufficient amount of grace, of her body and mind, which make her ultimately mentally prepared to pardon much of Jone's sins and accept him as the partner of her life. Even any of Shakespeare's romantic tragedies could not assimilate and absorb so much desperate elements in the character of a hero or heroine.

Shakespeare is the perfect model of tragic art. Huxley takes the example of Macduff who could have eaten his supper even though mentally so bitterly shocked at the murder of his wife and child, and with eye lashes still wet dropped off to sleep. There it would have been true to life and worthy of the Whole Truth, but would not fit in at all with the tragic design. Here is another truth to pin-point, and Shakespeare is after that.

Tragedy and the Whole Truth have their respective areas and specific truth, Huxley seems to say, and both have their roles to play in literature.

The Two Romanticisms: Definition and acceptability

Huxley starts the essay by defining the critics' attack on the Romantics. The lines of attack are varied, and Huxley's interest in the Romantic principle is mainly due to their variety and variableness. He does not consider it as a perfect principle of art, nor its critics either, but betrays his interest in the principle itself. He finds two opposite reactions of the same principles in the two far flung stages of literature and culture.

The contemporary scene of literature, Huxley says, is a picture of confusion, we have already left the solid ground of belief or faith, as Arnold tells us, the faith in Romantic values. The modern period has not yet filled in the vacuum. In his close study of this confusion in his age he finds an overall trend of modern Romanticism which he finally calls new Romanticism.

The modern Romanticism is not in the least like the Romanticism of Moore or de Messet, nor anything of the Romanticism of Shelley, Victor Hugo or Beethoven; it is exactly the opposite of it. 'Modern

Romanticism is the old romanticism turned inside out, with all its values reversed.' He tells us 'our romanticism is the photographic negative of what flourished during the corresponding years last century.'

Huxley believes the difference between these two Romanticisms is most strikingly apparent in the sphere of politics. The revolutionaries a hundred years ago were democrats and individualists. The supreme value of their revolution was personal liberty which Mussolini has described as a 'putrefying corpse' and the Bolshevicks derided as 'an ideal invented for the leisured bourgeoisie.' The aim of the English Reform Bill of 1832 and the Parisian Revolution of 1830 was individualism and freedom. The aim of the Communist Revolution in Russia was to deprive the individual of every right, every vestige of personal liberty and to transform him into a component cell of the great 'Collective Man'.

Huxley takes his example from the Russian Revolution to illustrate the modern romantic trend in politics. To the Bolshevicks an individual with a soul, his personal taste and special talents is extremely repugnant. The Bolshevick's earthly Paradise is a machine Paradise. Back to literature Huxley notes the political doctrines elaborated by Lenin are the direct antithesis of Godwin's and Sheley's revolutionary liberalism. Godwin and Shelley believed in pure individualism and Lenin in pure collectivism. One is equally romantic like the other.

Huxley finds both extravagant and one-sided. Man cannot live apart from society and without organization; cannot again live without a certain modicum of privacy and personal liberty. Huxley has noted the modern trend away from the human soul and a step closer to the concept of community life. Even the 'cubist' tendency in modern art is the reflection of this overall preoccupation of this collective life. Modern age is a soulless mechanic age. Maiakovaski's description of the Chicago city is absolutely that - a city 'built upon a screw', 'on steel disk'.

The passion for machines, so characteristic of modern art is a kind of regression to a second boyhood, Huxley tells us. Huxley has no great liking for either of the romanticisms. He frankly tells the world, if he has to make a choice between them he must choose the older one. The New Romanticism is headed straight towards death, he says. He is rightly for a middle course between the two extremes, that is the realistic golden mean, viable for mankind all the time, old and modern.

New Romanticism : Definition and choice

Huxley defines new Romanticism as the other extreme of the Romantic principle of the 19th century, a trend he has noted in the modern times, in everything we are attempting in art and literature, in political precepts of the day. The 19th century Romanticism is concentrated upon the soul of man, the New Romanticism is a soulless machine outlook on life and civilization.

Huxley is mainly concerned with modern collective outlook which finds favour with the younger generation who are after an artificial civilization, an artificial man-made world. D.H. Lawrence is against it, Huxley is a severe critic of this unnatural externalism. His *Brave New World* is an irony of this extremism. He does not at all find it a healthy development, civilization is now at its dead end. Modern Romanticism evolves only out of a confusion of undirected stray search after external values, when nothing avails, creative force becomes exceptionally romantic with a craze for material gain.

He defines the present trend of romantic withdrawal as from the spiritual centre to the social circumference, from individual liberty to the welfare of the 'Collective Man'. In this connection he explores the political scenes of Russia, the secrets of the Bolshevick Revolution. They estimated life in terms of collective utility and completely ignored individual uniqueness, the existence of soul in man. Life was so rigidly regimented that it left no scope for individual liberty or exceptional evolution of talents. Man is cut to the size of the 'Collective Man'.

The whole 'cubist' tendency in modern art is of the same withdrawal from the soul, from the inner vision and impulses of the individual. Huxley does not say the modern concept of art and literature is altogether wrong, but the exclusive concentration on the outer plan of life, man's social and economic programme to the absolute indifference to the other more important values of life is essentially wrong, Huxley tells us. Huxley is an author of the Whole Truth, and therefore more interested in life than in any particular province of it however brilliant it is.

Young writers have conceived a civilization highly mechanized, even the soul of man has only the granite grind, gone granite hard. The plan of a modern city in their vision, the city of Chicago, is the extreme point of fantasy no less romantic than the Romantic fancy of the 19th century, perhaps even more unrealistically romantic than the Romantic imagination. Huxley quotes Maiakovski's lines in translation:

City built upon a screw
Electro-dynamo-mechanical city!
...The squares
Mile high, they gallop to heaven,
Crawling with millions of men...

Huxley finds it no less fantastic than the Hatchery and Conditioning Centre of his *Brave New World*. He would not have it so, this is not life, its Whole Truth neither. It is only the unrealistic other end. If he is allowed any choice he would side with the other less unrealistic extreme of a personal truth of emotion, passion and all those freaks and foibles, which at least have bearing upon human life.

Huxley would have a balance between the two extremes, would have a life sense that can ignore neither, just the Whole Truth view of life in a still wider sense.

CHAPTER XVI
MODERN DRAMA (SHAW)

Shaw's Candida: An antiromantic comedy

Shaw is realist who is out to discard all illusions of life. He is belligerently antiromantic, because the romantic view of life is all too illusory. He describes his play *Arms and the Man* as an antiromantic comedy, but it is not alone, all Shavian plays are in fact antiromantic in nature and purpose. He adopts the traditional themes and deals with them in a new way. In *Arms and the Man,* for example, Shaw takes up the themes of love and war, but he views both from a different angle. He exposes the hollowness of the romantic conception of love and war.

In *Candida* Shaw deals with the eternal love triangle, the love of two men for the same woman. Mr. Morell is a Christian socialist. His wife Candida is a practical, clear-headed, sympathetic woman. The young poet Marchbanks is in love with her. This love triangle is the main theme of the play. The central conflict is thus of a conventional nature, dealing with intrigues of love. In a typical story of this sort, the wife carries on her love affair behind the back of her husband.

The pattern of the love story is only apparently of a conventional character, Shaw has ultimately made it absolutely unconventional. the conclusion of the intricate love affair dispel all illusions of romantic love. Candida declares her love for her husband and her home even to the serious discomfiture of the romantic lover.

Not only the conclusion of the story is highly significant but Shaw has made fun enough of this love triangle also in a sort of love auction, which is more modernized than the auction sale of a wife in Hardy's novel *The Mayor of Casterbridge.* Candida does not, of course, sell her husband for a lover. What she does in the play is quite characteristic of Shaw, she only dispels the curtain of mist in the minds of both Morell her husband and Marchbanks her lover, one aged 45, the other only 18, when Candida herself 33. Candida practically throws none of them, but keeps both in their right place, the lover must know that his romantic love is not real enough to survive the throes of realities, and the husband should also learn that his wife's role in his home is a highly complex role, too complex to be plainly understood as he sought. He must know that

Candida was not only his wife, she includes in her wifely role all the duties and responsibilities of mother and sister to the man she makes the partner of her life.

Candida is the model of the Shavian concept of personality as it is to be adjusted in a woman. She is the central pool of wisdom in the drama. She stands for Shavian commonsense which enables one to see things in their proper perspective. Mr. Morell thinks that he is a powerful preacher drawing a large crowd on every occasion. Candida makes him understand that he is not so influential a preacher as he thinks himself to be. He again gives the poet his due, but helps him only to get rid of false notion.

Shaw belongs to the realistic tradition of the English drama. As an able interpreter of Ibsen (*The Quintessence of Ibsenism,* 1891), he deals with the sociological matter without any illusion or predisposition. In his endeavour to reach the hard-core of reality he has discarded the traditional approach to life. He has evolved purely an unbiased line of inquiry into all modern preoccupations and some episodes of history to reach the truth of the matter.

Shaw's Candida: Minor characters

Shaw's *Candida* was published in 1895 and included in the collection, significantly, called *Plays Pleasant.* In all these plays Shaw, although satiric at times, did not at all tend to unpleasant consequence. Shaw is more pleasant in dealing with the minor characters in his plays. Whether major or minor all Shaw's characters served his own artistic or other thematic purpose as they do in the present play.

In the play of *Candida* we do not come across a large number of characters. We have only three major characters and three minor, the minor characters are not simply massed up in the outflanking areas of the action. The three minor characters are Proserpine, aged 30, Alexander Mill, a gentleman from the University and Mr. Burges, an old man of 60.

These three minor characters are so closely implicated in the affairs of the major characters of the play that they can hardly be detached from the plot and the action and obviously from the evolution of the subject matter in hand. The play is a comedy in which domestic love is closely set beside romantic love, all the which do not however keep themselves clearly apart from the moral and social outlook given to different major and minor characters.

We have barely two women characters in the play; Candida the heroine is a little over 33, and is, of course, contrasted with another lady character Proserpine Garnett. The latter is the typist secretary of Candida's husband who is a 'Christian socialist clergyman of the Church.' Now these two woman characters are contrasted in such a manner that one is to be regarded a little closer to idealism and the other closer to realism of life. The fun of Miss Proserpine's position in-between husband and wife is so very restrained yet so effectively painted in the play that it has been far above mere satire, which might have been attributed to the playwright.

Proserpine blurs her very clearly defined position as a typist secretary in Mr. Morell's home. The next character, an Oxfordman, picked up by Mr. Morell to serve as his curate, got a little mixed up with the family, and a little more intimately with the typist secretary, although does not definitely develop into a clear episode of love. Proserpine moves a little closer to Mr. Morell who was not only the husband of Candida, a man of 45, but in a sense a drudge. In Shaw's hand Alexander is a satire on University product. He may be compared to some of good for nothing intellectuals of the modern civilization.

Burgess is Mr. Morell's elderly father-in-law who comes to visit Mr. Morell's home over three years after. He is a man from a different sphere of life, an employer and a man of business, a man of wealth too. With Mr. Burgess Shaw's purpose is completely different. He is not only painted here as an unloved and unregarded father-in-law but painted definitely as a half-humoured, half-satirised social crank. He knows his interest but knows nothing else. In the play Burgess is not painted at all as a loving father but as a dull and insipid exploiter. In Shaw's story Mr. Burgess is an exceptional case of the mixed effect of satire and humour.

Shaw perhaps leads in the field of guarded humour very close to satire with most of his minor characters. The minor characters in his plays are not men of broken limbs, deficient of vigour and energy, they are rather full-blooded personalities, some of them are well-knit texture of all the viable qualities only a little misplaced. Louka in *Arms and The Man* is one such. In the present play Proserpine is another, Burgess and Alexander are two other such portraits, only in their respective fields of activities. Alexander is a neat picture of dull intellectualism when placed beside another young man in the play, Candida's romantic lover Marchbanks.

Shaw in his handling of minor characters thoroughly maintains his sense of comedy although never obscuring his serious purpose in the play. His comedy is quite distinct from the comedy of Shakespeare, his treatment of minor characters in this respect is also a distinct feature from the treatment of Shakespeare. He takes clear note of the changed perspective of social and industrial culture.

CHAPTER XVII

CRITICISM

Sidney's Defence of Poetry

Stephen Gosson calls the poets 'the Fathers of Lyes' in his *School of Abuse* (1579) and dedicates this work to Sidney. Sidney wrote his *Defence of Poesie* in reply to Gosson's adverse remarks on the poets, which was published later in 1595 long after his death. This is no doubt the first serious critical attempt in defence of poetry as a supreme measure of art.

First of all Sidney upholds the antiquity and universality of poetry. According to him, poetry was the first light given to the primitive ignorant people. The earliest books of, say, for example, Greek philosophers and historians were in verse. Sidney thinks that any attack on poetry is an act of unpardonable ingratitude. Sidney thinks that poets were held in reverence also in history. The Romans called their poets 'vates' by which they meant prophets and the Greek word for poet was 'Maker' or Creator. In Hebrew the psalms of David were considered holy.

Sidney breaks fresh grounds when he contrasts poetry with other arts or branches of learning and speaks of its superiority over the rest. Every other branch of knowledge depends upon the work of nature but poetry is not subject to nature. The poet is lifted up with the vigour of his invention, grows virtually into another nature. The poet is, and makes things, different from, and sometimes better than the objects of nature. The world of nature, says Sidney, is brazen but the poet makes it golden. Sidney's originality appears in the recognition of the fact that poetry transcends nature, in an idealized representation, an ennobling of the object imitated. It may be argued that Sidney is there a true Aristotelian in the exposition of the concept of poetic imitation. But he then makes explicit what was in Aristotle only implicit and his elaboration proceeds along independent lines.

Sidney's originality comes out as he passed from the defence of poetry along the traditional lines to the defence of a subtler nature. For example he mentions four specific charges against poetry and offer his defence of each of them. To the charge that the study of poetry is only waste of time, Sidney replies that poetry teaches man and moves him into virtues better than any other branch of learning.

To the second charge that poets are liars, Sidney pleads that of all writers under the sun poets are least liable to prevarication on the ground that all other men affirm something and therefore run some risk of making false statement but the poet never affirms, his concern being invention.

To the third charge that poetry abuses the wit of man 'training it to sinfulness and lustful love' Sidney replies that 'man's wit abuseth poetry' rather than 'poetry abuseth man's wit'.

Lastly Sidney refers to Plato and his adverse view of the poets of his time. Sidney's answer to this is a clear understanding of Plato. He feels Plato was misinterpreted; his charge was not against poetry, 'of all philosophers, he is most poetical. Plato's criticism was rightly directed against the abuse of poetry. He simply wanted to banish those poets who made the wrong use of poetry to misguide the unformed young minds. He was right to do it for the stability of his Republic. Sidney answers the last charge against poetry by saying simply 'Plato banishing the abuse, not the thing, not banishing it, but giving unto it, shall be our patron and not our adversary.'

Sidney considers poetry in relation to the other branches of human learning, in course of which he demonstrates that poetry exceeds all others. It is poetry that serves best to promote the supreme purpose of life. For Aristotle, not merely knowing but doing is the ultimate end of all knowledge, which poetry alone can ensure by its capacity to move men not merely to high theoretical principle, but to noble living or noble action.

Philip Sidney : The poet never lies

Philip Sidney is out and out an Aristotelian. So in 1595 he wrote an apology for poetry as generally a defence of poets against that very ancient attack against them. Sidney tries to refute the charges brought against poets by Plato. Aristotle has already done it quite in an artistic way. Sidney seems to be a little more elaborate on the same line.

Plato's main charge against poets, was they were purveyors of lies. Sidney does not at all agree with Plato, although he did not exactly understand what Plato meant by it. Plato himself was a little poetic in his exposition of philosophic thoughts, but yet he found no use for poets in his Republic. Sidney puts the matter like this: Poets do not cultivate any fruitful knowledge, there might be better avenues for knowledge than poetry. The second charge levelled against poets is that 'it is the mother of lies'. The third charge is, 'it is the nurse of abuse infecting us with many pestilent desires'.

Plato said these but why, Sidney took no particular care to know. In his defence of poetry Sidney only answers all these charges. How he does it in this part of his essay is very interesting. Sidney has already defined the special role of history, which is primarily factual, based upon the known happenings of human life. Philosophy differs from it, and poetry differs even more essentially. Sidney's view is simply that the province of poetry is not that of facts, not of course that of history. When poetry does not deal with facts at all how can it hold out anything that belies facts? A historian can be a liar, he may say something that is not true and falsified by facts. But a poet does not at all enter into a question of truth or falsehood. Sidney feels "of all writers under the sun the poet is the least liar", what he would be lying about? A geometrician, an astronomer can be a liar, his theory can be proved false; but a poet's subject is far beyond that scope.

Sidney tells us in his part of this essay 'the poet never affirmeth'. His world is purely a world of imagination, a world of passion, which is never well-defined by any set limitation, "The sweet Muses to inspire into him a good invention." The poet's is only a world of invention which far exceeds the boundary of our daily life and establishes the truth that has no parallel to the factual truth of our known world. Sidney takes the example of Aesop who never lied in the tales of his beasts realistically. He made them only the vehicle of his ideas, the emblem of some moral principles. When a poet writes Thebes upon the doors of a theatre house, he does not mean the place to be that real land of ancient Greece. He means simply things which could happen in that place without limiting the imagination of his audience within the four walls of the theatre house.

Poets are inventive but not prescriptive. They tell things, not exactly those which really happened, but which could happen under some special circumstances. Poets are therefore allegorically true, and their poetry allegories of truth, and not facts. Poets cultivate an art essentially 'figurative' in which there is a wide scope for fancy and imagination of the human mind.

Sidney ultimately defended poetry against that charge of falsehood by ultimately making a distinction between poetry and history. "And therefore, as in history, looking for truth, they go away full fraught falsehood, so in poetry, looking for fiction, they shall use the narration but as an imaginative ground plot of a profitable invention."

Aristotle: Plot *versus* Character

In his definition of tragedy Aristotle pointed out the imitation of an action which naturally implies personal agents who necessarily possess certain distinctive qualities of character and thought. So in Aristotle's *Poetics* the plot is the first principle of action and character the second. A tragedy is mainly defined by means of plot and character. Of course reinforced by some thought or idea.

Aristotle's plot consists mainly in Peripeteia and Anagnorisis. In this Aristitole is mainly guided by the Greek tragic poets before him. A tragedy is the imitation of an action by means of the human agents. So plot and character are inseparable elements in a tragic reconstruction of life.

The persons who are to take part in the action are mainly above the common level of life in a tragedy and below it in a comedy. This is mainly Aristotle's stipulation about character, although he does not see any reason why people either higher or lower cannot take part in the action, whether it is simple or complex.

Aristotle's view of action is either complex or simple. In the *Poetics* plot is Muthos and character is Ethos, and the thought element is called Dianoia. Any tragic view of life, if it is to be translated into a serious action will have all these three elements absolutely inseparable in their existence.

Aristotle has defined all these terms closely in the *Poetics;* the plot is according to Aristotle the kernal of the action. The Ethos and Dianoia are respectively the human agents and the principle and idea they illustrate.

Every character is inseparable from the action in which he takes part, again he is inseparable from the quality of thought or idea that he represents. Aristotle's view of plot and character relationship is like the relationship between action, agent and idea which is also an essential element making the first two elements absolutely indispensable in their inseparable existence.

Aristotle differs from the modern idea of the plot and character relationship, plot is today differentiated from the element of story, and character is today made more or less a psychological symbol. Aristotle makes no such distinction, but in his view plot and character are in the same company, one indispensably linked up with the other and given motion by a third element which he does not call psychology but an idea or at best the will.

In the ultimate analysis Aristotle's view of tragedy as an action requires to be interpreted by character or defined by it. Drama is an objective art in which the human agents are not described but given to define themselves by means of their words and actions. The action itself, when brought into a consolidated form of expression mainly defined by Aristotle as peripeteia and anagnorisis, is the plot which is all through brought to a conclusion through phases of development from one stage to another thoroughly linked up by means of the third element call it will or idea or thought.

Aristotle writing in the long past does not yet become obsolete in the enormous development of ideas and technique till today. Aristotle remains yet valid although his interpretation all through the ages shows some difference.

Aristotle's notion of Catharsis

Aristotle defined tragedy as an imitation of an action in which he saw the scope of proper 'Catharsis' of tragic emotion through pity and fear. Aristotle did not clearly define what he really meant by this Catharsis. May be both the teacher and the taught took it for granted and did not care to elaborate the idea just then.

Critics all through the centuries veered round this word and saw the different ideas at different stages of their attempts.. It is of course taken as a metaphoric expression, and confusion arose simply owing to the word used as a metaphor. It is of course clear that by this theory of Catharsis Aristotle sought to refute Plato's charge against the poets. So the idea behind this metaphor is all the more important.

Regarding the true meaning of the word and Aristotle's own idea behind it there has been a constant debate; author's like Corneille, Racine and Lessing offered different solutions assuming, of course, the purely ethical intention of the drama. Goethe differed from them, although his theory is not ultimately acceptable. Burnays took it to be a medical metaphor 'purgation'. So he entertained the view that Aristotle meant a pathological effect on the soul analogous to the effect of medicine on the body.

Even before Burnays Milton justly appreciated Aristotle's meaning of Catharsis in his Preface to *Samson Agonistis*. Milton is the first Englishman who actually conceived a form of homeopathic treatment of the soul of man which must have been Aristotle's idea. Aristotle may have sought the cure of excess of emotion by means of exciting a similar emotion in the human mind. Aristotle has elsewhere left a clue to his idea of Catharsis as Bucher has pointed out. Aristotle in his *Politics* has suggested the meaning of Catharsis by means of his idea of the role of music and tumultuous melodies. It is a physical stimulus which provides an outlet for religious fervour.

Even Aristotle has used in this context of *Politics* the very word 'Catharsis' - 'all undergo a Catharsis of some kind'. The word has therefore been metaphorically explained as 'illustration', 'purification' and 'purgation'; the last is a pathological word, although the two are either moral or ethical in their ultimate sense.

Abercrombie holds the view like many other critics, including an Indian critic S.C. Sengupta, that Aristotle used the word as a metaphor, so he did not mean the literal pathological sense of the word. His idea must have been purification, or purgation in the metaphoric sense, as in the homeopathic principle, "like cures like is".

In Aristotle's use of Catharsis most of the critics saw this metaphoric sense of purgation, the evacuation of the excess of human passions and emotions to restore balance in human disposition. Plato exactly sought to maintain this balance in young minds, in the mind of every citizen of his *Republic;* and wanted to banish all poets from his ideal state because it was they who disturbed this healthy balance of mind. Aristotle's vindication of the cause of poetry and poets was by means of this doctrine of Catharsis.

Aristotle clearly noted that the poetry like music, and the drama upon the stage like all other arts, did not really disturb the balance but restored man's mind to reason by means of this purgation or voiding of the excess of emotions and passions simply through excitement of similar emotions and passions on the stage.

Aristotle has ultimately refuted Plato's charge against poetry and poets and taken an artistic view of all such things like drama, music and fine arts that serve better a moral end than morality itself can.

Plato's Charge against poetry

Plato's own method is highly poetic, perhaps no philosopher is more poetic in his exposition of themes than Plato. It is an irony of fate that he should bring about some charges against poetry and poets. Plato's *Ion* was written some time in the first decade of the 4th century B.C. It is in this book that he introduced the subject particularly in the form of a dialogue between Socrates and a rhapsode of the name of Ion.

Ion is undoubtedly in favour of poetry, himself skilled in reading Homer and deeply interested in the technique of Homer's writings. Plato himself at time gave praise to poetic inspiration, for example, in the *Meno* he caused poetic persons 'all divinely inspired'.

The same trend is to be noted even in the *Phaedres* in which the poets rank only 6th in a hierarchy of the elite. Plato's mistrust of poetry definitely begins from the *Ion*. Again it recurs in Book II and III of *The Republic*, once again Book X in a more metaphysical context, and also in the *Laws*, the compromise *Republic* of Plato's old age. We encounter his well-known objection to moral effects of poetry.

Plato is of the view that 'poetry feeds and waters the passions' creating division an unsteadiness in the heart, of producing the opposite of civic virtue.

Plato points out the basic difference between the poet and the philosopher. In Book II and III of the *Republic* Plato's view is that poetry is engaged in fiction, often in wicked fiction, that is dangerous lies. He hurls his gauntlet to Homer and Hesiod, these poets, he tells us, shows heroes as emotional and cowardly, wicked men as prosperous just men as wretched.

Plato is definitely against all these poets' making fun of the gods and goddesses and thereby setting bad examples of moral instability. Even the dramatists of that period often painted the great gods of ancient origin as weak-principled. Plato did not think all these very healthy for his ideal Republic and any individual member of it.

Plato's final charge against the poets that they act against the moral principles and spread untruths by means of their imitation practically developed from this.

The greatest charge against the poets in all Plato's writings is a charge of false imitation. Whether it is tragedy or comedy the poets like all other artists attempts only an imitation of an imitation. Plato clears his points by means of the attempt of a carpenter making a bed. The carpenter makes it from his idea of a bed, and the painter only paints it from his knowledge of the bed already made by the carpenter. Plato tells us God is the ultimate maker of the bed, and the painter is only an odd imitator. So the poet is twice removed from the original.

According to Plato the poet's role in his Republic is not only inessential but also inimical to the moral principle of State and individual. He practically came to share the view of the Athenian people who brought a similar charge against Socrates. Plato's theory of *mimesis* is a well-known theory which is taken up by Aristotle in his *Poetics* for a clear answer.

The Distinction Coleridge makes between Fancy and Imagination

In 1817 Coleridge wrote his *Biographia Literaria* simply to define what Wordsworth has already introduced in his *Lyrical Ballads* Preface and other critical writings, [illegible]y dealing with his concept of metrical verse, diction, and the idea of the Imagination and Fancy.

Wordsworth took up the 18th century Fancy and Imagination and raised them to a higher level of creative principle. Wordsworth wrote a note to *The Thorn* in the 1800 edition of *Lyrical Ballads*. To define these two words Fancy and Imagination, rather to discriminate between them Coleridge perhaps took note of this interpretation of Wordsworth.

In Chapter XII of *Biographia Literaria* Coleridge comes down on Wordsworth's venture with a heavy hand:

> 'If by the power of evoking and combining, Mr. Wordsworth means the same...I meant by the aggregative and associative I continue to deny that it belongs at all to the imagination...'

In Chapter IV of the same book *Biographia Literaria* Coleridge gives clear hints as to where he differs from Wordsworth, he is really for the 'seminal principle'. In Chapters V-IX Coleridge traces the growth and the psychology of the two terms, and defines Imagination and Fancy as no one has done it, neither Wordsworth nor any of the 18th century English literature.

Coleridge classifies the Imagination into two groups, the primary and the secondary Imagination. Coleridge's concern is mainly with the secondary Imagination which he considers as an 'echo of the former'. The ultimate work of this Imagination is to 'dissolve, diffuse, dissipate in order to recreate.' So secondary Imagination is creative in essence.

Fancy is a sharp contrast to the secondary Imagination, which Wordsworth forgot to signify. Coleridge tells us: 'The fancy is indeed no other than a mode of Memory emancipated from the order of time and space.' So for Coleridge fancy does rarely enter into creative activity, it is evocative, 'that empirical phenomenon of the will,' we express it by the word 'choice'.

Wordsworth of course gave indication of Coleridge's idea in the more informal and literary statement of the 1815 Preface. Coleridge, however, gives it a more profound dimension of meaning. Coleridge is not so much indebted to Wordsworth as he is to the German philosophers. The sharp difference between Wordsworth and Coleridge is to be noted here. Coleridge takes essentially a philosophic view of the concept of imagination and Wordsworth does not.

Coleridge tells us about what he means by essemplastic Imagination. Perhaps here Coleridge is indebted to German philosophers like Kant and Schelling. Chapter XIII of *Biographia Literaria* deals with this 'essemplastic' or unifying nature of the Imagination. There it differs substantially from the act of Fancy.

The secondary Imagination as Colerdige defines it is a higher plastic power. It reworks the perpetual products of primary Imagination into concrete expressions where the artist's own self acts as the original Creator's own will for creation itself. It is therefore in other words the transcendental view of the Reason. The ideas are realities (nounmena) and the Reason is the faculty of philosophic insight into them ultimately giving them symbolic embodiment. Fancy has of course no such essentially creative role.

Coleridge is really in line with the German philosophers in his theory of Imagination and Fancy. Although he took the clue from Wordsworth in his analysis and elaboration he essentially maintains the standard of German transcendentalism and deviates much from Wordsworth's view.

Eliot's concept of Tradition and Individual Talents

T.S. Eliot has always an end in view even as a critic. Criticism itself has always been to him the 'elucidation of works of art and the correction of the taste'. His conception of tradition has a close relevance to this ultimate end of criticism. In one sense Eliot belongs to the tradition of earlier three critics—Dryden, Johnson and Arnold.

Tradition, as it is defined by Eliot, is not simply 'the maintenance of certain dogmatic beliefs'; it does, so far as creative genius is concerned, keep in touch with what went before in a manner almost inescapable for an original artist if he is at all to be so. Eliot tries to give his idea in as many words as are found indispensable. It is not simply a link with the past somehow established, tradition in creative activities always includes some sort of intellectual seiving.

The uniqueness of Eliot's critical view is to be noted in a proper adjustment of tradition and individual talent. Eliot speaks of the European tradition against which the evolution of individual excellence in any field and in any form is properly to be judged. Eliot is very clear about the impossibility of individual uniqueness completely out of touch with the wider background of values already established either in the remote past or in the immediate traditional evolutions that shape into the present.

The question of tradition in all creative activities is estimated just in a historical background of values. Eliot speaks of Homer and all those classical writers who form the basis of ideas and values for their further development in their curiously unique proliferations. The individual talent of course makes this peculiarity of adjustment in evolution possible although yet in the very lap of the traditional standard of outlook and evocation.

In clear terms Eliot tells us 'No poet, no artist of any art, has its complete meaning alone.' His significance is in the proper appreciation of his relation to the poets and artists who set the tradition for him. Just in this context Eliot states his principle of 'comparison and analysis' as the proper tools of criticism.

Eliot of course does not mean that an artist or poet should always repeat the ideas and values of the past, and should only have an independent colour of his outlook to it. What an artist is to do is to make an inevitable readjustment possible - the readjustment of the past in relation to the present uniqueness of resolution, thereby readjusting the whole into a new order of implication which neither the past nor the present alone could boast of.

Eliot is very subtle in defining the close inseparable link between the past and the present in the evolution of creative activity. He is very clear about the well-defined reasons of the past and of the present, but he does not mean simply the pastness of the past or simply the presentness of the present, but in his idea he readjusts the presence of the past and past in the present. In his idea a genius is he who can fashion everything into a new validity out of close link with the past standard of values. In poetry at least he does not think that there is 'complete originality owing nothing to the past'; when a Virgil, a Dante, a Shakespeare or a Goethe is born there is a unique achievement of altered values in the European tradition.

Eliot speaks of the individual talent thoroughly releasing itself in the depersonalised generalization in which all his subjective quality is lost but lost in such a way that it is regained in a unique form almost irrecognisible. Eliot makes it clear by means of an analogy of 'a bit of finely filiated platinum introduced into a chamber containing oxygen and sulpher dioxide'. The poet's individuality is newly rescued just like the filament of platinum in that glow of light.

Eliot introduces again the analogy of the catalyst. The poet's individuality as we have noted already is that shred of platinum. The poet's mind is just like a catalytic medium for a unique synthesis of all the materials gathered either from the past or from the present, of all kinds, sublime or trivial, for complete assimilation and transmutation by means of the creative energy and passion that are purely the artist's own into a new form and shape and expression in which nothing of the material nor of the gross personal element is kept intact.

Eliot defines the poet's mind in a language that fully supports this view,

> 'The poet's mind is in fact a receptacle for seizing and storing up numberless feelings, phrases, images, which remain there until all the particles which can unite to form a new compound are present together.'

Eliot of course does not accept Wordsworth's view of poetry as 'emotion recollected in tranquility.' For him it is an inexact formula. This way of reviving the past in the present is not Eliot's meaning as he has elaborated it under the title *Tradition and the Individual Talent.* Eliot reasonably discards gross subjectivity, even its refined version as in the Romantic Movement. Eliot is for a unique kind of objectivity in which the personality of the artist is entirely lost, it is 'an escape from personality' although the creative mind is the mind of a person. Eliot's idea of tradition and the individual talent points to a rare synthesis in which neither the tradition nor the individuality of the creator is ultimately the matter, it is simply an object of art with a prospect of revolution of all values of life.

Aristotle's Theory of Imitation

Aristotle and Plato met not always as preceptor and pupil, they were the two Greeks of two different bent of mind, so were often locked in unending debates over philosophic and literary subjects. Aristotle fundamentally differs from Plato on his theory of imitation.

It was Plato who remarkably raised the philosophy of mimesis, his theory gained ground until it was debated by his pupil Aristotle. Aristotle of course did not write his *Poetics* simply to refute the essential principles of imitation as propounded by Plato. *His Poetics* is in the nature of short notes to aid his Lectures to his scholars. In that unelaborated note Aristotle virtually defends poetry and poets and gives a new lease of life to the theory of imitation.

To Plato we owe the first statement of the mimetic or imitative character of art. A painter or a poet only imitates what we call reality and what Plato called 'phenomena'. Plato considered the visible universe as the simple transfiguration of idea, so the concrete physical existence is only an imitation of that idea. Art then in any form is an imitation of an imitation, and twice removed from what Plato termed as reality.

Aristotle's interpretation of imitation completely differs from this theory of imitation of an imitation. Plato may say, when a carpenter makes a bed he makes it out of his idea of it, when a painter paints it he still differs from that idea, but draws it out of that concrete shape of a bed. So what's the necessity of such an art? Aristotle differs completely from this notion of thrice removed imitation.

Aristotle's idea of imitation is essentially creative and imaginative. Imitation is not simply a copy, it is an act of artistic creation by means of all those rare faculties of imagination and passion under the two essential conditions of truth and beauty.

Imitation for Aristotle 'the objective representation of life', not meaning the exact copy, but 'the imaginative reconstruction of it', so it is something different from what we call reality. In that sense mimesis is not at all an unnecessary redundant process, as Plato may have considered it.

In such a concept of artistic creation lies Aristotle's whole contribution to the theory of imitation. Aristotle tries to say whatever expression the Greek may have attempted in poetry, sculpture and music was by means of selection, concentration and reorganization of the experience of their life, which was the creative act of the artist— out of life but not exactly life.

Plato in his concept of phenomenon imitated into a form of art quite overlooked or escaped this secret principle of artistic creation, which is an act of imagination, and an act of imitation by means of an exceptional application of imagination. Thus in Greek concept poets were 'vates'.

Aristotle of course viewed the act of imitation as scientifically an act of rare synthesis of the three different stages as the object of imitation, the medium in which it is imitated and the various modes of imitation. When we can achieve the secret harmony of these three it becomes an act of creation.

Plato as Theorist of Poetry

Before Plato Aristophanes introduced in his comedy *The Frogs* almost the same debate carried on further by Plato a few years later. Plato in *Ion* took up the debate only a few years after the death of his master Socrates. Again like the Agon in *The Frogs* Plato's debate takes the dramatic form – the same debate of the ultimate source of poetry and the power of the poet – a debate between a rhapsode Ion and the philosopher Socrates.

Plato is of the view in his *Ion* that the traditional theory of the source of poetry is not all true. Socrates appears in the dialogue a little too ironically critical of the view that the rhapsode elaborates the ultimate source of poetry - 'the poet is a light and winged and holy thing, and there is no invention in him until he has been inspired.'

Plato does not explain the question raised by Socrates in the *Ion* - what does poetry tell us, what is the source of a poet's power? Plato took it up for a clear analysis in his *Republic,* particularly Book II, III and Book X as also in the *Laws*, a compromise sort of *Republic* of Plato's old age.

The quarrel between the poet and the philosopher is the deep end of the quarrel between the poet and the moralist. Plato does proper justice to this issue in the middle and late stage of his writing. In Book II and III of the *Republic* it appears that poetry is engaged in fiction, often wicked fiction leading to wicked lies. Plato refers to Homer and Hesiod and some of the dramatists of his age, who misrepresent God and give us 'an anthropomorphic wrangling deceitful and revengeful crowd of deceits'.

Plato has so far deepened his mistrust of poetry already shown in his earlier work (*Ion*). At this stage of the argument appears the incidental concept of mimesis (imitation). Plato observes Book III that certain poems simply tell us what happened, others actually imitate what happened, and this latter he considers to be the most dangerous, because the most contagious.

In Book X of the *Republic* Plato develops his view of imitation, no doubt written some years after Book II and III. Plato's words are 'all poetical imitations are ruinous to the knowledge of their hearers, and that the knowledge of their true nature is the only antidote to them.'

The reasoning is made clear in a very explicit analogy between a poet and the illusionist painter of a bed. Plato knows behind all the creations of the bed either by a painter or made by a carpenter, there was only one bed, the idea of it. So there are three artists who superintend the bed: God, the maker of the bed (carpenter), and the painter. God gave the idea, that is the original of all these beds, the carpenter made the bed, so he imitated the original idea of it, then the painter imitated the bed made by the carpenter. So both the carpenter and painter were imitators.

Plato in his analysis of this analogy gives the essence of his idea of imitation and the work of a poet. The poet is according to Plato an imitator, but an imitator of an imitation, so he cannot be called a creator which he claims for himself. It is twice removed from the truth. Plato's objection to the works of the poets lies here.

With the allusion to the ideal bed, the work of God, we are involved in the Platonic metaphysics of transcendental reality, where Aristotle, his pupil, shows a marked difference. Plato sends poets into exile from his *Republic* because he takes a moral view of poetry. Aristotle's difference from Plato lies here that he does not at all take a moral view but an artistic view of poetry and poets. Aristotle refutes indirectly all those charges of Plato against poetry and poets in his *Poetics*. Sidney also does it much later in 1595 in his *Apology for Poetry*.

It is very clear that Plato objects to the seductive effect of poetry. He tells us that it can be perilous in effect for a sensitive and unstable character deficient in the intellectual or rational side. Plato is a mystic in the proper sense of the term, and to some extent puritanic in view of a modern term if at all to be applied. He follows a true mystic inclination when he condemns the arts. He is in the true climate of his own times when all arts were subservient to moral purpose. Aristotle later took exception to this view.

CHAPTER XVIII

GREEK DRAMA

Aeschylus as a dramatist

In ancient Greece Drama was not simply a form of art, it was what is religion to the modern man. The evolution of the tragedy in ancient Greece was closely related to the festival of Dionysus, called the spring god. Tragedy was a form of goat song, accompanying an elaborate rhythmic dance. Aeschylus took it at a stage like this.

In the oldest times the choral hymn, then called 'dithyramb', was the only form of tragic art. Afterwards to give rest to the chorus Thespis added one actor distinct form the singer. Then Aeschylus added a second, and Sophocles a third, which completed the development of tragedy.

Aeschylus then made a significant contribution to the evolution of the dramatic art on the Athenian stage. It is again Aeschylus who gave particular attention to the dance. He introduced buskins and also masks which not only added to the solemnity of the scene but gave it a spectacular effect.

It is again Aeschylus who took particular care to elaborate the theological view of life which was then current among the Athenian populace. By means of orchestra (dancing ground) and the altar of Dionysus (Thymele) Aeschylus pinpointed the essence of religious inculcation which was the ultimate end of tragedy. In those days the tragedy took simply the form of a three-tier evolution in a group of three plays performed in a series. The trilogy of *Oresteis* upheld the sombre view of monotheism. For Aeschylus even Zeus himself was but an instrument of 'an overriding law'.

The *Oresteia* trilogy opens with *Agamemnon* which is followed by the two other plays *Choephoroe* an *Eumenides*. It simply marks a development of a moral order, Clytemnestra's killing of Agamemnon is at the same time justice and sin that gave rise to a complex order of human necessity that is given in dramatic form in the other two plays in the series. The ultimate impression of the whole series is the overriding of an unknown invisible power that heeds no human complaint, as it does not in the case of Clytemnestra in *Choephoroe*.

Aeschylus is a theologian in the guise of a dramatist who has improved upon the already known form of drama upon the Athenian stage; but his successors Sophocles is a lesser theologian and a greater artist than his predecessor and ultimately introduced the original form of irony. The next stage of evolution in Greek tragedy is Euripides who took proper count of the human prospect more realistically than any of his predecessors within the framework of tragedy.

Aeschylus is neither like Sophocles nor like Euripides a pure artist or purely human in outlook; but it is he who developed the form of tragedy to accommodate both the planes of the divine and human in the art which he took so much seriously as no other artist of his land did earlier.

Some of his characters particularly in *Agamemnon* are not simply sketches, they are living men and women who did not think themselves completely free from the power that overruled them. Aeschylus gave perhaps more importance to this power as Euripides to the living men and women in his plays.

Antigone: Plot construction

From Aeschylus to Sophocles is a great improvement so far as the plot construction is concerned. Aeschylus gave dithyramb a true dramatic turn, and Sophocles gave drama into a good plot. Sophocles' excellence on quite obvious from, a close comparison between Aeschylus' *Agamemnon* and Sophocles' *Antigone*.

Agamemnon practically ends in the murder of the hero on return, all that is left after it is only an exposition of Greek theological belief, even before the act of murder the action lay in the straight development of the story of return. But *Antigone* is of a relatively complex pattern, the pieced out materials from an already known legend are given a compact dramatic design. The hamartia is clearly marked and its effect close after it is still grimly contracted.

The story is well-balanced between the two successive phases of peripetia and anagnorisis, the two phases taken particular note of by Aristotle. No other plot is so neatly poised between them as it is. Creon committed a great wrong not only against an individual but to a moral law then so seriously considered binding upon man in Greek Society.

Out of this committed blunder arose a phase of bitter sufferings when it ended in a true awakening of the benighted soul of the ruler, the ending is in true Greek tradition.

The play starts with Antigone's unilateral decision and single minded conviction of her role to act against a royal prerogative obedient to a moral law. The dead body cannot be left to the mercy and greed of the wild animals, Creon ventured to assault this moral law and provoked nature to pronounce her punishment, in Greek belief in those days the god of the underworld. The provocation was so sharp that Creon was in no time punished by the death of his son and wife.

Aeschylus would have constructed the plot on such a structure if only he did take a little more interest in the side of art than in the thought elements in his plays; but Sophocles could not remain satisfied with this structural neatness. He made art serve the interest of a complex design, so Creon's folly is made still more blind and foolish by ignoring a triple alliance of Tiresias, Antigone and Haeman - moral law, love and mercy.

Sophocles kept those three quite apart from each other in the story, but made them artistically contribute to the effect grievously against Creon, a man who wrecked the happiness of others life and thereby drew upon him a wreaked load of misery. To this the Chorus of Theban Senators are only disinterested observers or at best serves as interpreters.

The story and plot stand out distinct in most of Sophocles' plays especially in *Antigone*. The story is taken from a Greek legend, the plot is made out of the source materials for a contrived effect, made to contribute to the playwright's plan of art more than in any other playwrights of his age.

Irony in Antigone

Irony is a great invention of Sophocles, a conscious application of it in all his plays, mostly in his *Oedipus Rex*, although there was an unconscious and fortuitous use in Aeschylus too. Sophoclean irony is a type by itself, a little different from the modern dramatic irony. Sophoclean irony occurs in-between the two stages of 'peripetia' and 'anagnorists'. Practically it connects them, and all the dramatic effects depend on it.

Antigone's tragic effect is really an irony, Creon went against the moral law when he denied the dead body its proper burial. This first step led to another cruelty, hauling a young woman to living burial because she acted against the unjust prerogative of the king to observe the rites of the dead. This is no doubt the reversal of the fortune for the cursed house of Dedipus, Creon must have noted it; but the next stage of development in the action is an evident irony in which Creon makes the discovery of his fault, a very sad discovery.

Irony is also linked up with the theodicy of the ancient Greek belief. Destiny works through irony, irony is the instrument of divine punishment which is meted out and rightly apportioned to Creon. The Greek concept of moral order in which destiny rules the human world has irony as its instrument; Sophocles is a master artist, because he could make his art serve this need. *Antigone* is highly ironical because it is deeply spiritual in outlook and action. Any modern use of irony, say in Shakespeare, differs from this overall ethical and theological prepossession.

Irony in *Macbeth* is almost entirely divested of any moral outlook although apparently the action runs parallel to that of *Antigone*. Creon does not die, but he is given to view the diametrical change in the situation in which he stands alone a prey to the crime he committed in complete disregard of the established laws of life and death. He punished a dead man and also a living woman, brother and sister in relation, but he did not know that the same measure of punishment is still due to him. He thought Antigone should be parted from his son through death, but he did not know that love is a stronger force than hatred.

Irony is only a device of destiny in the Greek Drama, it was so even when playwrights did not consciously use it as a conscious expedient of their art. Sophocles is a greater artist because he made a fuller use of it consciously in his plays as pre-eminently in *Antigone*. The play comes to an end when the king is informed of the hapless death of his own son and the son's mother. Irony ends in anagnorisis; Creon now knows:

'Woe is me! to none else can they lay it,
This guilt, but to me! .
I, I was the slayer I say it,
Unhappy, of thee!'

The Chorus in Antigone

The chorus in the Greek drama serves as a crucial factor in their art and philosophical outlook. It was an inseparable link between literature and religion in the Greek society. Drama was in ancient Greece subservient to what religion they had then. In Sophocles it is still more significant, because he is a fully developed artist. In his play the chorus is an art that yet serves their theological principles and conviction.

In *Antigone* the Theban Senators form the chorus, normally the chorus here is a responsible segment of society and is expected to act a responsible role in the action. But the responsibility of the chorus in the Greek drama is of a different order, not limited to the design of the play though it also serves well the design. The chorus in *Antigone* also appears in a role like that. The senators of the State have their roles to play in a political move like that, and in that sense they are an integral part of the play and its plot.

The king follows a political line, but he ignores a moral principle. The Senators, as the chorus of the play, play an uninvolved role in both, the role of an ideal observer and guide in act and ideas. But they are not unfeeling instructors, rather feeling spectators we must say. They understand Antigone as also Creon though not meant to guide the course. They understand his error and wait for the consequence impartially without taking any side.

The appearance of the chorus in the play for the first time is when the audience may claim a bit of the background of the story and has it already from Antigone, but has not yet got the depth of the blunder being committed in a fit of insolence. The Senators are called for consultation of state affairs in an unwanted hour, the urgency of the situation called for it. But ultimately Creon gives them no authority to advise, they are left purely in their passive role:

I Senator: Then what else is there, besides, which you would lay on us?

Creon: Not to connive at disobedience.

The chorus remains in that position, the ideal position of the Greek chorus, with keen observation, appreciation and interpretation of the whole course of action.

The Greek drama provides song through the chorus, often it is in unique form of deportments through dance and in ode and epode, strophe and antistrophe, all helping to connect the mortal world with the immortal moral order. The second choric song in *Antigone* is an excellent piece of that order, a fragment is here to explain therein the human roles:

Man, abound in wiles
Entangles in his toils
And carries captive away...

The chorus does not ignore the specific case, the insolence of Creon and so the reference:

Now bends he to the good, now to the ill,
With craft of art, subtle past reach of sight;
Wresting his country's laws to his own will,
Spurning the sanctions of celestial right;

The chorus in almost all Sophocles' plays, especially in *Antigone*, is divided into the individuals who compose it for short comments. Here they are Senators and well-accommodated to the roles of individual observations. This role of individual comment is sharply contrasted with their voice in unison explaining the already believed principle of the Universal law, the overruling authority of God with his seat on Mount Olympus:

...Thy throne, is founded fast,
High on Olympus, in great brilliancy,
Far beyond time's annoy

The chorus takes part in the action not simply as a warning voice, nor as song providing relief in the misfortunes of the world, but also as an explanatory note to the action for the audience, providing a good philosophic lesson to the people who went there to be taught in life. Creon's whole family is wrecked and the chorus offers the reason why 'Love, thou art victor in fight'. The whole play is a victory of love, the moral order is another form of love ruling over everything.

The chorus in the Greek drama makes all the difference in form and spirit of their art. That drama is only one remove from the divine with only an added duty of art is firmly ratified by the use of the chorus the

Greek dramatists made, more significantly by Sophocles than any others of his age, thereby art given to dole out the beatitude of heaven to mankind.

Agamemnon a tragedy of silence

Aeschylus is closer to the Greek view of life than the other two great tragedians of his age, he is only a step farther from the Greek dithyramb and Dionysus rituals, the ultimate source of Greek drama. The tragic view of Aeschylus is not practically his own invention, it is dressed up in the traditional theodicy of the land. *Agamemnon* is the close representation of this view, the complete picture, is however, gained in the trilogy in which it is only the first piece.

The Greek drama as a whole, Aeschylus specially and his *Agamemnon* more particularly, contrasts sharply with the Elizabethan drama in the demonstration of the tragic conflict. The conflict is not only enacted in a British drama but often spectacular demonstration is made of all their bloody acts, even dead bodies are piled upon the stage to make it purple. But in a Greek tragedy no such act is allowed on the stage, in *Agamemnon* a little exceptionally the dead bodies of *Agamemnon* and Cassandra are open to the view of the audience. In Sophocles' *Antigone* such scenes are avoided, because Sophocles is more artistic than Aeschylus.

In *Agamemnon* the tragic death of the hero occurs completely in silence, there was only a shriek within the palace 'Oh, I am wounded with a mortal wound!' And after a minute's pause there only a despairing gasp. 'Again! O God!'. Complete silence thereafter. The other death, no less pathetic than this, is still more silent, if the victim's presentiment is not taken into consideration. Cassandra died a death she knew to be inescapable. She entered the palace after Agamemnon and did not even cry the awe and woe of a death blow.

Agamemnon is more like a revenge play but the revenge is taken without many words, the conflict is on the moral plane, not communicated to the other side. Agamemnon did not know at all what was being plotted against him. Cassandra knew through prophetic vision, but could not communicate to Agamemnon who brought her a captive from Troy. She shared the same chariot with him but had no word passing beyond her lips for him. She is an image of silence and volubility, a contrast both in one. All her ravings were not meant for Agamemnon but for the chorus. She is otherwise a riddle or enigma.

Agamemnon came home a hero, his booty of the great war is a woman, but to woman again he pays a silent price, not knowing at all that he is to. The Trojan hero died an unarmed death at the hand that he expected would hug him with love. He died altogether an unheroic death, to expiate for the blood of their own daughter and for another remote crime in his family.

The whole tragedy is a blood tragedy to which cuckoldry has been added and which makes the tragic gloom accumulate within the portals of the palace beyond the knowledge of the all too prying choric band of Argive Elders, completely in silence. Clytemnestra commits a double sin and plots against all moral rules and springs an unanticipated unprovoked attack upon her husband and Cassandra, no one knew she would do except that Trojan prophetess. The tragedy that occurs in the play occurs as far silently as it is possible.

***Agamemnon* : A representative Aeschylean play**

Aeschylus breaks new grounds in the tradition of Greek tragedy, from goat-song in the form of dithyramb to an action with an extra character to share the action with the singer, so it is left to Sophocles to introduce a third actor for a complete picture. Aeschylus is less artistic than Sophocles as Sophocles is less interested in human values than Euripides. Aeschylus is closer to the Greek philosophical principles than anybody else of the masters of tragedy. He is in tragedy what Pindar is in lyrical composition.

Agamemnon is a close representation of Aeschylus as an artist and thinker. He used his art to illustrate his view and his materials to form into a design that could reveal himself most. *Agamemnon* does. Aeschylus personality is closely behind it. The tragedy is Aeschylean, not caused by the character but by some other forces beyond his personal knowledge and scope. Here Agamemnon is not a hero who fights, but one who falls to unheroic, clandestine assault. Only his passage to Argive palace is somewhat heroic, a return home with a glory of a victory, yet there he does not enter the city at the head of the army, but accompanied by a captive lady. All that happens thereafter is quite unheroic.

A tragedy like this is in the right measure of Aeschylus' view of tragedy. A hero who falls, falls by the laws of the moral order in which he acts not always a positive role, but yet acts a role all the same for a fall otherwise morally deserved though not individually so much. The tragic waste and pity involved in it lies in this individually unmerited punishment. And fear is due to this massive force that can cause that waste in the form of expiation. Aeschylus' interest seems to be more in that unpronounced force. In this play too more interest is in that invisible undeclared war in which the hero of the Trojan war falls at his doorstep.

Clytemnestra and Aegisthus are only the visible instruments of that great conquering power, the excellence of the art is, even they do not know that they are only instruments to be used here and left out and crushed in the next stage in the cycle of the moral order. Exactly for this I am tempted to say Aeschylus is better judged in the complete trilogy as for example here the *Oresteia trilogy.*

The chorus has a dominant role in every play of Aeschylus mainly because of this secret force in the action. In *Agamemnon* it is the chorus of Argive Elders that explains the secret force not all too clearly, but as far as it is humanly possible to seize the air in the grip of the palm. The members of the chorus, or the band as a whole can only suggest the existence of a force, which is only supplemented by a yet clearer vision of a Prophetess. Agamemnon's bringing her home is another unique stroke of fate and the trick of the playwright's art to throw light on that dark region, the region Aeschylus knows moulds the tragic world from that unpenetrated unexplored existence.

Chorus in *Agamemnon*

The chorus plays a vital part in the Greek concept of tragedy. Gilbert Murray defines, the chorus forms the vulnerable borderline between the known human world and the unknown world of destiny. Drama in ancient Greece was really an interpretation of man's relationship with a moral order of which very little is known to mankind. It took the place of the modern Bible and the performance of a play of the pulpit.

Aeschylus makes more elaborate use of the chorus than any other play-wrights of his age, because he is a little closer to the original Greek tradition of faith. *Agamemnon* is the first piece of the Oresteia trilogy and full of choric hymns. The chorus is formed of the Argive Elders who represent the city public. They are ready to receive their king after long years of absence in the capital. They do not know what fate is awaiting him in his own home. They are contrasted with the Trojan Prophetess in that. Aeschylus has made them individuals and attributed to them all human limitations.

The Greek convention is, the chorus acts as an ideal spectator, they may not know everything, but they are expected to understand the true implication of things and communicate it to the audience. The chorus in *Agamemnon* does exactly that. Cassandra points an accusing finger to the home and declares her destiny and *Agamemnon's* much earlier than they occur. The Argive Elders do not do it, but explain the implication of the Queen's act, not all as seers, but as men of an extended power of understanding.

The chorus tells Cassandra: 'I have small skill in oracles but something evil I divine.' In the unusual hush they apprehend something ominous. They explain all the work of fate in the happenings and even in the prophecy of the Trojan Sibyl. They know things when they occur, they know when Agamemnon falls with a shriek. The whole choric band is divided into all those individuals who compose it, they argue as Elders of the city the issue in hand and argue with the murderer Queen her course of action. They form the body of observers of the action without serious involvement in it.

This is the general trend of the role of chorus in Aeschylus's plays, in *Agamemnon* the members of the choric band, as many as twelve, have reason to represent the people as Elders of the city and take interest in the palace intrigue and in the state affairs. But they are far different from the four representatives of the people in Shakespeare's *Julius Caesar*. Shakespeare's Roman Mob has no higher purpose to serve, they are deeply involved in the immediate turn of the situation and act in time or out of it with the instant impact upon them. The Elders of the Argive city have no such involvement but have correct discernment to judge rightly not only the action but also its bearing upon the moral order in which the Greek world had deep faith.

The chorus in *Agamemnon* makes this ancient belief sufficiently concrete in their acceptance of a divine head of this law. It is clear here:

> For Zeus abides upon His throne,
> And, through all times, all tides,
> The Law that quits the Doer,
> The changeless Law abides.

This supreme God of all gods, this Law of all laws, are the essence of this moral order and the chorus is the true interpreter of them for the general mass of the Greek society. The chorus has feelings and emotions but their discernments and true moral purpose are never beclouded by them.

Agamemnon: Aeschylean tragic vision

Aeschylus initiated the major phase of tragic drama in ancient Greece, and therefore more concretely the early Greek view of life than any of the other tragedians of his time. Aeschylus' is essentially a tragic view of life, a view which is Greek in origin and well entrenched in their tradition.

Agamemnon is the first of the Aeschylean trilogy and bears closely upon the playwright's view and vision of a theodicy that served then as an unpreached faith in absence of any preached one. Tragedy in ancient Greece evolved out of the rituals of their spring God Dionysus. A Single play in the series does not give us the complete picture of Aeschylus' vision, yet *Agamemnon* represents a significant related issue. In Greek tragedy greatest respect is due to the law that operates through 'hubris' and 'adikia' - pride and injustice. 'Arete' (virtue) is the highest point of attainment, disturbed by hubris or adikia.

In *Agamemnon* Aeschylus has shown the fall of a great hero at his doorstep, people fall like that owing to hubris or adikia. Agamemnon must have committed both, his pride of the victory must have been substantiated by the taking captive of a prophetess young lady and taking her to his palace, and to her death. The whole process is adikia. But Aeschylus differs a little from the Greek tradition in introducing the theme of blood revenge which gets the better of the direct Arete principle. Clytemnestra avenges her daughter's blood in *Agamemnon*, in the other two plays in the series the Greek theme returns, the sin of the parents implicating the children.

All his plays betray Aeschylus as believing in a moral order in which his characters play their unavailing parts finally to be controlled and decided by destiny. In *Agamemnon* there are at least a few characters who have clear vision of this truth / Argive Elders who form the chorus, and Cassandra who lately arrived from Troy the destroyed city. In the whole panoply of truth Zeus rules supreme over man and god. Final security of man lies in his submission to his power. Even in *Agamemnon* the whole course of the action conveys this idea of a central supreme rule.

The tragic concept of life and this universe derived out of Aeschylus' plays is ultimately a gloomy view - man is born destined and overruled. He plays his part, acts apparently freely as Agamemnon does, but is merely striking in the trap already laid. Laid by whom? This enquiry leads one to search for a supreme authority, to a concrete symbol called in Greek convention Zeus who apportions duties to other gods and moulds human destinies thereby in *Agamemnon* the destiny is overruled. There human roles, however desperate, never offer the final victory. Both Agamemnon and Cassandra come to the same sad end, one acting, significantly the other not acting at all.

In perfect agreement with the Greek tradition Aeschylus always recognises a higher plane above the human plane to rule over it. The tragedy on the human plane is not all independent of higher interference. The human world is properly linked with the moral world governed by the God of their conceptions.

Agamemnon : The tragic doom and Hamartia

Aeschylus is closer to the original Greek belief in a higher order that controls the lower human order. The idea of tragedy is ultimately derived from the gap between these two orders or planes, so it widely differs from the modern conception of tragedy and from also the Elizabethan, mainly Shakespearean view of it. So far as Aeschylus is concerned *Agamemnon* may categorically illustrate it, although for a total view the whole of the oresteia trilogy must be taken into consideration.

Shakespearean concept of Hamartia (tragic flaw) is not applicable to the Greek drama, far less to Aeschylean drama, Agamemnon, as it is in the play does not fall for any personal flaw or blunder, but yet he is in a trap of fate in which he acts only to precipitate the already laid snare; he can in no way escape it. In this play silence is almost all, the hero does not act at all, or say anything. He is given no power of action of speech. By the Elizabethan standard tragedy here is undeserved, but Greek tragedy has a different standard. The tragedy of Agamemnon must not be judged by that standard.

Agamemnon need not commit any personal blunder, he has practically no such grievous tragic flaw as Macbeth, Othello, Hamlet and King Lear are found to have. He is an exemplary case of ancient tragedy, even without a personal flaw he is to expiate for the sin of his parents, particularly his father, the trail of sin raises ripples of sin for further complication and still graver atonement in future. Aegisthus avenges his father's wrong done by Atreus, Agamemnon's father, but avenges with no less grievous a wrong which requires atonment on a plane further off. In this way wrong begetting wrong passes one after another inviting expiation in their turns. *Agamemnon* only takes the case of one, very preliminary.

Fate visited the sin of his father upon him it did not require his blunder or any defect of character. Yet Agamemnon had some responsibility which is not covered here in the action, only Clytemnestra brought this charge against him, of course silently. It was his shedding blood of Iphigenia their child, that blood cried for revenge, not exactly as Horatio's or Hamlet's father's blood did. Even blood revenge in Greek tragedy was a part of their theology. Blood once shed must have blood, no matter it is in personal interest or for a general cause.

Agamemnon came to the Argive capital to pay the price of that sin, but those who took revenge committed the same crime which again required to be punished and was punished. Hamartia in *Agamemnon* is quite Aeschylean and far from being solely a defect of the character or a tragic error, the only avoidable error in Agamemnon was his bringing Cassandra to the Capital from Troy and bringing her seated by his side in the same chariot, which doubly inflamed Clytemnestra's anger, made her decide in her mind to murder her too along with her husband.

In Aeschylus character's individuality is not so important as the accepted moral laws of life. So hamartia need not be explained in terms of the individuality of character but in terms of the law. This is particularly to be noted in the tale of *Agamemnon*. He is a victim of all those errors banded together against him. Those errors take not only his life but are relegated to a plane further down for a similar fate for the righting agents, here Clytemnestra and Aegisthus.

Hippolytus: A Revenge Tragedy: The role of the characters

Revenge tragedy is not new in Greek drama, but it takes a new turn in the hands of Euripides. *Media* is also a revenge tragedy., but in these two plays Euripides takes two different stands as to the cause of revenge, yet both are a clear departure from the traditional blood revenge in ancient Greece, so from Aeschylus; it differs strikingly from later developments in the Roman and Elizabethan periods.

Euripides has deeply involved the roles of the gods and goddesses in the revenge tragedy of man. He more than anybody else of his age makes frequent use of the weaknesses and freaks of the gods, often he humanizes their roles in his deep respect for human values. That is perhaps the reason why Plato took exception to such use of the gods by the poets, he must have had Euripides in mind mainly. Euripides does it in the *Hippolytus*. Here is a revenge not exactly taken by one man upon another as in Aeschylus' trilogy, but one god against another, the impact, of course, is laid on man.

Hippolytus is protected by Artemis the goddess of hunting and sport but antagonized by another goddess, Aphrodite, only because he does not worship her. The goddess lays the trap for his destruction, and out of a spirit of revenge, of course humanly unmerited. This play has thus for its subject matter. Aphrodite infected the mind of Phaedra, the young wife of his father, for which he was not at all responsible, but proved an unlucky victim. It is not blood for blood principle of tragedy, it is a tragedy of gods' interference in the affairs of man. It is almost the original fate of man, falling victim to Satan's plan of revenge upon God.

Tragedy occurs and both Phaedra and Hippolytus die, one in shame, the other again by arrangement of a god. Hippolytus dies but not before clearing him of the curse of his father and of the alleged sins. Theseus his father repents his folly when the messenger relates what he saw.

The Greek drama, when it deals with a tragic revenge, differs from modern, particularly Elizabethan revenge tragedy, in its essentially religious character, as in this case, although Euripides is considered less religious than Aeschylus. So after Hippolytus's death, although revenge is complete, the course of the action does not come to an end. Artemis takes the foreground to explain to Theseus the underlying secret force of the tragedy. The play, therefore, when it comes to an end, ends like a requiem:

> 'Rain down O ye fast-falling tears of our mourning!
> When the mighty are fallen, their burial oblation
> Is the wail of a nation.'

It is, therefore, clear that the taking part in the action are mainly acted upon. The whole of the Greek drama is religious in character, the human roles are often overshadowed by an overall moral order with an idea of fate. *Hippolytus* clearly bears it out. The characters, particularly Phaedra and Hippolytus; are trapped in a revenge design of a goddess, only the nurse in the play has some independence of action but her independent choice is also remotely controlled by destiny or better say by the wrath of the avenging goddess.

The other characters, mainly three, Theseus, Hippolytus, and Phaedra are within the ambient of higher control but within that area they are left free to act their roles obviously not knowing the mysterious overruling force. In Greek tragedy things are like, that even Euripides could not escape it. Character planning in the play requires a judicious apportioning of the human and the divine in their idea of life. The human and the divine have their own area of independence. *Hippolytus* is a tragedy that is perfectly in this tradition.

Hippolytus: Plot realistic or Adventitious

Euripides takes note of the human values of life in his plays, more eagerly than the side of form. In point of form Sophocles is more skilful than Euripides no doubt, but lesser skill is due to his greater interest in respect of human values. All the stories of Greek tragedies are taken from the legends and myths of the land and are common knowledge to the audience, the plot out of the known material is the credit of the playwrights. While dealing with the same legend the playwright differ from each other. The difference that Euripides marks from his immediate predecessors is quite interesting. The difference is due to the choice and personal predilection of the playwright.

The plot of *Hippolytus* is not as well-knit as any of Sophocles' plays, as for example the conflict between Creon and Antigone is well-defined but the conflict in relation to Hippolytus and Phaedra is rather not be called conflict at all and not well-defined; it is not, because conflict is not Euripides' object. His object is a human problem and deeper psychology involved in it, a kind of Shakespearean inner conflict. The outer force of the plot is the wrath of a goddess against the protege of another goddess, the conflict or contest must have been between these two goddesses, and there is a little of a conflict but the contest is not sharp enough, not sharp enough because Euripides has humanized it and made it realistic.

Before the nurse discloses Phaedra's consuming love for Hippolytus there is no real conflict of two different forces actuating two individuals on the human plane, love one and sport another. These are the two natural human passions, only realistically a little antagonized. The two individuals are kept apart although one mentally wanted to come closer, kept apart by the hatred of the other. It is quite a human problem. Euripides has made it psychologically realistic.

It is very difficult to explain Euripide, plot in terms of peripeteia and anagnorisis, easier to explain Sophocles' plots. Euripides' plot in this play follows a human evolution, first a conflict between two goddesses then between two moral principles - love and adventure – and last of all between father and child, between Theseus and Hippolytus, all leading to an impression of human crisis, human tragedy to which only the first push was given by a supra-human force which Greek drama as a whole could not avoid. Only the last stage of conflict can be explained by the reversal of the fortune and discovery theory of plot. Hippolytus' supposed sin, sin that has been attributed to him by his father, is cleared in the successive stage of evolution in a sort of *deus ex machina*, which was also an accepted pattern of denouement in Greek drama. The rest of the plot, particularly the part played by Phaedra in it along with her nurse is better explained by psycho-machina, in which Euripides excels. Phaedra embraces death, before she could disclose the secret of her passion, the passion that came in conflict with her culture and moral sense.

The plot has only a three stage development, at the last stage the tragedy occurs, the hero dies, here not by his own hand. The sublimated stage of the action is ruled by a divine grace, by a sanity of outlook, a sort of resignation, theological resignation, which again forms part of the

Greek outlook given vent to in their drama. The contest on the plane of the gods leads to the lower human plane for a contest between Hippolytus and Phaedra, which again leads to still another plane of filio-parental relationship embittered first and then fully reconciled after tragic waste. Viewed like that the playwright does not seem to be with no sense of art or design, but he is deeply interested in human values and sometimes that interest attains more distinction than the other.

Agamemnon: Clytemnestra's role and character

Agamemnon is the first of a trilogy that Aeschylus wrote in the contemporary convention of semi-philosophic semi-dramatic production. The play is based upon an already known Greek myth in which Agamemnon the great hero met his death when came safe from a long war in Troy. Clytemnestra is his Queen and daughter of Tyndareus. Her mother was Leda. All the characters are ultimately drawn from Greek myth.

While dealing with all those already known characters Aeschylus had to take into consideration the legendary value of their lives and lessons they might offer to the contemporary Greek society. Aeschylus does not of course deal with them as purely for artistic excellence as Sophocles is famed to do, or simply to deal with the human prospects as Euripides has done. Aeschylus in his treatment of characters is well within the scope of the contemporary theological conception.

Clytemnestra is a character who is regarded by Professor Gilbert Murray as most prospective in the whole play. Clytemnestra is most outstanding in the play not simply because she illustrates the Greek theology better than any other character, but because she betrays some human qualities which even the most theological of playwrights in ancient Greece could not ignore. Clytemnestra is represented here as a human character with her excellence and defects, her strength and weaknesses, both are well adjusted in her human nature.

Sophocles and Euripides have also painted Clytemnestra, but Aeschylus' portrait is something different although not out of the Greek convention, rather she is more steeped in it in this play than she is outside.

Clytemnestra is painted by Aeschylus as a cruel murderess. Of course Aeschylus based his account upon the myth, but the trick and the cruelty of the act are perhaps his own creation. The watchman described Clytemnestra as a woman with a 'woman's heart strong with a man's resolve'. The chorus of Argive Elders too describes her in similar terms.

Clytemnestra is not only painted as a lady with a man's resolve, which Shakespeare's lady Macbeth also was; she is given a vision which Lady Macbeth had not. Lady Macbeth ultimately collapsed because she could not foresee the violent reaction in her nature after the deed was done. Clytemnestra has no such untoward prospect. She has a vision of all that happened in Troy, a vision that Shakespeare has given to Margaret in *Richard III.* At times of course Clytemnestra attains a choric character in her view of the unknown past and of the unborn future.

Clytemnestra is extremely tricky and simply guided by the strong resolve to take revenge of her daughter's death. It is interesting to note how she received the Herald at the gate of the palace, how she acted the fidelity of a devoted wife, as if to receive her husband within the portals of the palace with all the sweetness of a loving wife. She acted like Penelope though she was not at all.

Clytemnestra is full of her infidelity to the marriage bond. She is already with Aegisthus. She killed Agamemnon even when she simply acted as a loving spouse. She has her reason of course, Agamemnon killed her only daughter, Iphigenia, Agamemnon killed her of course for a greater cause which Euripides paints significantly well in his play. But that was not the only reason that Clytemnestra should kill Agamemnon. She is no doubt a depraved woman even more depraved than the proverbial Cleopatra. Shakespeare's Cleopatra delineates the mystery of her spell cast upon a great hero like Antony. Clytemnestra's life with Aegisthus in her husband's absence is no doubt prompted by her depraved nature.

Aeschylus of course has not given a fuller account of the side in the play, but he has definitely suggested it. Lady Macbeth surely love Macbeth and did the wrong thing to share the bliss of kingship with her husband. Clytemnestra is just the opposite.

Clytemnestra is again very envious of the prospect of Cassandra, of course it was wrongly constructed prospect of no existence. Cassandra was brought down to the gate of the palace in the same chariot with her husband, and she was inflamed with jealousy as any woman would have been, but she was not at all a beloved wife having no love lost for Agamemnon, although he has returned home after long ten years of hard labour and bloody war.

Clytemnestra in Aeschylus' *Agamemnon* is the only woman character that has shown deeply all those responses and reactions, right or wrong, quite natural in a lady of her position. Aeschylus has sharply contrasted Clytemnestra with Cassandra who ultimately fell victim to her wrath.

CHAPTER XIX

LANGUAGE

Early Latin influx

English belonged to the West Germanic group of languages. From late 7th century onwards the language of the already settled Germanic tribes in Britain came under the domination one after another of three major invading races and was subjected to changes and new acquisitions from their exotic sources, as the ruled could be by the rulers. Hence the three main influences in the development of English.

The earliest is the Latin influx into the English vocabulary. Driven by the Huns the Germanic tribes, Jute, Angle and Saxon, came from the Elbe and Oder valley area with their native tongue intact, and made a wholesale massacre of the Britons and the almost total annihilation of their language. That is why only a dozen words of Celtic origin are found in the language. That serves as a clue to what happened to the people and their language in the pre-Christian period.

In the next stage when Britain was named after the majority of the tribes and thereafter came within the conversion campaign of the Christian missionaries from the two sides, from Rome as from Ireland, the already settled Germanic tribes came into contact with a new culture and a new language and of course received some of the words during their contact with Roman traders years before the Christian cultural invasion and again later from the missionaries, a good deal.

In the pre-Christian period the German tribes, still of Pagan outlook and habit, picked up from their Roman counterpart words of commercial interest like 'wine' Lat. vinum, 'calicem' (cup), 'caupones' (wine dealers) OE ceapian (to buy) modern cheap. Another word of this period is 'monger' OE mangere (retailer), 'moneta' OE mynet (coin) mod. mint.

It gives an idea that among the Roman rulers a section dominated trade and commerce, however long before that might be, and gave the language some of the common terms of their profession. Roman rule in the land provided the barbarians with greater amenities, improved condition of the city, and gave it their own words, for example Lat. strata (original meaning via) supplanted OE straet and assumed the modern meaning of paved road. The word castra OE ceaster which survives in so many names of places ending in-chester, -chaster or -caster, Roman word castra means camp, the Roman garrison towns were called legionis castra (the legion's camp), OE lega ceastter.

After the preaching of Christianity in the whole land a good number of Latin words are introduced, their number far exceeded the number of loans under Roman invasions thrice over, one before the Christian era, twice after it and before the official conversion of the people. Some of the words are 'minster' OE mynster, from Lat. monasterium, 'monk' OE munuc Lat. monachus, 'bishop' OE biscop Lat. episcopus, 'priest' OE preost Lat. presbyter, 'Mass' OE maesse Lat. missa, 'church' OE cyrice Lat. cyriacum. Many of these words were originally Greek.

In some cases the existing pagan customs and conventions had their names which attained new implications under the impact of the new culture and ideas of the Roman missionaries, such as the pre-Christian Anglo-Saxon term Eastru, Eastron, remaining in the language as Easter with the changed background of Christian celebration of The Resurrection, although in the pagan custom it was only the worship of the Goddess of dawn, the symbol of the revival of life and energy, as in Greece the spring festival. Another such word is 'bless', the modern meaning is due to the Christian meaning, the original pagan meaning 'to sprinkle with blood' after animal sacrifice is supplanted.

The largest number of Latin words, however, is not due to Latin Christianity but due to Latin learning which held its sway over England in later 10th century Benedictine revival. But of the four hundred and odd number of Latin words thus taken in at this stage only about a score still remain in the language.

In imitation of Latin compound the native elements developed a new power of composition, for example Gōdspell, gōd and spell — these two elements joined exactly as the two Lat. (ultimately Skt.) elements Eu (well) and agelion (news) of the compound Euangelium. Gōdspell is the origin of gospel. Likewise Trinity (threeness) is modelled on Lat. Trinitatem OE thryness.

Later borrowing from Latin had a completely different character. The ME period was essentially a period of French domination in English. So Latin interpolation is very difficult to trace accurately, such interpolation is mostly through French. But the influx of Latin during the Renascence is a predominant feature in the language history, and mainly due to the classical learning and translation of literary monuments in the past. Even English authors often wrote in Latin in this period, for example Bacon, and still later Milton. Swift also wrote in Latin as did Newton in science. Still later Latin intake has still varied reasons both in literature and in science studies.

Scandinavian Element

From the settlement of the Germanic tribes in England down to the invasion of the land by the Northmen the language had only Latin influx; from the first batch of the Danes coming to the English shore the language history had yet another turning point. Their contribution to the English language has only a sisterly effect, because it notably differed from the contributions of Latin and French in its streaming ultimately from the same stock as the Germanic tribes, undergoing only local changes and modifications as a result of their migration farther away to the North centuries ago. So when they permanently settled in England after their long viking career (the treaty of Wedmore 878 gave them that opportunity) they could easily accommodate themselves and their language either with their English neighbours, there was hardly any prolonged language conflict as it was after the Norman conquest in the Middle English period between the conqueror and the conquered races.

The word viking is a reminiscence of this settlement , OE wicing has a narrower sense of something about settlement (OE wic settlement, -ing pertaining to), the ON word viking means 'one who crossed the sea from Norway for plunder or for founding a new era of contact etc.'. The history of this word gives the true nature of their inroads, ultimately the word stood for Northern plunders. The word Dane came to be a word of reproach for heathen.

However bitter this attitude might be the English people received them finally well and never behaved as they did to the Britons nor the marauders did to the island people. The interchange of languages was smooth. Even a Dane became their king in 1017. Their custom, religion and social order were almost the same. The conformity between these two languages is well authenticated from a vast number of common words practically with no change in inflection such as man, wife, father, folk, house, thing, life, sorrow, winter, summer, will, can, meet, hear, see, think, ride, stand, sit, wise, wait, better, all of common everyday currency and relationship sometimes with only a slight change of sound as in OE swan ON svein – a changed into ei, OE leas ON laus – ea changed into au, OE shyrt ON skyrt – sk changed into sh.

In some cases both the forms, English and Norse, are extant in the language with only a slight difference of meaning, such as whole–hale, no–nay, raise - rear, from –fro, shirt–skirt, shot–scot, screak–screach, edge - egg.

Very often both Scandinavian and English forms of the same word survive, one in dialect and the other in literary use, as for example church –kirk, mouth – mun, yard – garth. Often the two different forms are in competition for survival, and often the Norse word wins the race, such as the pronouns they, their, them; the word take OE niman is another example. The curious competition between egg and ey, has a history of battle for survival, any book on philology, particularly Jespersen's, has quoted the actual passage that shows it.

There are good many cases where the native form survive as for example yarn–garn, star–sterne; sometimes both the forms make a pair *e.g.*, nook and corner; at other times the native word adopts the Scandinavian sense *e.g.*, Dream in OE meant joy, in ME the modern meaning was taken from ON draumr, Dan. drom; bread OE sense fragment, mod. sense from ON; bloom OE bloma (mass of metal), mod meaning is due to Norse nuance of meaning; very significant is the word earl OE eorl (noble man), in Knute's time it took over the meaning of Norse jarl (under king). OE gift meant price paid by a suiter for a woman taken to wife, modern meaning is due to Scandinavian. OE dwellan meant only to lead astray, the modern meaning is derived from Scandinavian. Death and dead are OE words, the corresponding verb was steorfan, sweltan, mod. die is Scandinavian; the result was sweltan was discarded and steorfan acquired a different meaning starve.

Most of the judicial and administrative terms are French, yet there are a few taken from Scandinavian, law itself a Scandinavian term, by-law, crave, thrall are some others.

The scandinavian settlers were not like the Norman lords far above the native, population in social status, which Scott has noted in his *Ivanhoe*, if they were above the English they were at least in the master and servant relationship. Their contribution was quite brotherly, and in their life habit almost on their own level. The contribution is not aristocratic in character, but democratic in nature. They fought like brothers and amicably also settled like brothers, they could also accommodate their language between themselves, and never felt like an imposition as the Saxons felt about the incursion of French into their stronghold and felt the necessity of replacing it by their own about 1367. Scandinavian was no such imposition, was neither new to them. So the blending was easy and uneventful. French produced Chaucer but Scandinavian contribution made none, rather silently settled. Jespersen's observation is therefore quite suggestive – "An Englishman cannot 'thrive' or be 'ill' or 'die' without Scandinavian words; they are to the language what 'bread' and 'eggs' are to the daily fare".

French influence in English

Since the Norman conquest of England in 1066 the English people came to be receiving an easy flow of French words through French domination of England, the native language being replaced by French in schools, colleges and law courts and also in Parliament. French settlement in England and French domination in the administration brought English under the direct impact of French.

Most of the administrative words are French, words like 'crown', 'state', 'government', 'sovereign', 'minister' and 'parliament'. Native 'king' and 'queen' of course remained.

Feudalism was imported from France, and along with the system some words of description of the ranks as 'vassal', 'liege' and some words to express ideas of the principle, as 'fief', 'feudal'. Some ranks of aristocracy are designated by the French words such as 'prince', 'peer', 'duke', 'duchess', 'baron', 'viscount', 'marquis', but native 'lord' and 'lady' are retained as also 'earl'. But the wife of the Earl is denoted by a French word 'countess'.

The upper classes took into their hands the management of military matters. So most of the military ranks and activities were given French names, such as 'war', 'peace', 'battle', 'captain', 'colonel', 'lieutenant', 'admiral' etc. Some words now used in a slightly changed meaning were originally well within the military jurisdiction and were due to French influx. Such words are 'challenge', 'enemy', 'danger', 'escape', 'espy', 'prison', etc.

Another direct impact of Norman upper classes upon the English language is a good number of French words in the vocabulary, words like 'justice', 'judge', 'just', 'jury', 'court', 'suit', 'sue', 'plaintiff', 'defendant', 'summon', 'assize', 'session', 'attorney', 'fee', 'cause', 'felony', 'traitor' etc. Up to 1362 French remained the official language of the law court, it retained its hold upon the proceedings of Parliament even up to a few years later. So already French introduced a good number of other categories of words not directly related to law, such as 'marry', 'case', 'rest', 'prove', 'false', 'heir', 'prison'. The French word 'puis ne' in its legal sense remains 'puisne'— younger or inferior in rank— originally 'later born', but in ordinary sense appears with a different spelling 'puny'. Similar other instances of French borrowing in the strict legal use and still surviving native words for general use side by side, as for example 'larceny' used by the lawyers, 'theft' and 'steal' of common use are not yet displanted.

Ecclesiastic matters were also in the conduct of the upper class French landed gentry, so a good number of French words are connected with the Church, such as 'religion', 'service', 'trinity', 'saviour', 'virgin', 'angel', 'saint', 'abbey', 'cloister', 'friar', 'clergy', 'sacrifice', 'Psalter', 'homily', 'sermon', 'prayer'. A related series of words to describe moral ideas were also introduced in the language from French origin. Such words are 'virtue', 'vice', 'chaste', 'charity', 'grace', 'cruel', 'lechery', 'mercy', 'pity', 'discipline' etc.

It is curious to note a significant remark made by John Wallis and then still more significantly made use of in Scott's *Ivanhoe* to define the relationship between the Norman masters and the Saxon servants. The native servants addressed their Norman lords and ladies in their language 'sir', 'madame', 'master', 'mistress'. They 'command' in their language and the Saxon servants 'obey', the words themselves represent their side of the language. Scott's Womba jestingly defined the relationship in terms of the language they used, 'cow', 'ox', 'calf', 'sheep', 'swine', 'boar', 'deer', when they were under the protection of the Saxon servants, were called by English names, and when those animals were dressed into items of food for the table of the Norman lords the items were given French names like 'beef', 'veal', 'mutton', 'pork', 'bacon', 'brawn', 'venison' etc.

Likewise superiority of French cuisine gave the language words like 'sauce', 'boil', 'fry', 'roast', 'toast', 'pastry', 'soup', 'jelly'; the word 'dainty' is French; the humbler 'breakfast' remained English while the more sumptuous meal 'dinner', 'supper' as well as 'feast' were French.

The clear definition between these two classes, the French rulers and the ruled native populace gave an aristocratic character to the actual French loan, while the Scandinavian loans were essentially democratic in nature. All comforts of life seem to be reserved for the ruling class, and words to describe them were from French, such as 'joy', 'pleasure', 'delight', 'ease', 'comfort'; all sports were mainly described in French terms such as 'sports', 'deport', 'chase', 'dice', 'scent', 'quarry'; French 'chase' could not displace native 'bunt'.

The French were teachers of art to the English as almost in everything, so a good number of words related to art were taken over from French, the examples are: 'art', 'beauty', 'colour', 'image', de-sign', figure', 'ornament' etc. So also are words related to architecture, such as 'arch', 'tower', 'pillar', 'vault', 'porch', 'column', aisle', 'chapel', 'cloister'; the architects were also named in French, as for example 'tailor', 'mason', 'painter', 'carpenter', joiner etc. The articles of furniture were also given French names as 'chair', 'table', 'furniture', but the humbler 'stool' is native. The great period of influx of French words was 1251-1400, there are other periods of influx later, of course with obvious differences of the nature of loan. Jespersen has noted one very significant difference, the sound of ch- as in 'change' and 'chaunt' of the earlier period and in 'châmpagne' of the later loan, evidently flowing from different regions of France.

Index

For economy of space this Index only supplements the elaborate contents of the book

D

E

F

G

H

I

J

K

L

M

N

O

P

Q

R

S

T

U

V

W

Y

Z